HOLLYWOOD GOLD
THE AWARD WINNING MOVIES

HOLLYWOOD GOLD

The
Award Winning Movies

Roy Pickard

TAPLINGER PUBLISHING COMPANY
NEW YORK

First published in the United States in 1979 by
TAPLINGER PUBLISHING CO. INC.
New York, New York.

Library of Congress Catalog Card No.: 78-63445

ISBN 0-8008-3919-6 (cloth)
ISBN 0-8008-3920-X (paper)

Printed in Great Britain

Preface

It is probably true to say that just about the only 'traditional' part of Hollywood still remaining from the great days of the past is Oscar Night.

Each year, in the early spring at one of Hollywood's largest theatres, all the razzamatazz and glamour is suddenly brought out on display once more. Stars and starlets try to outdress each other, the searchlights soar high above the famous neon streets and crowds jostle with each other to catch a glimpse of their favourite stars as they arrive for the film capital's most glamorous ceremony.

For a few hours it really is like old times. The clock is turned back to a time when Hollywood really was Hollywood. Only the fashions give any indication that it is the 70s. Otherwise it could easily be the 40s or 50s or almost any period in the history of the Academy Awards. The studios, the star system, the films themselves may have changed, but not the Oscars.

Inside the theatre a tension always seeps through the audience even when hot favourites are expected to take the top awards. There is always the possibility of a surprise. As the envelope is torn open and the words 'And the winner is. . .' announced, the TV cameras swing cruelly across the faces of the five nominees sitting in the auditorium, zooming in close to reveal their nervous smiles, strains and apprehensions.

It is a noisy, glittering, vulgar and exciting occasion. And it is always news. The Oscars always make the front pages of the world no matter who wins.

It's been that way since the first award winners — for the year 1927/28 — were presented at a banquet on May 16, 1929. Doubtless it will remain so in the years ahead.

The actual birth of the Academy of Motion Picture Arts and Sciences — the organization that each year hands out the Oscars — occurred on May 4, 1927 when 36 people from various areas of film production met to organize a non-profit making corporation dedicated to the ideal of improving the artistic quality of the film medium. Among those first three dozen members were Douglas Fairbanks, who was the Academy's first president, actors Richard Barthelmess, Mary Pickford and Conrad Nagel, directors Raoul Walsh, Henry King, Frank Lloyd and Fred Niblo, studio executives Louis B. Mayer and Irving Thalberg, and art director Cedric Gibbons.

The latter was the man responsible for the design of Oscar himself. At a banquet at Hollywood's Biltmore Hotel, just after the formation of the Academy, he responded to a call for a symbol which would depict continuing progress in the industry and which was both militant and dynamic. His pencil quickly sketched across the table cloth in front of him and in a few minutes the design for Oscar as we know him today was complete.

It was not until four years later, however, in 1931, that he finally got his name. Margaret Herrick, late president director of the Academy, spotted a copy of the statuette on an executive's desk and exclaimed: "Why, he looks like my uncle Oscar!"

Every movie that has been awarded an 'Uncle Oscar' over the last fifty years is here in this book, no matter whether it is a multiple Oscar winner like *Ben-Hur* or *West Side Story* or a single best song winner like *Shaft*, or just a special effects winner like *The War Of The Worlds* or *Mighty Joe Young*.

Within these pages the famous and the nearly forgotten mingle with each other side by side, but all have that one single crowning achievement in common. All have been awarded that prized bronze statuette which stands no more than 13½ inches high, weighs just over 8lbs and is covered with a gleaming finish of 14 carat gold.

In this volume, for ease of reference, the winners have been listed in alphabetical order. Under each entry is the year of release, the number of Oscars won — and in what category, a brief synopsis of the plot, the production company, director, cast, colour and technical process and running time.

Unusual aspects of the Oscar winning movies are also included, such as *The Godfather Part II* being the first sequel to be a best picture winner or *The Exorcist* being the only horror movie ever to be nominated in the best film category. Or, again, Walter Brennan being the only actor to win three supporting Academy Awards or Charles Laughton being the first British actor to win for a performance in a British film — *The Private Life Of Henry VIII*.

Included in the synopses of the films which won acting awards are descriptions of the various roles played by the winning performers and where they figured in the story line. All major and supporting performances are treated in this fashion.

The only absentees are documentaries and short films. In the case of the foreign language film award all winners since 1956 have been included, as that is the date when the Academy first made the category a competitive one with five yearly nominees. Earlier, the award had been selected by the Academy Board of Governors and was not a 'winner' in the accepted sense.

At the rear of the book, for quick checking purposes, is a list in year order of the top six Oscar winners (film director, the four acting awards) and a companion list, also in year order, of all the nominees in the same six categories. There are also three additional appendices, one listing a hundred famous films, which never won a single Oscar nomination, another listing a separate hundred which *were* nominated but didn't win a single award betwen them and a third listing all the special and honorary awards presented by the Academy, including the Irving G. Thalberg and Jean Hersholt Humanitarian Awards.

As far as Oscar books go *Hollywood Gold* is unique. There have been other books on the Academy Awards in the past but mainly they have been photographic records or straightforward listings by year of the winners. This, I believe, is the only book to deal lucidly and precisely with *all* the Oscar winning movies.

Extensively illustrated, it is to be hoped that it makes interesting and useful reading.

Roy Pickard

The Adventures of Don Juan (1949)

Oscars (1) best colour costume   Leah Rhodes, Travilla and
          design   Marjorie Best

Lavish Technicolor swashbuckler, set in 17th century Spain with Errol
Flynn as the legendary lover saving Queen Viveca Lindfors from the
evil machinations of the King's first minister, Robert Douglas.

A Warner Bros. Picture, directed by Vincent Sherman. With Errol
Flynn, Viveca Lindfors, Robert Douglas, Alan Hale, Romney Brent,
Ann Rutherford. Technicolor. 110 mins.

The Adventures of Robin Hood (1938)

Oscars (3) best art direction   Carl Weyl
          best editing   Ralph Dawson
          best music: Erich Wolfgang Korngold
             original score

The first Technicolored version of the Robin Hood legend with Flynn
duelling to the death with Basil Rathbone around the shadowy walls of
Nottingham castle. A silken Claude Rains adds a purring Prince John, a
lovely Olivia de Havilland beauty and adoration. Along with *Captain
Blood* (35) the only swashbuckler ever to be nominated for the best
picture award.

A Warner Bros. Picture, directed by Michael Curtiz & William
Keighley. With Errol Flynn, Olivia de Havilland, Claude Rains, Basil
Rathbone, Ian Hunter, Eugene Pallette, Alan Hale, Melville Cooper.
Technicolor. 105 mins.

The African Queen (1951)

Oscars (1) best actor   Humphrey Bogart

C. S. Forester World War I adventure about a grizzled old Canadian tug-boat skipper (Bogart) who takes his ramshackle launch and a spinster missionary (Katharine Hepburn) down a treacherous African river in order to sabotage a German gunboat.

A Romulus Film, directed by John Huston. With Humphrey Bogart, Katharine Hepburn, Robert Morley, Peter Bull, Theodore Bikel. Technicolor. 106 mins.

Air Force (1943)

Oscars (1) best editing   George Amy

Howard Hawks' World War II account of the flight of a single flying fortress and her crew from take-off in San Francisco on December 6, 1941, to the battles above the South Pacific.

A Warner Bros. Picture, directed by Howard Hawks. With John Garfield, John Ridgely, Gig Young, Arthur Kennedy, Charles Drake, Harry Carey, George Tobias. 124 mins.

Airport (1970)

Oscars (1) best supporting actress   Helen Hayes

One of the most troublesome nights in movie aviation history with all the runways of Lincoln International Airport snowed up in a blizzard and Van Heflin as a mad bomber blowing an airliner half to bits in midflight. Pilot Dean Martin brings 'em back alive including aged stowaway Helen Hayes — the first actress to win a supporting award as well as a major acting Oscar (see also *The Sin of Madelon Claudet*).

A Universal Picture, directed by George Seaton. With Burt Lancaster, Dean Martin, Jean Seberg, Jacqueline Bisset, George Kennedy, Helen Hayes, Van Heflin, Maureen Stapleton, Barry Nelson, Dana Wynter, Lloyd Nolan. Technicolor. 136 mins.

The Alamo (1960)

Oscars (1) best sound   Gordon E. Sawyer & Fred Hynes

The full story of how, in 1836, a handful of assorted Americans defended a broken down mission against the full might of the Mexican Army. Wayne, as well as directing, stars as Davy Crockett, Richard Widmark as Jim Bowie, Laurence Harvey as the commander of the mission, William Travis.

A United Artists Picture, directed by John Wayne. With John Wayne, Richard Widmark, Laurence Harvey, Richard Boone, Frankie Avalon. Todd-AO/Technicolor. 192 mins.

Alexander's Ragtime Band (1938)

Oscars (1) best music score   Alfred Newman

Large-scale Fox show-biz epic covering the period 1911 to 1938. Plenty of three-way romance (Power, Faye, Ameche) and plenty of Irving Berlin melodies, the latter helping the film win its solitary Oscar. Songs include 'Easter Parade', 'Blue Skies', and 'A Pretty Girl Is Like A Melody.'
   A 20th Century-Fox Picture, directed by Henry King. With Tyrone Power, Alice Faye, Don Ameche, Ethel Merman, Jack Haley, Jean Hersholt, Helen Westley, John Carradine. 105 mins.

Alice Doesn't Live Here Any More (1974)

Oscars (1) best acress   Ellen Burstyn

Ellen Burstyn as a widow with a teenage son trying to make an independent life for herself but finding just how difficult it can be.
   A Warner Bros. Picture, directed by Martin Scorsese. With Ellen Burstyn, Kris Kristofferson, Billy Green Bush, Diane Ladd, Lelia Goldoni, Lane Bradbury, Jodie Foster. Technicolor. 112 mins.

All About Eve (1950)

Oscars (6) best film   Darryl F. Zanuck, (producer)
            best direction   Joseph L. Mankiewicz
            best supporting actor George Sanders
            best screenplay   Joseph L. Mankiewicz
            best b/w costume design Edith Head & Charles LeMaire
            best sound recording   W. D. Flick & Roger Heman

Backstage movie about New York's theatre world with Bette Davis at the peak of her powers as fading actress Margo Channing warning everybody that 'its going to be a bumpy night.' Also on hand: Anne Baxter as her scheming understudy and critic George Sanders, cynically amused by the whole thing. With 14 nominations the most nominated film in the history of the Academy.
   A 20th Century-Fox Picture, directed by Joseph L. Mankiewicz. With Bette Davis, Anne Baxter, George Sanders, Celeste Holm, Gary Merrill, Hugh Marlowe, Thelma Ritter, Marilyn Monroe. 138 mins.

All Quiet on the Western Front (1929/30)

Oscars (2) best film   Carl Laemmle, Jr (producer)
            best direction   Lewis Milestone

Wholly pacifist movie following the experiences of a group of German schoolboys who, in World War I, volunteer to serve their fatherland for death and glory only to find their romantic illusions shattered at the front.

A Universal Picture, directed by Lewis Milestone. With Lew Ayres, Louis Wolheim, John Wray, Raymond Griffith, Slim Summerville, Russell Gleason. 140 mins.

All That Money Can Buy (1941)

Oscars (1) best music: Bernard Herrmann
            scoring of a dramatic
            picture

An adaptation of Stephen Vincent Benet's story 'The Devil & Daniel Webster', a parallel of the Faust story in a New Hampshire setting with James Craig as a young farmer signing a contract with the Devil (Walter Huston) and selling his soul for a pot of gold.

An RKO Picture, directed by William Dieterle. With Edward Arnold, Walter Huston, James Craig, Anne Shirley, Jane Darwell, Simone Simon, Gene Lockhart. 112 mins.

All The King's Men (1949)

Oscars (3) best film   Robert Rossen (producer)
            best actor   Broderick Crawford
            best supporting actress   Mercedes McCambridge

The rise and fall of 'hick' politician Willie Stark (Crawford) who becomes corrupted on his rise to power and finishes up the ruthless self-styled dictator of his home State. Adapted from the Pulitzer Prize-winning novel by Robert Penn Warren which, in turn, was based on the career of Huey 'Kingfish' Long, the Louisiana presidential contender assassinated in the mid-30s. Mercedes McCambridge's Oscar was for her debut performance as Crawford's vixenish campaign manager.

A Columbia Picture, directed by Robert Rossen. With Broderick Crawford, John Derek, Joanne Dru, John Ireland, Mercedes McCambridge, Shepperd Strudwick. 109 mins.

All The President's Men (1976)

Oscars (4) best supporting actor   Jason Robards
            best screenplay   William Goldman
            best art direction   George Jenkins
               set decoration   George Gaines
            best sound   Arthur Piantadosi, Les Fresholtz,
                                      Dick Alexander & Jim Webb

The Watergate scandal — as exposed by Washington Post reporters Bob
Woodward (Robert Redford) and Carl Bernstein (Dustin Hoffman) —
meticulously transferred to the screen by Alan Pakula and proving that
politics, providing they are sensational enough, can be both a critical
and box-office success. Jason Robards won his supporting Oscar for his
portrait of Washington Post editor, Ben Bradlee.

A Warner Bros. Picture, directed by Alan J. Pakula. With Dustin
Hoffman, Robert Redford, Jack Warden, Martin Balsam, Hal Holbrook,
Jason Robards, Jane Alexander, Meredith Baxter, Ned Beatty. Tech-
nicolor. 138 mins.

Amarcord (1974)

Oscars (1) best foreign language   Italy/France
               film

Federico Fellini reminisces about the people and day-to-day events that
occurred in a small North Italian town under the fascists in the thirties.
Fellini's fourth foreign language film award — see also *La Strada, The
Nights of Cabiria* and *8½*.

F. C. Produzioni (Rome), P. E. C. F. (Paris), directed by Federico
Fellini. With Puppela Maggio, Magali Noel, Armando Brancia, Ciccio
Ingrassia, Nandino Orfei, Luigi Rossi. Technicolor. 123 mins.

America, America (1963)

Oscars (1) best b/w art direction   Gene Callahan

Elia Kazan's basically factual account of how his Greek immigrant
uncle struggled to leave oppressed Turkey at the turn-of-the-century
and make the long journey to the promised land of America.

A Warner Bros. Picture, directed by Elia Kazan. With Stathis Giallelis,
Frank Wolff, Harry Davis, Elena Karam, Estelle Hemsley, Gregory
Rozakis. 174 mins.

An American in Paris (1951)

Oscars (6)	best film	Arthur Freed (producer)
	best story & screenplay	Alan Jay Lerner
	best colour cinematography	Alfred Gilks & John Alton
	best colour art direction colour set decoration	Cedric Gibbons & Preston Ames Edwin B. Willis & Keogh Gleason
	best colour costume design	Orry-Kelly, Walter Plunkett & Irene Sharaff
	best scoring of a musical	Johnny Green & Saul Chaplin

Gershwin musical about a footloose American painter (Gene Kelly) pursuing delightful French girl Leslie Caron and being pursued by wealthy American art promoter Nina Foch in post-war Paris.

An MGM Picture, directed by Vincente Minnelli. With Gene Kelly, Leslie Caron, Oscar Levant, Georges Guetary, Nina Foch. Technicolor. 113 mins.

Anastasia (1956)

Oscars (1)   best actress   Ingrid Bergman

Ingrid Bergman as an amnesiac refugee chosen by scheming conman Yul Brynner as the woman to be passed off as the last surviving daughter of Tsar Nicholas and Alexandra of Russia. Bergman's second Oscar, her first having been won twelve years earlier for *Gaslight*.

A 20th Century-Fox Picture, directed by Anatole Litvak. With Ingrid Bergman, Yul Brynner, Helen Hayes, Akim Tamiroff, Martita Hunt, Felix Aylmer. CinemaScope/De Luxe Color. 105 mins.

Anchors Aweigh (1945)

Oscars (1)   best scoring of a musical   Georgie Stoll

Kelly and Sinatra teamed for the first time as two sailors on shore leave in Hollywood. The film's highlight, however, is that of another teaming – Kelly and cartoon mouse Jerry who danced together in a combined live-action animated sequence.

An MGM Picture, directed by George Sidney. With Gene Kelly, Frank Sinatra, Kathryn Grayson, Jose Iturbi, Dean Stockwell. Technicolor. 140 mins.

Anna and the King of Siam (1946)

Oscars (2)   best b/w cinematography Arthur Miller
            best b/w art direction   Lyle Wheeler & William Darling
                b/w interior   Thomas Little & Frank E. Hughes
            decoration

The true story of a 19th century British governess (Irene Dunne) who took on the job of tutor to the Royal children of the King of Siam (Rex Harrison). Rodgers & Hammerstein's musical version of the story, *The King And I*, was a bigger award winner when it was released ten years later.

A 20th Century-Fox Picture, directed by John Cromwell. With Irene Dunne, Rex Harrison, Linda Darnell, Lee J. Cobb, Gale Sondergaard. 128 mins.

Anne of the 1000 Days (1969)

Oscars (1)   best costume design   Margaret Furse

The love affair and tragic marriage of Henry VIII (Richard Burton) and the young Anne Boleyn (Genevieve Bujold) who failed to give him his much desired male heir and finished, as did several others, with her head on the executioner's block.

A Universal Picture, directed by Charles Jarrott. With Richard Burton, Genevieve Bujold, Irene Papas, Anthony Quayle, John Colicos, Michael Hordern. Panavision/Technicolor. 146 mins.

Annie Get Your Gun (1950)

Oscars (1)   best scoring of a musical Adolph Deutsch & Roger Edens

MGM version of Irving Berlin's musical stage hit about the rise to fame of backwoods sharpshooting gal Annie Oakley (Betty Hutton). Howard Keel co-stars as rival sharpshooter Frank Butler, Louis Calhern as Buffalo Bill.

An MGM Picture, directed by George Sidney. With Betty Hutton, Howard Keel, Louis Calhern, J. Carrol Naish, Edward Arnold, Keenan Wynn. Technicolor. 107 mins.

Annie Hall (1977)

Oscars (4)   best film   Charles H. Joffe (producer)
            best direction   Woody Allen
            best actress   Diane Keaton
            best original
                screenplay   Woody Allen and Marshall
                                   Brickman

Autobiographical comedy by Woody Allen following the up-down relationship between a TV nightclub comic (Allen) and a young singer (Diane Keaton) who meet, fall in love, quarrel, finally break up. Like Orson Welles for *Citizen Kane,* Woody Allen was nominated in three categories - acting, writing, direction. Welles emerged the victor in only the writing category, Allen won for writing and direction. No-one has yet accomplished the hat trick. The film marked the first occasion that a studio had won the best picture award in three successive years, United Artists having won in 75 for *One Flew Over The Cuckoo's Nest* and 76 for *Rocky.*

A United Artists Picture, directed by Woody Allen. With Woody Allen, Diane Keaton, Tony Roberts, Carol Kane, Paul Simon, Shelley Duvall, Janet Margolin. De Luxe Color. 93 mins.

Anthony Adverse (1936)

Oscars (4)	best supporting actress	Gale Sondergaard
	best cinematography	Tony Gaudio
	best editing	Ralph Dawson
	best music score	Leo Forbstein

Fredric March as a young Napoleonic adventurer finding love and excitement wherever his travels take him — America, Cuba, Mexico, France, Africa. Adapted from the best-seller by Hervey Allen. Gale Sondergaard (she was the first winner in the supporting actress category) features as the friend and associate of Scottish born merchant Edmund Gwenn.*

A Warner Bros. Picture, directed by Mervyn LeRoy. With Fredric March, Olivia de Havilland, Anita Louise, Edmund Gwenn, Claude Rains, Donald Woods, Louis Hayward, Gale Sondergaard, Akim Tamiroff. 136 mins.

*Note: Erich Wolfgang Korngold composed the score for *Anthony Adverse* and by rights should have been awarded the Oscar. Leo Forbstein was only music director on the movie.

The Apartment (1960)

Oscars (5)	best film	Billy Wilder (producer)
	best direction	Billy Wilder
	best story & screenplay	Billy Wilder & I. A. L. Diamond
	best b/w art direction	Alexander Trauner
	b/w set decoration	Edward G. Boyle
	best editing	Daniel Mandell

Billy Wilder's acid comedy about a young, stuck-in-the-groove executive (Jack Lemmon) who advances his prospects of promotion by letting out his apartment to fellow executives and their girl friends. The last best picture winner to be filmed in black-and-white.

A United Artists Picture, directed by Billy Wilder. With Jack Lemmon, Shirley MacLaine, Fred MacMurray, Ray Walston, David Lewis, Jack Kruschen, Joan Shawlee, Edie Adams, Panavision. 125 mins.

Arise My Love (1940)

Oscars (1) best original story   Benjamin Glazer & John S. Toldy

Paramount wartime propaganda piece with Claudette Colbert involved with imprisoned flier Ray Milland in the latter days of the Spanish Civil War.

A Paramount Picture, directed by Mitchell Leisen. With Claudette Colbert, Ray Milland, Dennis O'Keefe, Walter Abel, Dick Purcell, George Zucco. 100 mins.

Around the World in Eighty Days (1956)

Oscars (5)	best film	Michael Todd (producer)
	best screenplay: adapted	James Poe, John Farrow & S. J. Perelman
	best colour cinematography	Lionel Lindon
	best editing	Gene Ruggiero & Paul Weatherwax
	best music score of a drama or comedy	Victor Young

Can Jules Verne's staid, confident Englishman Phineas Fogg (David Niven) win his bet and go round the world in 80 days at the turn-of-the-century. He can and does in exactly that time and the equal of 165 screen minutes. Victor Young's Oscar (his only one after 19 nominations) was awarded posthumously, the composer having died just four months before the '56 awards were presented.

A Todd-United Artists Picture, directed by Michael Anderson. With David Niven, Cantinflas, Robert Newton, Shirley MacLaine and all-star cast. Todd-AO/Eastman Color. 165 mins.

The Awful Truth (1937)

Oscars (1) best direction   Leo McCarey

Irene Dunne and Cary Grant, about to get divorced, find that they love each other after all and ultimately link up again. Wild matrimonial farce expertly directed by McCarey who snatched the director's prize from William Dieterle, maker of 1937's best picture, *The Life of Emile Zola*.

A Columbia Picture, directed by Leo McCarey. With Irene Dunne, Cary Grant, Ralph Bellamy, Alexander D'Arcy, Cecil Cunningham. 90 mins.

The Bachelor and the Bobby-Soxer (1947)

Oscars (1) best original screenplay   Sidney Sheldon

RKO comedy of the late 40's with artist-playboy Cary Grant finding himself as an embarrassed knight-in-shining armour of lovesick, 17-year-old Shirley Temple. Myrna Loy as a lady judge adds grace, elegance and common sense.

An RKO Picture, directed by Irving Reis. With Cary Grant, Myrna Loy, Shirley Temple, Rudy Vallee, Ray Collins, Harry Davenport. 95 mins.

The Bad and the Beautiful (1952)

Oscars (5) best supporting actress   Gloria Grahame
best screenplay   Charles Schnee
best b/w cinematography Robert Surtees
best b/w art direction   Cedric Gibbons & Edward Carfagno
b/w set decoration   Edwin B. Willis & Keogh Gleason
best b/w costume design Helen Rose

Ruthless Hollywood film producer Kirk Douglas reaches the top by double-crossing each of his three closest colleagues — hardworking young director Barry Sullivan, Pulitzer-Prize winning author Dick Powell and alcoholic star Lana Turner. Hard-hitting Hollywood movie said to be based partly on the career of David Selznick.

An MGM Picture, directed by Vincente Minnelli. With Lana Turner, Kirk Douglas, Walter Pidgeon, Dick Powell, Barry Sullivan, Gloria Grahame. 118 mins.

Bad Girl (1931/32)

Oscars (2) best direction   Frank Borzage
best writing: adaptation Edwin Burke

Part melodrama, part comedy, spanning one year in the life of store clerk James Dunn and the girl he has to marry after they have spent one night together.

A Fox Picture, directed by Frank Borzage. With James Dunn, Sally Eilers, Minna Gombell, Frank Darien, William Pawley. 88 mins.

The Barefoot Contessa (1954)

Oscars (1) best supporting actor   Edmond O'Brien

Earthy Spanish flamenco dancer, discovered in a Madrid night club, becomes a major Hollywood star and then rejects the tinsel world she has conquered. Ava Gardner is the dancer, Bogie a cynical movie director, Edmond O'Brien (memorable) a high-powered, sweating press agent.

A United Artists Picture, directed by Joseph L. Mankiewicz. With Humphrey Bogart, Ava Gardner, Edmond O'Brien, Marius Goring, Valentina Cortesa, Rossano Brazzi. Technicolor. 128 mins.

Barry Lyndon (1975)

Oscars (4) best cinematography   John Alcott
best art direction   Ken Adam & Roy Walker
set decoration   Vernon Dixon
best costume design   Ulla-Britt Soderlund &
Milena Canonero
best music scoring: Leonard Rosenman
adaptation

The rise to power and eventual fall from grace of an amorous young Irish adventurer (Ryan O'Neal). Based on Thackeray's novel *The Memoirs of Barry Lyndon, Esq* and set in 18th century Ireland and Europe.

A Warner Bros. Picture, directed by Stanley Kubrick. With Ryan O'Neal, Marisa Berenson, Patrick Magee, Hardy Kruger, Steven Berkoff, Gay Hamilton. Eastman Color. 187 mins.

Battleground (1949)

Oscars (2) best story & screenplay   Robert Pirosh
best b/w cinematography Paul C. Vogel

The Battle of the Bulge — the Germans' last great offensive of World War II — as experienced by the men of an American Airborne Infantry division in the bleak, snow-covered Ardennes near Bastogne.

An MGM Picture, directed by William A. Wellman. With Van Johnson, Ricardo Montalban, John Hodiak, George Murphy, Marshall Thompson. 118 mins.

Becket (1964)

Oscars (1) best screenplay: Edward Anhalt

Film version of Anouilh's stage play *Becket* about the relationship between church and politics in twelfth century England and, more dramatically, the conflict between two men — the Norman King Henry II (Peter O'Toole) and his former Saxon companion (Richard Burton), later Archbishop of Canterbury.

A Paramount Picture, directed by Peter Glenville, With Richard Burton, Peter O'Toole, Sir Donald Wolfit, Sir John Gielgud, Martita Hunt. Panavision/Technicolor. 148 mins.

Bedknobs and Broomsticks (1971)

Oscars (1) best special visual effects   Danny Lee, Eustace Lycett & Alan Maley

'Mary Poppins' country revisited by Disney with apprentice witch Angela Lansbury delighting the three evacuee children in her care by doing most of her travelling on a magic bedstead. The Oscar winning special effects included a live action/animated football game in Noboombu Land refereed by an unlucky David Tomlinson.

A Walt Disney Picture, directed by Robert Stevenson. With Angela Lansbury, David Tomlinson, Roddy McDowall, Sam Jaffe, John Ericson, Bruce Forsyth. Technicolor. 117 mins.

The Bells of St. Mary's (1945)

Oscars (1) best sound recording   Stephen Dunn

Leo McCarey's attempt to cash in on the success of *Going My Way*. Bing Crosby again as a priest (Father Chuck), Ingrid Bergman as a tubercular nun — but, alas, no Barry Fitzgerald.

An RKO Picture, directed by Leo McCarey. With Bing Crosby, Ingrid Bergman, Henry Travers, Joan Carroll, Martha Sleeper. 126 mins.

Ben-Hur (1959)

Oscars (11)	best film	Sam Zimbalist (producer)
	best direction	William Wyler
	best actor	Charlton Heston
	best supporting actor	Hugh Griffith
	best colour cinematography	Robert Surtees
	best colour art direction	William A. Horning & Edward Carfagno
	colour set decoration	Hugh Hunt
	best colour costume design	Elizabeth Haffenden
	best editing	Ralph E. Winters & John D. Dunning
	best sound	Franklin E. Milton
	best sound effects	A. Arnold Gillespie
	visual effects	Robert MacDonald
	audible effects	Milo Lory
	best music score of a drama or comedy	Miklos Rozsa

General Lew Wallace's famous novel of how Christianity gradually made inroads into the pagan civilization of ancient Rome. Ends in a spectacular blood bath in the chariot arena with converted Christian Ben-Hur (Charlton Heston) defeating Roman commander and former boyhood friend Messala (Stephen Boyd) in one of the most spectacular screen races of all time. The only remake to win the best picture Academy Award and with 11 Oscars the all-time Academy record holder.

An MGM Picture, directed by William Wyler. With Charlton Heston, Jack Hawkins, Hugh Griffith, Martha Scott, Cathy O'Donnell, Haya Hayareet, Stephen Boyd, Sam Jaffe, Finlay Currie. Camera 65/ Panavision/Technicolor. 217 mins.

Best Years of Our Lives (1946)

Oscars (7)	best film	Samuel Goldwyn (producer)
	best direction	William Wyler
	best actor	Fredric March
	best supporting actor	Harold Russell
	best screenplay	Robert E. Sherwood
	best editing	Daniel Mandell
	best music score of a drama or comedy	Hugo Friedhofer

Sam Goldwyn's classic about the problems facing three ex-servicemen — a sergeant (Fredric March), a captain (Dana Andrews) and a handless sailor (Harold Russell) — when they return to their home town at the end of World War II.

A Sam Goldwyn Production (released through RKO Pictures), directed by William Wyler. With Myrna Loy, Fredric March, Dana Andrews, Teresa Wright, Virginia Mayo, Cathy O'Donnell, Hoagy Carmichael. 172 mins.

The Big Broadcast of 1938 (1938)

Oscars (1) best song   'Thanks For The Memory'
                                         (Ralph Rainger, music:
                                         Leo Robin, lyrics)

Fourth in Paramount's series of musical revues of the thirties and famous for introducing the song that became Bob Hope's theme tune on his radio and TV shows.

A Paramount Picture, directed by Mitchell Leisen. With W. C. Fields, Martha Raye, Dorothy Lamour, Shirley Ross, Lynne Overman, Bob Hope, Ben Blue. 97 mins.

The Big Country (1958)

Oscars (1) best supporting actor   Burl Ives

Large-scale western with two opposing landowners, wealthy Charles Bickford and patriarch Burl Ives, fighting over the grazing water known as Big Muddy. Stars Gregory Peck, Charlton Heston, Jean Simmons and Carroll Baker help settle the matter. The memorable music score by Jerome Moross was nominated but did not prove a winner, the Oscar going to Dimitri Tiomkin for *The Old Man and The Sea.*

A United Artists Picture, directed by William Wyler. With Gregory Peck, Jean Simmons, Carroll Baker, Charlton Heston, Burl Ives, Charles Bickford. Technirama/Technicolor. 165 mins.

The Big House (1929/30)

Oscars (2) best writing achievement   Frances Marion
            best sound recording   Douglas Shearer

One of the toughest and most realistic of the early prison dramas with Wallace Beery (in a role originally intended for Lon Chaney) as a condemned convict and Robert Montgomery as a cowardly informer.

Shearer's sound recording Oscar was the first to be awarded in the category.

An MGM Picture, directed by George Hill. With Chester Morris, Wallace Beery, Lewis Stone, Robert Montgomery, Leila Hyams, George F. Marion. 88 mins.

The Bishop's Wife (1947)

Oscars (1) best sound recording   Gordon Sawyer

Man-of-the-world angel (Cary Grant) comes to the aid of over-worked bishop David Niven in answer to the latter's prayer for funds for a new city cathedral. Goldwyn whimsy; the bishop's wife of the title is Loretta Young.

A Sam Goldwyn Production (released through RKO Pictures), directed by Henry Koster. With Cary Grant, Loretta Young, David Niven, Monty Woolley, James Gleason, Gladys Cooper, Elsa Lanchester. 105 mins.

Black and White in Colour (1976)

Oscars (1) best foreign language film Ivory Coast

A satirical look at racism, colonialism and imperialism in Africa during World War I when a handful of Frenchmen find belatedly that they are at war with Germany and attack some Germans living in a nearby European community — both sides eventually relying on native armies to fight their respective 'causes'.

An Arthur Cohn Production/Societe Ivoirienne De Cinema, directed by Jean Jaques Annaud. With Jean Carmet, Jacques Dufilho, Catherine Rouvel, Jacques Spiesser, Dora Doll, Maurice Barrier. Eastmancolor. 100 mins.

Black Narcissus (1947)

Oscars (2) best colour cinematography Jack Cardiff
            best colour art direction   Alfred Junge
                  set decoration   Alfred Junge

Rumer Godden's story of five British nuns, led by Deborah Kerr, who set up school and a hospital in the Himalayas. Historically important for its notable colour designs and photography, both honoured by the Academy.

An Archers Production, directed by Michael Powell & Emeric Pressburger. With Deborah Kerr, Sabu, David Farrar, Flora Robson, Esmond Knight, Jean Simmons, Kathleen Ryan. Technicolor. 100 mins.

Black Orpheus (1959)

Oscars (1) best foreign language film France/Italy

Updated version of the Orpheus legend with the doomed lovers playing out their game of inevitable death amid the riotous pageantry of a carnival in Rio de Janiero. Superb colour and bossa nova score.

Dispatfilm Paris, Gemma Cinematografica, directed by Marcel Camus. With Breno Mello, Marpessa Dawn, Lourdes De Oliveira, Lea Garcia. Eastman Color. 98 mins.

The Black Swan (1942)

Oscars (1) best colour cinematography   Leon Shamroy

Pirate swashbuckler, based on the novel by Rafael Sabatini, with Tyrone Power as the athletic hero, George Sanders the red-bearded villain and Laird Cregar the real-life reformed pirate Sir Henry Morgan. The film earned the late Leon Shamroy the first of his four Academy Awards for colour cinematography, a record that still stands to this day. Shamroy's other wins: *Wilson* (44), *Leave Her To Heaven* (45), *Cleopatra* (63).

A 20th Century-Fox Picture, directed by Henry King. With Tyrone Power, Maureen O'Hara, Laird Cregar, Thomas Mitchell, George Sanders, Anthony Quinn, George Zucco. Technicolor. 85 mins.

Blithe Spirit (1946)

Oscars (1) best special effects   Thomas Howard, photographic

Noel Coward's sophisticated stage play about a famous novelist (Rex Harrison) who finds his marriage to wife no. 2 (Constance Cummings) complicated by the return of his first wife's ghost (Kay Hammond). Not surprisingly, spiritualist Margaret Rutherford is the cause of all the trouble.

A Two Cities-Cineguild Picture, directed by David Lean. With Rex Harrison, Constance Cummings, Kay Hammond, Margaret Rutherford, Joyce Carey. Technicolor. 97 mins.

Blood and Sand (1941)

Oscars (1) best colour cinematography Ernest Palmer & Ray Rennahan

Tyrone Power as an innocent young bullfighter involved with dangers not only inside the bullring but also with those outside — Spanish aristocrat Rita Hayworth and childhood sweetheart Linda Darnell.

A 20th Century-Fox Picture, directed by Rouben Mamoulian. With Tyrone Power, Linda Darnell, Rita Hayworth, Nazimova, Anthony Quinn, J. Carrol Naish, John Carradine, Laird Cregar. Technicolor. 124 mins.

Blood on the Sun (1945)

Oscars (1) best b/w art direction   Wiard Ihnen
              int. decoration   A. Roland Fields

American newsman James Cagney back in Tokyo in the 20's fighting a one-man campaign against Japanese militarists planning world conquest.

A United Artists Picture, directed by Frank Lloyd. With James Cagney, Sylvia Sidney, Wallace Ford, Rosemary De Camp, Robert Armstrong, John Emery. 98 mins.

Blossoms in the Dust (1941)

Oscars (1) best colour art direction   Cedric Gibbons & Urie McCleary
              int. decoration Edwin B. Willis

Greer Garson as Edna Gladney, the famous child welfare worker who formed a Texas orphanage after the loss of her own child and did much to remove the 19th century social stigma from illegitimate children. Soap opera with a message and the film that made Garson a superstar.

An MGM Picture, directed by Mervyn LeRoy. With Greer Garson, Walter Pidgeon, Felix Bressart. Marsha Hunt, Fay Holden, Samuel S. Hinds. Technicolor. 100 mins.

Body and Soul (1947)

Oscars (1) best editing   Francis Lyon & Robert Parrish

One of the half-dozen most famous boxing films of all time with John Garfield fighting his way up from the Lower East Side to Middleweight Champion of the World only to find himself owned completely 'body and soul' by the shady characters who run his seedy racket.

A United Artists Picture, directed by Robert Rossen. With John Garfield, Lili Palmer, Hazel Brooks, Anne Revere, William Conrad, Joseph Pevney, Canada Lee. 104 mins.

Bonnie and Clyde (1967)

Oscars (2) best supporting actress   Estelle Parsons
             best colour cinematography Burnett Guffey

The real-life exploits of Bonnie Parker (Faye Dunaway) and Clyde
Barrow (Warren Beatty) who created a reign of terror and killed 18
people whilst robbing banks in the American South-West of the early
30's. Co-star Estelle Parsons won her Oscar for her preacher's daughter
wife of Barrow's brother Buck — played by Gene Hackman.

   A Warner Bros. Picture, directed by Arthur Penn. With Warren
Beatty, Faye Dunaway, Michael J. Pollard, Gene Hackman, Estelle
Parsons. Technicolor. 111 mins.

Born Free (1966)

Oscars (2) best original music score John Barry
             best song   'Born Free'
                                         (John Barry, music:
                                         Don Black, lyrics)

The true story of Joy Adamson's life with Elsa, the tame lioness she
raised from a cub in the African bush and then gradually reconditioned
to her normal wildlife existance.

   A Columbia Picture, directed by James Hill. With Virginia McKenna,
Bill Travers, Geoffrey Keen. Panavision/Technicolor. 95 mins.

Born Yesterday (1950)

Oscars (1) best actress   Judy Holliday

Judy Holliday as *the* dumb blonde of all time, taken to Washington on
a business trip by millionaire junk dealer Broderick Crawford and given
a crash course in culture by literate young journalist William Holden.
Based on the Broadway hit by Garson Kanin.

   A Columbia Picture, directed by George Cukor. With Judy Holliday,
William Holden, Broderick Crawford, Howard St. John, Frank Otto.
103 mins.

Bound for Glory (1976)

Oscars (2) best cinematography   Haskell Wexler
             best adaptation music   Leonard Rosenman
                score

The early career of Oklahoma-born folk singer Woody Guthrie, following him from his no-hope life in the depressed Southwest of the mid-30's to California where he successfully breaks into radio before eventually opting for a life on the open road. Based on Guthrie's autobiography and featuring David Carradine in the lead role.

A United Artists Picture, directed by Hal Ashby. With David Carradine, Ronny Cox, Melinda Dillon, Gail Strickland, John Lehne, Randy Quaid. Panavision/De Luxe Colour. 148 mins.

Boys' Town (1938)

Oscars (2)	best actor	Spencer Tracy
	best original story	Dore Schary & Eleanore Griffin

Spencer Tracy as Father Flanagan, the priest who helped create the first community for teenage boys regardless of race or creed. His biggest problem? Mickey Rooney as a tough, poker-playing aggressive rebel. With his performance in this film Tracy became the first actor to win two best acting Oscars having also won the previous year for *Captains Courageous*.

An MGM Picture, directed by Norman Taurog. With Spencer Tracy, Mickey Rooney, Henry Hull, Leslie Fenton, Addison Richards, Edward Norris. 96 mins.

The Brave One (1956)

Oscars (1) best motion picture story Harry Franklin & Merrill G. White
from an original story by Robert Rich

A young boy adopts a bull as a pet and then travels all the way to Mexico City to try to prevent it going into the ring for a duel to the death with Mexico's greatest toreador.

An RKO Picture, directed by Irving Rapper. With Michael Ray, Rodolfo Hoyos, Elsa Cardenas, Carlos Navarro, Joi Lansing, Fermin Rivera. CinemaScope/Technicolor. 94 mins.

Breakfast at Tiffanys (1961)

Oscars (2)	best music score of a drama or comedy	Henry Mancini
	best song	'Moon River' (Henry Mancini, music: Johnny Mercer, lyrics)

The adventures of bizarre 'super-tramp' Holly Golightly (Audrey Hepburn) with struggling writer George Peppard in New York's Manhattan. Adapted — and toned down — from Truman Capote's best-selling novella.

A Paramount Picture, directed by Blake Edwards. With Audrey Hepburn, George Peppard, Patricia Neal, Martin Balsam, Mickey Rooney, Buddy Ebsen, John McGiver. Technicolor. 115 mins.

Breaking the Sound Barrier (1952)

(*Original U.K. title: The Sound Barrier*)

Oscars (1) best sound recording   London Films Sound Dept.

David Lean's film about man's obsession with flying planes faster than the speed of sound. Appropriately enough it won the best sound recording award although Ralph Richardson, as a ruthless aircraft designer-pioneer, driven on by his vision of conquering the unknown, should well have been among the best actor nominees. He wasn't, which was surprising considering the New York critics had named him best actor of the year in their annual poll.

A London Films Production, directed by David Lean. With Ralph Richardson, Ann Todd, Nigel Patrick, John Justin, Dinah Sheridan, Joseph Tomelty, Denholm Elliott. 118 mins.

The Bridge of San Luis Rey (1928/29)

Oscars (1) best art direction   Cedric Gibbons

1929 version (remade in 1944) of Thornton Wilder's Pulitzer Prize-winning novel — set in 18th century Peru — about five people who meet their deaths when a rickety bridge collapses and hurtles them to their doom.

An MGM Picture, directed by Charles Brabin. With Lily Damita, Ernest Torrence, Raquel Torres, Don Alvarado, Duncan Renaldo, Henry B. Walthall. 10 reels.

The Bridge on the River Kwai (1957)

Oscars (7)	best film	(Sam Spiegel, producer)
	best direction	David Lean
	best actor	Alec Guinness
	best screenplay	Pierre Boulle
	best cinematography	Jack Hildyard
	best editing	Peter Taylor
	best music scoring	Malcolm Arnold

Pierre Boulle's famous story — set in the jungles of Siam during World War II — about the construction by British P.O.W.'s of a railway bridge on the murderous Bangkok to Rangoon railroad and of its subsequent destruction by a small commando unit. Guinness played the British colonel in charge of the bridge building; David Lean became the first-ever British director to win an American Oscar.

A Columbia Picture, directed by David Lean. With William Holden, Alec Guinness, Jack Hawkins, Sessue Hayakawa, James Donald, Geoffrey Horne. CinemaScope/Technicolor. 161 mins.

The Bridges at Toko-Ri (1955)

Oscars (1) best special effects   Paramount Studios

James A. Michener tale of the Korean War with jet pilots William Holden and Mickey Rooney performing heroically on a special mission against the communists. Grace Kelly is the wife who waits behind, Fredric March the admiral-in-chief. Notable special effects work in the climactic blowing of the North Korean bridges and the aerial photography.

A Paramount Picture, directed by Mark Robson. With William Holden, Grace Kelly, Fredric March, Mickey Rooney, Robert Strauss, Charles McGraw. Vista Vision/Technicolor. 103 mins.

The Broadway Melody (1928/29)

Oscars (1) best film   (Harry Rapf, producer)

The very first MGM musical with songs like 'Wedding of The Painted Doll' (presented as a big 2-colour Technicolor production number), 'Give My Regards to Broadway' and 'You Were Meant For Me.' Advertised with the words "All Talking, All Singing, All Dancing" it featured Charles King as an amorous songwriter who breaks up the show-biz sister act of Bessie Love and Anita Page.

An MGM Picture, directed by Harry Beaumont. With Bessie Love, Anita Page, Charles King, Jed Prouty, Kenneth Thompson, Mary Doran, Eddie Kane. Scenes in 2-colour Technicolor. 110 mins.

The Broadway Melody of 1936 (1935)

Oscars (1) best dance direction   David Gould
                for the 'I've Got a Feeling You're Fooling' number (Gould
                was also named the same year for his work on *Folies
                Bergere* — see page 50.)

The first of MGM's subsequent Broadway Melody series with Eleanor Powell at the top of her dancing form and Jack Benny stealing the acting honours as a Walter Winchell-type columnist always panning things he doesn't like. Robert Taylor features as a young producer.

An MGM Picture, directed by Roy Del Ruth. With Jack Benny, Eleanor Powell, Robert Taylor, June Knight, Una Merkel, Buddy Ebsen. 118 mins.

Broken Lance (1954)

Oscars (1) best motion picture story Philip Yordan

Spencer Tracy as a beef baron of the prairies, Katy Jurado as his Indian wife and Richard Widmark, Robert Wagner and Hugh O'Brian as his three sons. A 'King Lear' of the West and a remake of Joseph Mankie-wicz's *House of Strangers*.

A 20th Century-Fox Picture, directed by Edward Dmytryk. With Spencer Tracy, Richard Widmark, Katy Jurado, Jean Peters, Hugh O'Brian, Earl Holliman. CinemaScope/De Luxe Color. 96 mins.

Bullitt (1968)

Oscars (1) best editing   Frank P. Keller

Steve McQueen as a cop and Robert Vaughn as an opportunist politician after a well-organised underworld syndicate in the streets of San Francisco. Highspot — and the main reason it won the best editing award — the stunning up-and-down car chase over the deep 'Frisco hills.

A Warner Bros. Picture, directed by Peter Yates. With Steve McQueen, Robert Vaughn, Jacqueline Bisset, Don Gordon, Robert Duvall, Simon Oakland, Norman Fell. Technicolor. 114 mins.

Butch Cassidy and the Sundance Kid (1969)

Oscars (4) best story & screenplay   William Goldman
            best cinematography   Conrad Hall
            best original music score Burt Bacharach
            best song   'Raindrops Keep Fallin' On My
                                      Head'
                                      (Burt Bacharach, music:
                                      Hal David, lyrics)

The final years of two of the West's most legendary characters who, around the turn of the century, operated out of a place called 'Hole in

The Wall' and finished their days less than gloriously in the dusty towns of Bolivia. Newman is Cassidy, Robert Redford the Sundance Kid.

A 20th Century-Fox Picture, directed by George Roy Hill. With Paul Newman, Robert Redford, Katharine Ross, Strother Martin, Henry Jones, Jeff Corey, George Furth, Cloris Leachman. Panavision/De Luxe Color. 110 mins.

Butterfield 8 (1960)

Oscars (1) best actress   Elizabeth Taylor

Elizabeth Taylor as a New York whore caught up with the socially prominent and very much married Laurence Harvey. From the novel by John O'Hara. The intriguing title is simply Taylor's telephone number for those clients with the urge.

An MGM Picture, directed by Daniel Mann. With Elizabeth Taylor, Laurence Harvey, Eddie Fisher, Dina Merrill, Mildred Dunnock. Cinemascope/Metrocolor. 108 mins.

Butterflies are Free (1972)

Oscars (1) best supporting actress   Eileen Heckart

Bitter-sweet love story about a feckless would-be-actress (Goldie Hawn) and a blind young songwriter (Edward Albert) living in the same small apartment block. Adapted by Leonard Gershe from his own play and dominated by Eileen Heckart as Mr. Albert's overpowering ma!

A Columbia Picture, directed by Milton Katselas. With Goldie Hawn, Edward Albert, Eileen Heckart, Michael Glasser, Mike Warren. Eastman Color. 109 mins.

Cabaret (1972)

Oscars (8)	best direction	Bob Fosse
	best actress	Liza Minnelli
	best supporting actor	Joel Grey
	best cinematography	Geoffrey Unsworth
	best art direction	Rolf Zehetbauer & Jurgen Kiebach
	set direction	Herbert Strabl
	best editing	David Bretherton
	best sound	Robert Knudson & David Hildyard
	best scoring: adaptation & original song score	Ralph Burns

Sally Bowles' experiences as a night club singer in pre-war Berlin just prior to the country's take-over by the Nazis. A musical version of John Van Druten's play which, in turn, was based on the collected stories of Christopher Isherwood, 'Goodbye to Berlin.' Liza Minnelli is the 'divinely decadent' Sally, Joel Grey the lurid MC of the night club in which she works.

An Allied Artists Picture, directed by Bob Fosse. With Liza Minnelli, Michael York, Helmut Griem, Joel Grey, Fritz Weber, Marisa Berenson. Technicolor. 123 mins.

Cactus Flower (1969)

Oscars (1)	best supporting actress	Goldie Hawn

Broadway comedy-farce, set in Greenwich Village, and based on the misunderstandings between four people who eventually sort themselves out with the right partners. Walter Matthau is a goodtime bachelor dentist, Ingrid Bergman his secretary, Goldie Hawn his kooky blonde girl friend and Rick Lenz the struggling young writer with an apartment next door.

A Columbia Picture, directed by Gene Saks. With Walter Matthau, Ingrid Bergman, Goldie Hawn, Jack Weston, Rick Lenz. Technicolor. 104 mins.

Calamity Jane (1953)

Oscars (1) best song   'Secret Love'
                                       (Sammy Fain, music:
                                           Paul Francis Webster, lyrics)

Musical horse opera with an effervescent Doris Day clad in buckskin in the title role and Howard Keel as her deadshot singing lover Wild Bill Hickok. The fine Sammy Fain/Paul Francis Webster score included not only the Oscar-winning 'Secret Love' but also 'The Deadwood Stage', 'The Black Hills of Dakota' and 'I Just Blew In From The Windy City.'
   A Warner Bros. Picture, directed by David Butler. With Doris Day, Howard Keel, Allyn McLerie, Philip Carey, Dick Wesson. Technicolor. 101 mins.

Call Me Madam (1953)

Oscars (1) best scoring of a musical   Alfred Newman

Irving Berlin's satirical musical about socialite Perle Mesta's life as a Washington hostess and Lichtenburg ambassadress. Ethel Merman ('The Hostess with The Mostess') features as the Mesta character.
   A 20th Century-Fox Picture, directed by Walter Lang. With Ethel Merman, Donald O'Connor, Vera-Ellen, George Sanders, Billy De Wolfe, Helmut Dantine, Technicolor. 117 mins.

Camelot (1967)

Oscars (3) best colour art direction   John Truscott & Edward Carrere
                             set decoration John W. Brown
            best colour costume design John Truscott
            best music adaptation   Alfred Newman & Ken Darby
                or treatment

Arthurian legend and the stirring, romantic events of the days of the Knights of The Round Table set to music by Frederick Loewe and Alan Jay Lerner. Richard Harris is Arthur, Vanessa Redgrave Guenevere and Franco Nero, Lancelot du Lac. Based on T. H. White's 'The Once and Future King.'

A Warner Bros. Picture, directed by Joshua Logan. With Richard Harris, Vanessa Redgrave, Franco Nero, David Hemmings, Lionel Jeffries, Laurence Naismith. Panavision 70/Technicolor. 181 mins.

The Candidate (1972)

Oscars (1) best story and screenplay Jeremy Larner

The fortunes of a young lawyer-civil rights worker (Robert Redford) who is gradually turned, against his better judgement, into a Kennedy-style U.S. Senator by the party's campaign machine.

A Warner Bros. Picture, directed by Michael Ritchie. With Robert Redford, Peter Boyle, Don Porter, Allen Garfield, Karen Carlson, Melvyn Douglas. Technicolor. 110 mins.

Captain Carey, U.S.A. (1950)
(*G.B. title: After Midnight*)

Oscars (1) best song   'Mona Lisa'
                                          (Ray Evans & Jay Livingston:
                                          music & lyrics)

Alan Ladd involved in obscure intrigue in post-war Italy. The Oscar winning song (made famous by Nat King Cole) is now the only reason the film is remembered.

A Paramount Picture, directed by Mitchell Leisen. With Alan Ladd, Wanda Hendrix, Francis Lederer, Joseph Calleia, Celia Lovsky. 83 mins.

Captains Courageous (1937)

Oscars (1) best actor   Spencer Tracy

The spoilt son of a business tycoon finds humility and learns life's important lessons the hard way during his voyage on a small fishing boat and through his acquaintance with an understanding Portuguese fisherman (Spencer Tracy). Freddie Bartholomew stars as the boy; from the Kipling novel of the same name.

An MGM Picture, directed by Victor Fleming. With Freddie Bartholomew, Spencer Tracy, Lionel Barrymore, Melvyn Douglas, Mickey Rooney, Charley Grapewin, John Carradine. 115 mins.

Casablanca (1943)

Oscars (3) best film   (Hal B. Wallis, producer)
            best direction   Michael Curtiz
            best written screenplay   Julius J. Epstein, Philip G.
                                 Epstein & Howard Koch

One of the finest casts of all time sweat it out in the North African town of Casablanca — 'haven to the refugees fleeing persecution in Nazi Europe.' Cynicism, intrigue, disillusionment, old love rekindled and Humphrey Bogart as Rick ordering pianist Dooley Wilson to play 'As Time Goes By.'

A Warner Bros. Picture, directed by Michael Curtiz. With Humphrey Bogart, Ingrid Bergman, Paul Henreid, Claude Rains, Conrad Veidt, Sydney Greenstreet, Peter Lorre, S. Z. Sakall. 102 mins.

Cat Ballou (1965)

Oscars (1) best actor   Lee Marvin

Rare western parody with Jane Fonda as a well educated young lady who turns outlaw to avenge her father's death and Lee Marvin as the whiskey-sodden, has-been gunfighter she employs to help her in her task.

A Columbia Picture, directed by Elliott Silverstein. With Jane Fonda, Lee Marvin, Michael Callan, Dwayne Hickman, Nat King Cole, Stubby Kaye. Technicolor. 96 mins.

Cavalcade (1932/33)

Oscars (3) best film   (Winfield Sheehan, producer)
            best direction   Frank Lloyd
            best art direction   William S. Darling

Noel Coward's famous panorama of English history observed from the point of view of one family as they live through the period from 1899 to the Great War and its aftermath. Among the spectacular highlights: the celebrations at the Relief of Mafeking, the departure of the troops to the war, the Zeppelin raids, the sinking of the Titanic.

A Fox Picture, directed by Frank Lloyd. With Diana Wynyard, Clive Brook, Una O'Connor, Herbert Mundin, Beryl Mercer, Irene Browne, Tempe Pigott. 115 mins.

The Champ (1931/32)

Oscars (2) best actor   Wallace Beery
            best original story   Frances Marion

Wallace Beery splitting his Oscar with Fredric March (the only best actor tie in the history of the Academy) as a drunken broken-down boxer who makes a comeback for the sake of his idolizing young son, Jackie Cooper. March's award was for his performance as *Dr. Jekyll and Mr. Hyde*.

An MGM Picture, directed by King Vidor. With Wallace Beery, Jackie Cooper, Irene Rich, Jesse Scott, Roscoe Ates, Hale Hamilton. 87 mins.

Champion (1949)

Oscars (1) best editing   Harry Gerstad

Kirk Douglas in one of his early 'heel' parts as a young middleweight who tramples over his crippled brother, wife, assorted girl friends and long-suffering manager on the way to the top. The ferocious boxing scenes helped Gerstad win his Oscar for the best editing of the year.

A United Artists Picture, directed by Mark Robson. With Kirk Douglas, Marilyn Maxwell, Arthur Kennedy, Paul Stewart, Ruth Roman, Lola Albright. 99 mins.

The Charge of the Light Brigade (1936)

Oscars (1) best assistant direction   Jack Sullivan

$1,200,000 account of the famous charge by around 700 English cavalrymen — led on this occasion by Errol Flynn — against the Russian artillery in the Crimea in the 1850's.

A Warner Bros. Picture, directed by Michael Curtiz. With Errol Flynn, Olivia de Havilland, Patric Knowles, Henry Stephenson, Nigel Bruce, Donald Crisp, David Niven, 115 mins.

Charly (1968)

Oscars (1) best actor   Cliff Robertson

Provocative movie about a man with the mind of a child (Cliff Robertson) who becomes a genius virtually overnight after a brain operation only to slip back once more into his original feeble-minded state. Claire

Bloom features as the therapist who has an affair with the transformed man during his brief period of normality and then helplessly watches his deterioration.

A Selmur-Robertson Associates Production, directed by Ralph Nelson. With Cliff Robertson, Claire Bloom, Leon Janney, Lilia Skala, Dick Van Patton, William Dwyer. Techniscope/Technicolor. 103 mins.

Chinatown (1974)

Oscars (1) best original screenplay   Robert Towne

Many-layered private-eye thriller with brash matrimonial investigator Jack Nicholson involved with corruption, mystery, double-cross and murder in 1937 Los Angeles. Faye Dunaway is the enigmatic femme fatale, John Huston the embodiment of smiling villainy and, for a few seconds, Roman Polanski, a menacing little hood with a knife.

A Paramount Picture, directed by Roman Polanski. With Jack Nicholson, Faye Dunaway, John Huston, Perry Lopez, John Hillerman, Darrell Zwerling, Diane Ladd, Roman Polanski. Panavision/Technicolor. 131 mins.

Cimarron (1930/31)

Oscars (3) best film   (Louis Sarecky, Associate
                                          Producer)
            best writing adaptation   Howard Estabrook
            best art direction   Max Ree

Western epic by Edna Ferber (the only western ever to win a best picture Oscar) about the development of the small Oklahoma town of Osage from its foundations in the 1880's to its growth into a great modern industrial city. The films highlight: The frenzied Land Rush in which the first settlers race in covered wagons and on horseback to claim their land. Other westerns to have been nominated for best picture: *In Old Arizona* (28/29), *Stagecoach* (39), *The Ox-Bow Incident* (43), *High Noon* (52), *Shane* (53), *The Alamo* (60), *How The West Was Won* (63), *Butch Cassidy and The Sundance Kid* (69).

An RKO Picture, directed by Wesley Ruggles. With Richard Dix, Irene Dunne, Estelle Taylor. Nance O'Neil, William Collier Jr, Roscoe Ates, George E. Stone 130 mins.

Citizen Kane (1941)

Oscars (1) best original screenplay   Herman J. Mankiewicz &
                                                       Orson Welles

The rise to power of an American newspaper tycoon (Orson Welles), told in flashback through interviews with people who were close to him in his lifetime. Closely based on the career of William Randolph Hearst and generally regarded as the greatest film ever made but winner of only one Oscar — for writing. Its other eight nominations were for: — best film, direction, actor, photography (Gregg Toland), art direction, editing, sound, & music.

An RKO Picture, directed by Orson Welles. With Orson Welles, Dorothy Comingore, Joseph Cotten, Everett Sloane, George Coulouris, Ray Collins, Ruth Warrick, Erskine Sanford, Agnes Moorehead, Paul Stewart. 119 mins.

Cleopatra (1934)

Oscars (1) best cinematography   Victor Milner

Restrained (for DeMille) account of the Cleopatra-Caesar-Antony story with Claudette Colbert, Warren William and Henry Wilcoxon featuring as the doomed trio.

A Paramount Picture, directed by Cecil B. DeMille. With Claudette Colbert, Warren William, Henry Wilcoxon, Gertrude Michael, Joseph Schildkraut. 95 mins.

Cleopatra (1963)

Oscars (4) best colour cinematography Leon Shamroy
            best colour art direction   John DeCuir, Jack Martin Smith, Hilyard Brown, Herman Blumenthal, Elven Webb, Maurice Pelling and Boris Juraga
                    set decoration   Walter M. Scott, Paul S. Fox & Ray Moyer
            best colour costume design Irene Sharaff, Vittorio Nino Novarese & Renie
            best special effects   Emil Kosa, Jr

Multi-million dollar version of the same two love affairs, the first between Caesar (Rex Harrison) and Cleopatra (Elizabeth Taylor), the second between the same lady and Marc Antony (Richard Burton).

The film has been described as being 'conceived in a state of emergency,' 'shot in confusion' and 'winding up in blind panic.' Not surprisingly, at 37 million dollars, it nearly bankrupted the Fox Studio.

A 20th Century-Fox Picture, directed by Joseph L. Mankiewicz. With Elizabeth Taylor, Richard Burton, Rex Harrison, Pamela Brown, George Cole, Hume Cronyn, Cesare Danova, Kenneth Haigh, Roddy McDowall. Todd-AO/De Luxe Color. 243 mins.

Close Encounters of The Third Kind (1977)

Oscars (2) best cinematography   Vilmos Zsigmond

Special award to Frank Warner for sound effects editing

UFO science fiction drama from the director of *Jaws,* set in modern day America and following the experiences of an electrical linesman (Richard Dreyfuss) and a distraught mother (Melinda Dillon) when the latter's small child is kidnapped from his home by extraterrestrial visitors. Hokum, often camouflaged as serious cinema but with outstanding special effects. 'Outshone' at Academy Awards time by 7 Oscar winner *Star Wars.*

A Columbia Picture, directed by Steven Spielberg. With Richard Dreyfuss, François Truffaut, Teri Garr, Melinda Dillon, Bob Balaban, J. Patrick McNamara, Cary Guffey. Panavision/Metrocolor. 135 mins.

Closely Observed Trains (1967)

Oscars (1) best foreign language film Czechoslavakia

The experiences — sad, funny, tender by turn — of a young apprenticed railwayman at a sleepy country station in wartime Czechoslavakia.

A Ceskoslovensky Film, Barrandov Studio Production, directed by Jiri Menzel. With Vaclav Neckar, Jitka Bendova, Vladimir Valenta, Josef Somr, Libuse Havelkova. 92 mins.

Come and Get It (1936)

Oscars (1) best supporting actor   Walter Brennan

Edna Ferber tale of the Wisconsin lumber country and in particular of the life of lumber magnate Edward Arnold who becomes a rival with his son for the daughter of a woman he knew years before. The first supporting actor winner, Walter Brennan, featured as Arnold's faithful Swedish buddy Swan Bostrom. Also up for supporting Oscar nomination that year: Mischa Auer (*My Man Godfrey*), Stuart Erwin (*Pigskin Parade*), Basil Rathbone (*Romeo and Juliet*) and Akim Tamiroff (*The General Died at Dawn*).

A Sam Goldwyn Production (released through United Artists), directed by Howard Hawks & William Wyler. With Edward Arnold, Joel McCrea, Frances Farmer, Walter Brennan, Andrea Leeds. 105 mins.

Come Back Little Sheba (1952)

Oscars (1) best actress   Shirley Booth

William Inge's study of a marriage dying from resignation. Shirley Booth, in her screen debut, plays the slovenly, middle-aged housewife living in a pathetic make-believe world and Burt Lancaster her husband whose medical career was ruined years before when as a student he was forced to marry her.

A Paramount Picture, directed by Daniel Mann. With Burt Lancaster, Shirley Booth, Terry Moore, Richard Jaeckel, Philip Ober, Edwin Max. 99 mins.

Cool Hand Luke (1967)

Oscars (1) best supporting actor   George Kennedy

Modern chain-gang drama of the American South with Paul Newman as the indomitable boss baiter who stubbornly refuses to buckle under and becomes a hero to his fellow convicts. George Kennedy's supporting Oscar was for his performance as Dragline, until Newman's arrival the uncrowned king of the chain-gang.

A Warner Bros. Picture, directed by Stuart Rosenberg. With Paul Newman, George Kennedy, J. D. Cannon, Lou Antonio, Robert Drivas, Strother Martin, Jo Van Fleet, Clifton James. Panavision/Technicolor. 127 mins.

Coquette (1928/29)

Oscars (1) best actress   Mary Pickford

Mary Pickford's only Oscar role as the heartless belle of a Southern town whose love affair with a crude mountaineer ends in tragedy. The song, 'Coquette', used in the picture was composed by Irving Berlin.

A United Artists Picture, directed by Sam Taylor. With Mary Pickford, John Mack Brown, Matt Moore, John Sainpolis, William Janney, Henry Kolker. 9 reels.

The Country Girl (1954)

Oscars (2)   best actress   Grace Kelly
             best screenplay   George Seaton

Film version of Clifford Odet's poignant stage play about a faded, drunken stage star (Bing Crosby), his long suffering wife (Grace Kelly) and the young Broadway director (William Holden) who tries to help the actor recover some of his lost eminence by casting him in a big comeback role.

A Paramount Picture, directed by George Seaton. With Bing Crosby, Grace Kelly, William Holden, Anthony Ross, Gene Reynolds. 104 mins.

Cover Girl (1944)

Oscars (1)   best scoring of a musical   Morris Stoloff &
                                          Carmen Dragon

Rita Hayworth and Gene Kelly dancing together for the first and only time in Columbia's super backstage musical of the mid-40's. Rita rises from Brooklyn singer to cover girl of Vanity magazine, dancer Kelly is the honest guy in her life and Phil Silvers and Eve Arden provide the wisecracks. Numbers by Ira Gershwin and Jerome Kern include 'Long Ago and Far Away.'

A Columbia Picture, directed by Charles Vidor. With Gene Kelly, Rita Hayworth, Phil Silvers, Lee Bowman, Otto Kruger, Eve Arden. Technicolor. 107 mins.

The Cowboy and the Lady (1938)

Oscars (1)   best sound recording   Thomas T. Moulton

Typical 30's comedy from the Goldwyn stable with aristocratic, fun-loving Merle Oberon falling for lanky rodeo star Gary Cooper.

A Sam Goldwyn Picture (released through United Artists), directed by H. C. Potter. With Gary Cooper, Merle Oberon, Patsy Kelly, Walter Brennan, Fuzzy Knight, Mabel Todd, Henry Kolker, Harry Davenport. 91 mins.

Crash Dive (1943)

Oscars (1)   best special effects   Fred Sersen (photographic)
                                      Roger Heman (sound)

Technicolored war story centering around a submarine in the North Atlantic with Tyrone Power as a specialist in naval warfare (both in

PT boats and subs), Dana Andrews as the sub captain and Anne Baxter the girl they're both in love with.

A 20th Century-Fox Picture, directed by Archie Mayo. With Tyrone Power, Anne Baxter, Dana Andrews James Gleason, Dame May Whitty, Henry Morgan. Technicolor. 105 mins.

Cries and Whispers (1973)

Oscars (1) best cinematography   Sven Nykvist

The haunting memories of a young woman (Harriet Andersson) dying in the house where she was born and being cared for by her devoted servant (Kari Sylwan) and her married sisters (Ingrid Thulin, Liv Ullmann).

A Cinematograph-Svenska Filminstitutet Film, directed by Ingmar Bergman. With Harriet Andersson, Kari Sylwan, Ingrid Thulin, Liv Ullmann, Erland Josephson, Henning Moritzen. Eastman Color. 91 mins.

Cromwell (1970)

Oscars (1) best costume design   Nino Novarese

The rise of Oliver Cromwell, Puritan squire and Member of Parliament, to dictator of 17th century England. Richard Harris is the usurper, Alec Guinness the defiant Charles I.

A Columbia Picture, directed by Ken Hughes. With Richard Harris, Alec Guinness, Robert Morley, Dorothy Tutin, Frank Finlay, Timothy Dalton, Patrick Wymark, Patrick Magee. Panavision/Technicolor. 140 mins.

Cyrano De Bergerac (1950)

Oscars (1) best actor   Jose Ferrer

Jose Ferrer as the famous long nosed Gascon swordsman-poet who courts the woman he adores for another man. Based on the 1897 verse comedy by Edmond Rostand.

A United Artists Picture, directed by Michael Gordon. With Jose Ferrer, Mala Powers, William Prince, Morris Carnovsky, Ralph Clanton, Lloyd Corrigan. 112 mins.

A Damsel in Distress (1937)

Oscars (1) best dance direction   Hermes Pan
                                                for the 'Fun House' number

Gershwin musical, set in London society, with Joan Fontaine as an heiress Fred Astaire mistakes for a chorus girl. Songs include 'A Foggy Day in London Town' and 'Nice Work If You Can Get It.' The number 'Fun House' for which Hermes Pan won his Oscar is an elaborate and inventive routine full of distorting mirrors, revolving drums, etc.

An RKO Picture, directed by George Stevens. With Fred Astaire, George Burns, Gracie Allen, Joan Fontaine, Reginald Gardiner, Ray Noble, Constance Collier. 100 mins.

Dangerous (1935)

Oscars (1) best actress   Bette Davis

Bette Davis, in the first of her two Oscar winning roles, as a once famous Broadway actress who has fallen to the depths, and Franchot Tone as the young architect who helps her rise from the gutter to a successful comeback. The film made Davis an international star and helped compensate for her missing out on the Oscar the year before when she was hotly fancied for *Of Human Bondage*.

A Warner Bros. Picture, directed by Alfred E. Green. With Bette Davis, Franchot Tone, Margaret Lindsay, Alison Skipworth, John Eldredge, Dick Foran. 78 mins.

The Dark Angel (1935)

Oscars (1) best art direction   Richard Day

Goldwyn soap-opera with Merle Oberon and Fredric March as a pair of lovers whose lives are almost destroyed when the latter is blinded in the trenches in World War I. Herbert Marshall features as the other suitor for Miss Oberon's hand.

A Sam Goldwyn Picture (released through United Artists), directed by Sidney Franklin. With Fredric March, Merle Oberon, Herbert Marshall, Janet Beecher, John Halliday, Henrietta Crosman, Frieda Inescort. 105 mins.

Darling (1965)

Oscars (3) best actress   Julie Christie
     best story and screenplay Frederic Raphael
     best b/w costume design Julie Harris

The career of a vain, man-eating advertisement model (Julie Christie) who soars up the social scale by using all the men she comes in contact with — a young TV interviewer (Dirk Bogarde), a suave business executive (Laurence Harvey) and an Italian prince (Jose-Luis de Villalonga) who finally traps and frustrates her in a loveless marriage. A cold, hard look into the empty heart (and mind) of a girl living in London in the swinging 60's.

A Warner-Pathe-Anglo Amalgamated Picture, directed by John Schlesinger. With Dirk Bogarde, Laurence Harvey, Julie Christie, Roland Curram, Alex Scott, Basil Henson. 127 mins.

The Dawn Patrol (1930/31)

Oscars (1) best original story   John Monk Saunders

Howard Hawks' first sound film, set in World War I and concerning the strains on inexperienced British fliers who live with almost certain death as they do daily battle above the trenches at the front line.

A Warner Bros. Picture, directed by Howard Hawks. With Richard Barthelmess, Douglas Fairbanks Jr, Neil Hamilton, William Janney, James Finlayson. 95 mins.

Day for Night (1973)

Oscars (1) best foreign language film France/Italy

A film within a film with Francois Truffaut (as a fictional film director) beset with difficulties of all kinds — the love affairs and emotional problems of his international cast — as he works his way through his latest production.

Les Films Du Carosse-P.E.C.F.-P.I.C., directed by Francois Truffaut. With Jacqueline Bisset, Jean Pierre Leaud, Francois Truffaut, Valentina Cortese, Jean-Pierre Aumont. Technicolor. 116 mins.

Days of Wine and Roses (1962)

Oscars (1) best song   'Days of Wine and Roses'
                                      Henry Mancini, music:
                                      Johnny Mercer, lyrics

The harrowing account of two seemingly normal young people — a hard-pressed advertising executive (Jack Lemmon) and his wife (Lee Remick) — whose lives are shattered by drink as they sink deeper and deeper into alcoholism.

A Warner Bros. Picture, directed by Blake Edwards. With Jack Lemmon, Lee Remick, Charles Bickford, Jack Klugman, Alan Hewitt, Tom Palmer, Jack Albertson. 117 mins.

The Defiant Ones (1958)

Oscars (2) best story & screenplay   Nathan E. Douglas &
                                       Harold Jacob Smith
            best cinematography   Sam Leavitt

Two convicts, one white, one black, make their escape from a police van in the American South but have to spend their short-lived freedom together chained by the wrist. Stanley Kramer's optimistic movie about racial tolerance with Tony Curtis and Sidney Poitier as the two convicts.

A United Artists Picture, directed by Stanley Kramer. With Tony Curtis, Sidney Poitier, Theodore Bikel, Charles McGraw, Lon Chaney, King Donovan, Claude Akins. 97 mins.

Dersu Uzala (1975)

Oscars (1) best foreign language film Russia/Japan

Akira Kurosawa adventure, set at the turn-of-the-century, and centering on a Siberian trapper and a hunter-explorer who form a deep, inseparable friendship while surveying the unexplored forests of Eastern Siberia and Taiga Land.

Mosfilm, Moscow-Toho, Tokyo, directed by Akira Kurosawa. With Maxim Munzuk, Yuri Solomin. Colour. 137 mins.

Designing Woman (1957)

Oscars (1) best story & screenplay   George Wells

Sports writer Gregory Peck and successful dress designer Lauren Bacall find, after their marriage, unforseen difficulties as they try to adapt to each other's friends and habits. Sophisticated updating of the 1942 hit *Woman of The Year* which also won a writing Oscar.

An MGM Picture, directed by Vincente Minnelli. With Gregory Peck, Lauren Bacall, Dolores Gray, Sam Levene, Tom Helmore, Mickey Shaughnessy, Jesse White. CinemaScope/Metrocolor. 118 mins.

Destination Moon (1950)

Oscars (1) best special effects   Lee Zavitz & George Pal

The first of the big post-war science-fiction movies, based on scientific knowledge of the time and showing how four men journey to the moon and back in an atomic rocket. Set designer Ernst Fegte's intriguing moonscapes helped win the film its special effects award.

An Eagle Lion Picture, directed by Irving Pichel. With John Archer, Warner Anderson, Tom Powers, Dick Wesson, Erin O'Brien Moore. Technicolor. 90 mins.

The Diary of Anne Frank (1959)

Oscars (3)	best supporting actress	Shelley Winters
	best b/w cinematography	William C. Mellor
	best b/w art direction	Lyle R. Wheeler & George W. Davis
	set decoration	Walter M. Scott & Stuart A. Reiss

The story of how in World War II two Jewish families and a garrulous old dentist lived in unbearably cramped conditions above an attic in an Amsterdam warehouse. Found by the Nazis just 9 months before the liberation of Holland, only the father of Anne Frank (the young girl through whose diary the world heard the story) survived.

A 20th Century-Fox Picture, directed by George Stevens. With Millie Perkins, Joseph Schildkraut, Shelley Winters, Richard Beymer, Gusti Huber, Lou Jacobi, Ed Wynn. CinemaScope. 170 mins.

The Dirty Dozen (1967)

Oscars (1) best sound effects   John Poyner

Twelve misfits, rapists, murderers, psycopaths, are turned by Major Lee Marvin into a bloodthirsty commando group to perform a dangerous mission in World War 2 — proving themselves heroes in the process.

An MGM Picture, directed by Robert Aldrich. With Lee Marvin, Ernest Borgnine, Charles Bronson, John Cassavetes, Richard Jaeckel, Robert Ryan, Telly Savalas, Donald Sutherland, George Kennedy. 70mm Widescreen/Metrocolor. 150 mins.

The Discreet Charm of the Bourgeoisie (1972)

Oscars (1) best foreign language film France

Superficially the tale of the inability of six rich people to get through an elusive meal without interruption but basically yet another blistering attack by the cinema's master anarchist Luis Bunuel on the stupidities of the world's bourgeoisie.

A Greenwich Film Production, directed by Luis Bunuel. With Fernando Rey, Delphine Seyrig, Stephane Audran, Bulle Ogier, Jean-Pierre Cassel, Paul Frankeur. Eastman Color. 105 mins.

Disraeli (1929/30)

Oscars (1) best actor   George Arliss

George Arliss' sound debut (at 61 years of age), recreating the role he played silently 9 years earlier and becoming the first British actor, albeit in an American film, to win a best actor Oscar. As Britain's wily Prime Minister Benjamin Disraeli he thwarts a group of Russian agents and at the same time raises money to purchase the Suez Canal.

A Warner Bros. Picture, directed by Alfred E. Green. With George Arliss, Joan Bennett, Florence Arliss, Anthony Bushell, David Torrence, Ivan Simpson, Doris Lloyd. 9 reels.

The Divine Lady (1928/29)

Oscars (1) best direction   Frank Lloyd

None other than the lowly born Emma Hamilton who rises to a position of some distinction by marrying the British Ambassador at the Court of Naples and then achieves considerable notoriety by falling in love with Britain's greatest hero Horatio Nelson. Corinne Griffith is Emma,

Victor Varconi Nelson and H. B. Warner the luckless Sir William Hamilton.

A First National Picture, directed by Frank Lloyd. With Corinne Griffith, Victor Varconi, H. B. Warner, Ian Keith, William Conklin, Marie Dressler. 12 reels.

The Divorcee (1929/30)

Oscars (1) best actress   Norma Shearer

Norma Shearer's Oscar-winning role and the first of several wayward wives she was to play on the screen in subsequent years. In this one she plays one of the first women's libbers — a woman who discards her newspaper husband (Chester Morris) when she disovers he's been cheating on her, emulates his sexual freedom, and finally takes him back.

An MGM Picture, directed by Robert Z. Leonard. With Norma Shearer, Chester Morris, Conrad Nagel, Robert Montgomery, Florence Eldridge, Helene Millard. 9 reels.

Divorce Italian Style (1962)

Oscars (1) best story & screenplay   Ennio De Concini, Alfredo
                                        Giannetti & Pietro Germi

Black comedy about the vanishing Sicilian aristocracy with Marcello Mastroianni as an impoverished Sicilian nobleman finding that the only way he can court his beautiful young cousin is by murdering his amiable but demanding wife.

A Lux-Vides-Galatea Picture (Italy), directed by Pietro Germi. With Marcello Mastroianni, Daniella Rocca, Stefania Sandrelli, Leopoldo Trieste. 104 mins.

Doctor Dolittle (1967)

Oscars (2) best song   'Talk To The Animals'
                                        (music & lyrics: Leslie Bricusse)
            best special visual effects L. B. Abbott

Musical version of Hugh Lofting's stories with Rex Harrison as the irascible Dr. John Dolittle (taught some 500 animal dialects by his sagacious parrot) off in search of the elusive Great Pink Sea Snail.

A 20th Century-Fox Picture, directed by Richard Fleischer. With Rex Harrison, Samantha Eggar, Anthony Newley, Richard Attenborough, Peter Bull, Todd-AO/De Luxe Color. 152 mins.

Doctor Zhivago (1965)

Oscars (5) best screenplay from   Robert Bolt
                another medium
            best colour cinematography Freddie Young
            best colour art direction   John Box & Terry Marsh
                set decoration   Dario Simoni
            best colour costume   Phyllis Dalton
                design
            best music score   Maurice Jarre

Idealistic Russian doctor-poet (Omar Sharif), in sympathy with the
ideals of the Revolution, finds himself unable to adjust to the new
society when the Revolution finally occurs. Boris Paternak's classic
statement of the liberal bourgeois position, set in the revolutionary
period and hinging on the doomed romance between Zhivago and his
beautiful mistress Lara (Julie Christie).
    An MGM Picture, directed by David Lean. With Omar Sharif, Julie
Christie, Geraldine Chaplin, Tom Courtenay, Alec Guinness, Siobhan
McKenna, Ralph Richardson, Rod Steiger, Rita Tushingham. Panavision/
Metrocolor. 197 mins.

Dodsworth (1936)

Oscars (1) best art direction   Richard Day

Mid-western industrialist Sam Dodsworth (Walter Huston), married to
an immature and restless wife, finds a new set of values on a trip to the
Continent where an American widow teaches him to appreciate the
traditions of Europe. William Wyler's version of the novel by Sinclair
Lewis.
    A Sam Goldwyn Picture (released through United Artists), directed
by William Wyler. With Walter Huston, Ruth Chatterton, Paul Lukas,
Mary Astor, David Niven, Maria Ouspenskaya. 90 mins.

Dog Day Afternoon (1975)

Oscars (1) best original screenplay   Frank Pierson

The story of three young men who hold up a Brooklyn bank in order
to get money to finance a sex-change operation. Based on real life
characters and events that occurred in a Chase Manhattan bank in 1972
and starring Al Pacino, John Cazale and Gary Springer as the gay
bank robbers.

A Warner Bros Picture, directed by Sidney Lumet. With Al Pacino, John Cazale, Sully Boyar, Penelope Allen, Beulah Garrick, Technicolor. 130 mins.

La Dolce Vita (1961)

Oscars (1) best b/w costume design   Piero Gherardi

The film that created a world sensation in the early 60's — a scorching look at the jet set life of Rome (especially at the decadence of the moneyed classes) as seen through the eyes of scandal reporter Marcello Mastroianni.

Riama Film (Italy/France), directed by Federico Fellini. With Marcello Mastroianni, Yvonne Furneaux, Anouk Aimee, Anita Ekberg, Alain Cuny, Annibale Ninchi, Magali Noel, Lex Barker, Nadia Gray. 175 mins.

A Double Life (1947)

Oscars (2) best actor   Ronald Colman
            best music score of a   Miklos Rozsa
            drama or comedy

Schizophrenic actor Ronald Colman, obsessed with the role of Othello he is playing on the Broadway stage, finds he is playing the part in real life, even to the point where he commits murder. Colman's only Oscar, and a belated one at that.

A Universal-International Picture, directed by George Cukor. With Ronald Colman, Signe Hasso, Edmond O'Brien, Shelley Winters, Ray Collins, Philip Loeb, Millard Mitchell. 103 mins.

The Dove (1927/28)

Oscars (1) best art direction   William Cameron Menzies

Romantic melodrama with Norma Talmadge as a dance hall girl ('The Dove' of the title) in love with gambler Gilbert Roland. Complicating things, and the third member of an eternal triangle, is wealthy caballero Noah Beery. Menzies was the first art director to win an Oscar and was also named for his work on *The Tempest* (see page 158) released the same year.

A United Artists Picture, directed by Roland West. With Norma Talmadge, Noah Beery, Gilbert Roland, Eddie Borden, Harry Myers. 9 reels.

Dr. Jekyll and Mr. Hyde (1931/32)

Oscars (1) best actor   Fredric March

The most successful of the many attempts to film Robert Louis Stevenson's nightmare tale of a Victorian doctor (March) who finds, by taking a special drug, that he can change into his other self — ruthless, cruel and bestial. Rose Hobart is the doctor's luckless fiancee,Miriam Hopkins, the cockney slut who arouses Hyde. March's acting award was shared with Wallace Berry for *The Champ*.

A Paramount Picture, directed by Rouben Mamoulian. With Fredric March, Miriam Hopkins, Rose Hobart, Holmes Herbert, Edgar Norton, Halliwell Hobbes. 90 mins.

Dumbo (1941)

Oscars (1) best scoring of a musical   Frank Churchill & Oliver Wallace
                 picture

Full length cartoon by Walt Disney (his fifth) about a baby elephant who learns to fly by using his enormous ears as wings. Songs include 'Casey Junior', 'Baby Mine' and 'When I See An Elephant Fly.'

A Walt Disney Picture, released by RKO. Supervising director, Ben Sharpsteen. Voices by Edward Brophy, Herman Bing, Verna Felton, Sterling Holloway, Cliff Edwards. Technicolor. 64 mins.

Earthquake (1974)

Oscars (2) best sound   Ronald Pierce &
Melvin Metcalfe Sr.

best visual effects   ('for realistic depiction of the
devastation of Los Angeles by
an earthquake')
Frank Brendel, Albert Whitlock,
& Glen Robinson

The biggest earthquake film since *San Francisco* with not one but two tremors as a massive quake hits Los Angeles, the first destroying most of the city, the second bursting the Hollywood Dam. Heroic efforts by L.A. engineer Charlton Heston and cop George Kennedy prove to be in vain.

A Universal Picture, directed by Mark Robson. With Charlton Heston, Ava Gardner, George Kennedy, Lorne Greene, Genevieve Bujold, Richard Roundtree. Panavision/Sensurround/Technicolor. 123 mins.

Easter Parade (1948)

Oscars (1) best scoring of a musical   Johnny Green & Roger Edens

Technicolor musical right off the MGM conveyor belt with Fred Astaire taking on chorus girl Judy Garland as his new dancing partner after clashing with ambitious Ann Miller. Set in the early 20's and with Astaire's 'Drum Crazy', Miller's 'Shakin' The Blues Away' and the Astaire-Garland duet 'We're a Couple of Swells' as the highlights.

An MGM Picture, directed by Charles Walters. With Fred Astaire, Judy Garland, Peter Lawford, Ann Miller, Dick Beavers, Jules Munshin, Clinton Sundberg. Technicolor. 103 mins.

East of Eden (1955)

Oscars (1) best supporting actress   Jo Van Fleet

Steinbeck's twentieth century allegory of the Cain and Abel story with rebellious James Dean and wholesome Richard Davalos as the two contrasted sons competing for the love of their patriarchal father Raymond Massey. Set in California in 1917 and co-starring Oscar winning Jo Van Fleet as the boys' mother who has broken free of her family and become the proprietress of a nearby brothel.

A Warner Bros. Picture, directed by Elia Kazan. With Julie Harris, James Dean, Raymond Massey, Richard Davalos, Burl Ives, Jo Van Fleet, Albert Dekker. CinemaScope/Warner Color. 115 mins.

$8\frac{1}{2}$ (1963)

Oscars (2) best foreign language film Italy
              best b/w costume design   Piero Gherardi

The memories, fantasies and desires of an artistically exhausted Italian film director (based on Fellini himself), as he rests his mind and body at a spa and searches frantically for a story for his new film. A vivid piece of cinematic self-analysis.

An Angelo Rizzoli Picture, directed by Federico Fellini. With Marcello Mastroianni, Claudia Cardinale, Anouk Aimee, Sandra Milo, Rosella Falk, Barbara Steele, Guido Alberti. 135 mins.

Elmer Gantry (1960)

Oscars (3) best actor   Burt Lancaster
              best supporting actress   Shirley Jones
              best screenplay   Richard Brooks

Burt Lancaster as Sinclair Lewis' whoring, whiskey-drinking salesman who joins up with evangelist Jean Simmons, exploits her tent-pitching revivalist group and unscrupulously turns it into big business. Based on Lewis' 1927 novel of the American Mid-West; Shirley Jones' supporting Oscar was for her portrayal of Gantry's former girl-friend turned prostitute.

A United Artists Picture, directed by Richard Brooks. With Burt Lancaster, Jean Simmons, Arthur Kennedy, Shirley Jones, Dean Jagger, Patti Page, Edward Andrews, John McIntire. Eastman Color. 146 mins.

The Enemy Below (1957)

Oscars (1) best special effects   Walter Rossi

The futile waste of human life in wartime revealed in a gripping duel between an American destroyer and a German U Boat who play cat and mouse in the Atlantic in World War II. Robert Mitchum commands the destroyer, Curt Jurgens the sub. Notable underwater effects.

A 20th Century-Fox Picture, directed by Dick Powell. With Robert Mitchum, Curt Jurgens, Al Hedison, Theodore Bikel, Russell Collins, Kurt Kreuger. CinemaScope/De Luxe Color. 98 mins.

Eskimo (1934)

Oscars (1) best editing   Conrad Nervig

Documentary feature about Eskimo life in the northernmost inhabited settlement in Alaska. Filmed on the spot by W. S. Van Dyke (who travelled with his technicians by whaling schooner to Alaska to get his footage) and edited into a magnificent whole by Conrad Nervig – the first editor to win an Oscar. The entire native cast spoke in the Eskimo tongue.

An MGM Picture, directed by W. S. Van Dyke from a script by John Lee Mahin. With a native cast headed by Mala. 117 mins.

Exodus (1960)

Oscars (1) best music score of a   Ernest Gold
            drama or comedy

The founding of the modern State of Israel in 1948, based partly on historical fact and partly on the fiction of the 600 page best-seller by Leon Uris. Ernest Gold's inspired score deservedly won the music award but, alas, sadly defeated Elmer Bernstein's music for *The Magnificent Seven* – a cert winner in any other year and one of the unluckiest music losers in the history of the awards.

A United Artists Picture, directed by Otto Preminger. With Paul Newman, Eva Marie Saint, Ralph Richardson, Peter Lawford, Lee J. Cobb, Sal Mineo, John Derek, Hugh Griffith. Super-Panavision 70/Technicolor. 213 mins.

The Exorcist (1973)

Oscars (2)	best screenplay	William Peter Blatty
	best sound	Robert Knudson & Chris Newman

The only horror film to be nominated as best picture of the year — the story of a twelve-year-old girl (Linda Blair), living in Washington with her actress mother (Ellen Burstyn), who suddenly finds herself in the power of the Devil and unable to free herself from the horrors that possess her. Mercedes McCambridge (never seen) is the rasping, hoarsely mocking voice of Satan. Rarely has a soundtrack Oscar been so well deserved.

A Warner Bros. Picture, directed by William Friedkin. With Ellen Burstyn, Max Von Sydow, Lee J. Cobb, Kitty Winn, Jack MacGowran, Jason Miller, Linda Blair. Metrocolor. 122 mins.

The Facts of Life (1960)

Oscars (1) best b/w costume design   Edith Head & Edward Stevenson

Bob Hope-Lucille Ball comedy, in more serious vein than usual, with the comic pair starring as two middle-aged marrieds who, despite doing their utmost to make adultery succeed, find it just too much trouble. Don DeFore and Ruth Hussey co-star as the shelved partners.

   A United Artists Picture, directed by Melvin Frank. With Bob Hope, Lucille Ball, Ruth Hussey, Don DeFore, Louis Nye, Philip Ober. 103 mins.

The Fair Co-Ed (1927/28)

Oscars (1) best title writing   Joseph Farnham

Silent American comedy-romance with John Mack Brown working his way through college as a basketball coach and Marion Davies as the girl who joins the team and becomes the star player. One of the three films to figure in the only title writing Oscar given by the Academy, Farnham also winning for his work on *Laugh, Clown, Laugh* and *Telling The World*.

   An MGM Picture, directed by Sam Wood. With Marion Davies, John Mack Brown, Jane Winton, Thelma Hill, Lillian Leighton. 7 reels.

Fantastic Voyage (1966)

Oscars (2) best colour art direction   Jack Martin Smith &
                                         Dale Hennesy
             set decoration Walter M. Scott &
                                         Stuart A. Reiss
             best special visual effects Art Cruickshank

Science fiction, set in the year 1995, about a four man (and one woman) scientific team who are miniaturised to microbe size and journey by submarine into a patient's bloodstream. Their task? To perform a difficult brain operation and save the life of a Czech scientist with vital secrets to tell.

A 20th Century-Fox Picture, directed by Richard Fleischer. With Stephen Boyd, Raquel Welch, Edmond O'Brien, Donald Pleasence, Arthur O'Connell, William Redfield, Arthur Kennedy, CinemaScope/ De Luxe Color. 100 mins.

A Farewell to Arms (1932/33)

Oscars (2) best cinematography   Charles B. Lang Jr.
            best sound recording   Harold C. Lewis

Ernest Hemingway's doomed romance between an American ambulance driver (Gary Cooper), wounded at the Italian front in World War 1, and the English Red Cross nurse (Helen Hayes) who nurses him back to health. The first of Hemingway's novels to reach the screen.

A Paramount Picture, directed by Frank Borzage. With Helen Hayes, Gary Cooper, Adolphe Menjou, Mary Philips, Jack La Rue, Blanche Frederici. 78 mins.

The Farmer's Daughter (1947)

Oscars (1) best actress   Loretta Young

Swedish maid Loretta Young, employed as a servant in the home of political patriarch Ethel Barrymore, quickly makes it big in Washington, winning not only a seat in Congress but a husband (Joseph Cotten), into the bargain. Cheerful comedy-drama which won Miss Young a somewhat surprising best actress Oscar, other nominees that year being Joan Crawford (*Possessed*), Susan Hayward (*Smash Up*), Rosalind Russell (*Mourning Becomes Electra*) and Dorothy McGuire (*Gentleman's Agreement*).

An RKO Picture, directed by H. C. Potter. With Loretta Young, Joseph Cotten, Ethel Barrymore, Charles Bickford, Rose Hobart, Rhys Williams, Harry Davenport. 97 mins.

Father Goose (1964)

Oscars (1) best story & screenplay   Peter Stone & Frank Tarloff
                                      (screenplay), S. H. Barnett
                                      (story)

Unshaven, boozy beachcomber (Cary Grant), tricked by the Australian navy into reporting on Japanese plane and ship movements in World War II, finds himself suddenly having to share his isolated outpost with a gaggle of stranded schoolchildren and their frosty teacher, Leslie Caron.

A Universal Picture, directed by Ralph Nelson. With Cary Grant, Leslie Caron, Trevor Howard, Jack Good, Verina Greenlaw, Pip Sparke. Technicolor. 115 mins.

Fellini's Casanova (1976)

Oscars (1) best costume design   Danilo Donati

Federico Fellini's visual treat — a stylised and very personal vision of the life of the celebrated 18th century lover. Donald Sutherland features in the lead.

A P.E.A. — Produzioni Europee Associate S.P.A. Production (Italy), directed by Federico Fellini. With Donald Sutherland, Tina Aumont, Cicely Browne, Olimpia Carlisi, Adele Angela Lojodice. Eastmancolor. 166 mins.

Fiddler on the Roof (1971)

Oscars (3)	best cinematography	Oswald Morris
	best sound	Gordon K. McCallum & David Hildyard
	best scoring: adaptation & original song score	John Williams

The Sheldon Harnick/Jerry Brock stage musical about traditional Jewish life in a small pre-revolutionary village in the Ukraine. Topol stars as the honest milkman Tevye determined to find good husbands for his five daughters.

A United Artists Picture, directed by Norman Jewison. With Topol, Norma Crane, Leonard Frey, Molly Picon, Paul Mann. Panavision 70/ Technicolor. 180 mins.

Folies Bergere (1935)

Oscars (1) best dance direction   Dave Gould for the 'Straw Hat' number (Gould was also named the same year for his work on *The Broadway Melody of 1936* — see page 21)

Lavish musical with a double identity plot with Folies Bergere entertainer Maurice Chevalier impersonating a look-alike baron who finds
his fortune suddenly in jeopardy.

A 20th Century Picture, directed by Roy Del Ruth. With Maurice
Chevalier, Merle Oberon, Ann Sothern, Walter Byron, Lumsden Hare,
Robert Grief, Eric Blore. 83 mins.

The Fortune Cookie (1966)
(*G.B. title: Meet Whiplash Willie*)

Oscars (1) best supporting actor   Walter Matthau

TV cameraman Jack Lemmon, slightly injured when filming a football
game, takes to his bed on the advice of his brother-in-law, shyster
lawyer Walter Matthau, so they can cook up a million dollar accident
insurance claim against all concerned. A prime example of a major
acting performance being slotted into the supporting category so that
the performer stood a better chance of winning an Oscar.

A United Artists Picture, directed by Billy Wilder. With Jack
Lemmon, Walter Matthau, Ron Rich, Cliff Osmond, Judi West, Lurene
Tuttle. Panavision. 126 mins.

For Whom the Bell Tolls (1943)

Oscars (1) best supporting actress   Katina Paxinou

Hemingway's 1940 novel of the Spanish Civil War with Gary Cooper (as
an American schoolteacher) and Ingrid Bergman (as a tortured orphan
girl) fighting for the loyalists and trying to blow a strategic bridge in a
heavily guarded mountain pass. Katina Paxinou's Oscar winning performance was for his fiery peasant leader, Pilar.

A Paramount Picture, directed by Sam Wood. With Gary Cooper,
Ingrid Bergman, Akim Tamiroff, Arturo de Cordova, Vladimr Sokoloff,
Katina Paxinou, Joseph Calleia. Technicolor. 170 mins.

A Free Soul (1930/31)

Oscars (1) best actor   Lionel Barrymore

Modern gal Norma Shearer, brought up by her drunken lawyer father
(Lionel Barrymore) to do exactly what she wants finds that what she
does want is a sordid love affair with Clark Gable whom she discovers,
too late, to be nothing more than a brutal underworld leader.

An MGM Picture, directed by Clarence Brown. With Norma Shearer, Lionel Barrymore, Clark Gable, Leslie Howard, James Gleason, Lucy Beaumont. 91 mins.

The French Connection (1971)

Oscars (5)		
	best film	Philip D'Antoni (producer)
	best direction	William Friedkin
	best actor	Gene Hackman
	best screenplay	Ernest Tidyman
	best editing	Jerry Greenberg

Based-on-fact thriller about two New York Narcotics Squad detectives (Gene Hackman and Roy Scheider) who play a long-shot hunch hoping to smash a 32 million dollar dope smuggling ring. Highlight: A reckless car chase in which Hackman speeds madly beneath an elevated railway after a runaway train.

A 20th Century-Fox Picture, directed by William Friedkin. With Gene Hackman, Fernando Rey, Roy Scheider, Tony LoBianco, Marcel Bozzuffi, Frederic de Pasquale. De Luxe Color. 104 mins.

Frenchman's Creek (1945)

Oscars (1)		
	best colour art direction	Hans Dreier & Ernst Fegte
	int. decoration	Sam Comer

Lavish Daphne Du Maurier romance about a young aristocratic Englishwoman (Joan Fontaine) who, when domiciled at her Cornish estate, finds herself involved with a handsome French pirate (Arturo de Cordova) plundering the Cornish coast. Set in the 17th century and among the most beautiful colour films to come out of America in the 40's.

A Paramount Picture, directed by Mitchell Leisen. With Joan Fontaine, Arturo de Cordova, Basil Rathbone, Nigel Bruce, Cecil Kellaway, Ralph Forbes. Technicolor. 113 mins.

From Here to Eternity (1953)

Oscars (8)		
	best film	Buddy Adler (producer)
	best direction	Fred Zinnemann
	best supporting actor	Frank Sinatra
	best supporting actress	Donna Reed
	best screenplay	Daniel Taradash
	best b/w cinematography	Burnett Guffey
	best sound recording	John P. Livadary
	best editing	William Lyon

The novel they said 'couldn't be filmed' — the sex lives and personal problems of the men of an American Army infantry outfit in Hawaii just prior to Pearl Harbour. The Oscar winners were in the supporting roles: Frank Sinatra as a cocky little G.I. and Donna Reed as a professional hostess 'two steps up from the pavement.' In the leads — Burt Lancaster as a tough Company Sergeant, Deborah Kerr as a shop soiled army wife and Montgomery Clift as the G.I. who refuses to box for the Company's team because he once blinded a man in the ring. With its eight Oscars the highest Academy Award winner since *Gone With The Wind* fourteen years earlier.

A Columbia Picture, directed by Fred Zinnemann. With Burt Lancaster, Montgomery Clift, Deborah Kerr, Frank Sinatra, Donna Reed, Philip Ober, Mickey Shaughnessy, Ernest Borgnine. 118 mins.

Funny Girl (1968)

Oscars (1) best actress   Barbra Streisand

The story of musical comedy star Fanny Brice (Barbra Streisand) the determined little girl from New York's Lower East Side who makes it to stardom on Broadway but suffers in her private life and in her marriage to gambler Nick Arnstein (Omar Sharif). Streisand's film debut and an Oscar winner first time out. The number 'Don't Rain On My Parade' is the film's musical tour-de-force. Streisand's best actress award was shared with Katharine Hepburn for *The Lion In Winter*, the only best actress tie in Oscar history.

A Columbia Picture, directed by William Wyler. With Barbra Streisand, Omar Sharif, Kay Medford, Anne Francis, Walter Pidgeon, Lee Allen. Panavision 70/Technicolor. 147 mins.

A Funny Thing Happened on the Way to the Forum (1966)

Oscars (1) best music: adaptation   Ken Thorne
            or treatment

Send-up of slave life in first century Rome with moon-faced Zero Mostel as a slave bent on gaining his freedom, Phil Silvers as a fast-talking brothel owner and a bevy of nubile, busty girls.

A United Artists Picture, directed by Richard Lester. With Zero Mostel, Phil Silvers, Jack Gilford, Buster Keaton, Michael Crawford, Annette Andre, Patricia Jessel, Michael Hordern. De Luxe Color. 98 mins.

The Garden of the Finzi Continis (1971)

Oscars (1) best foreign language film Italy/West Germany

Vittorio de Sica's major work of his later period — the story of an unrequited love affair, set in the Mussolini dominated Italy of 1938 and against the background of the country's decaying aristocratic Jewry.

A Documento Film, directed by Vittorio De Sica. With Dominique Sanda, Lino Capolicchio, Helmut Berger, Romolo Valli, Fabio Testi. Eastman Color. 95 mins.

Gaslight (1944)

Oscars (2)	best actress	Ingrid Bergman
	best b/w art direction	Cedric Gibbons & William Ferrari
	int. decoration	Edwin B. Willis &
		Paul Huldschinsky

Handsome Charles Boyer, cast against type as a ruthless murderer, marries his victim's niece (Ingrid Bergman) and then tries to gain her inheritance by driving her slowly insane. Set mainly within the confines of an old Victorian house and based on the psychological stage melo-drama by Patrick Hamilton. Joseph Cotton co-stars as a Scotland Yard man.

An MGM Picture, directed by George Cukor. With Charles Boyer, Ingrid Bergman, Joseph Cotton, Angela Lansbury, Dame May Whitty. 114 mins.

Gate of Hell (1954)

Oscars (1) best colour costume design Sanzo Wada

Exotic tragedy, set in 12th century Japan, about a married Japanese woman who finds herself loved not only by her husband but passionately and illicitly by a conquering Japanese warrior. Voted a special award as the best foreign language picture of the year, it was the first Japanese production to make use of a Western colour process.

A Daiei Picture, directed by Teinosuke Kinugasa. With Kazuo Hasegawa, Machiko Kyo, Isao Yamagata, Yataro Kurokawa, Kotaro Bando. Eastman Color. 90 mins.

The Gay Divorcee (1934)

Oscars (1) best song   'The Continental'
                                       (Con Conrad, music:
                                       Herb Magidson, lyrics)

The first musical in which Astaire and Rogers had the leading roles. Also the forerunner of things to come with the usual mistaken identity plot (dancer Fred is suspected by Ginger of being the hired correspondent in her divorce suit) and the usual magnificent numbers — 'Looking For A Needle In A Haystack', 'Night And Day' and the climactic Oscar-winning routine, 'The Continental', the first song to win an Academy Award.

An RKO Picture, directed by Mark Sandrich. With Fred Astaire, Ginger Rogers, Alice Brady, Edward Everett Horton, Erik Rhodes, Eric Blore. 107 mins.

Gentleman's Agreement (1947)

Oscars (3) best film   (Darryl F. Zanuck, producer)
            best direction   Elia Kazan
            best supporting actress   Celeste Holm

Journalist Gregory Peck, asked to write a series of magazine articles on anti-semitism, passes himself off as a Jew for six weeks and finds his eyes opened by the many hidden prejudices around him. One of the first of Hollywood's social message pictures of the post-war period and released in the same year as *Crossfire* which dealt with the same subject, was nominated for best picture but, rather undeservedly, finished up without an award to its name.

A 20th Century-Fox Picture, directed by Elia Kazan. With Gregory Peck, Dorothy McGuire, John Garfield, Celeste Holm, Anne Revere, June Havoc, Albert Dekker, Jane Wyatt. 118 mins.

Giant (1956)

Oscars (1) best direction   George Stevens

George Stevens' massive chronicle of a Texas land-rich family, spanning several generations and showing how huge empires were built by beef and oil. Based on the novel by Edna Ferber, it proved to be James Dean's last film before his death in a car crash. Both Dean (as a ranch hand who becomes an oil millionaire) and Rock Hudson (as a stubborn, old-style Texas rancher) received acting nominations.

A Warner Bros. Picture, directed by George Stevens. With Elizabeth Taylor, Rock Hudson, James Dean, Jane Withers, Chill Wills, Mercedes McCambridge, Carroll Baker, Dennis Hopper. Warner Color. 198 mins.

Gigi (1958)

Oscars (9) best film   (Arthur Freed, producer)
            best direction   Vincente Minnelli
            best screenplay   Alan Jay Lerner
            best colour   Joseph Ruttenberg
              cinematography
            best colour art direction   William A. Horning &
                                                 Preston Ames
                          set decoration Henry Grace & Keogh Gleason
            best colour costume   Cecil Beaton
              design
            best editing   Adrienne Fazan
            best scoring of a musical   Andre Previn
              picture
            best song   'Gigi'
                                               (Frederick Loewe, music:
                                               Alan Jay Lerner, lyrics)

Colette's turn-of-the-century Parisian fairy tale about an innocent little schoolgirl (Leslie Caron) who is carefully trained by her grandmother (Hermione Gingold) and aunt (Isabel Jeans) for the role of grand cocotte. An elegant musical which won awards in just about every category except acting and, at the time of its release, proved to be the biggest Oscar winner since the Academy was first formed thirty years earlier. A record that lasted no more than one year (see *Ben Hur*).

An MGM Picture, directed by Vincente Minnelli. With Leslie Caron, Maurice Chevalier, Louis Jourdan, Hermione Gingold, Eva Gabor, Jacques Bergerac, Isabel Jeans. CinemaScope/Metrocolor. 116 mins.

Humphrey Bogart in his Academy Award Winning role in 'THE AFRICAN QUEEN', 1951

'ALL ABOUT EVE', best film 1950. (Still by courtesy of Twentieth-Century Fox Film Company Limited.)

'ANNE OF THE THOUSAND DAYS', best costume design, 1969. (Universal Pictures)

From the MGM release 'AN AMERICAN IN PARIS'. © 1951 Loew's
Incorporated

Dana Andrews and Teresa Wright in 'THE BEST YEARS OF OUR LIVES',
best film of 1946 (RKO Pictures)

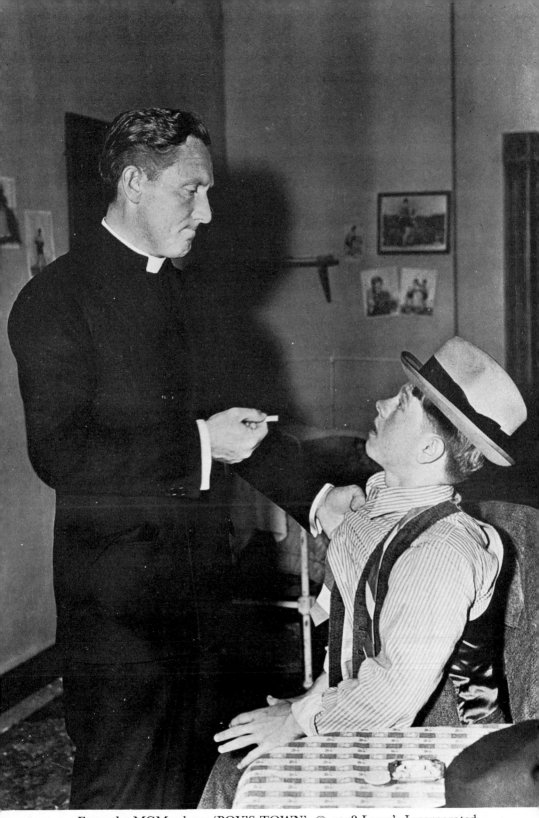

From the MGM release 'BOY'S TOWN'. © 1938 Loew's Incorporated.
Copyright renewed 1965 by Metro-Goldwyn-Mayer Inc.

Liza Minnelli (best actress) and Joel Grey (best supporting actor) in the award winning 'CABARET', 1972. (Allied Artists)

Judy Holliday, best actress 1950, for her dizzy blonde Billie Dawn in 'BORN YESTERDAY'. (Columbia Pictures Corporation Ltd)

'THE BRIDGE ON THE RIVER KWAI', winner of seven Oscars, 1957. (Columbia Pictures Corporation Ltd)

Lee Marvin receiving his 'CAT BALLOU' Oscar from Julie Andrews, 1965

'CITIZEN KANE', best original screenplay, 1941. (R.K.O. Pictures)

Richard Burton and Elizabeth Taylor in 'CLEOPATRA', 1963. (Still by
courtesy of Twentieth-Century Fox Film Company Limited)

'CAVALCADE', best picture winner, 1932/33. (Fox Film Company Limited)

From the MGM release 'THE BROADWAY MELODY'. © 1929 Metro-Goldwyn-Mayer Distributing Corporation. Copyright renewed 1956 by Loew's Incorporated

Ingmar Bergman's 'CRIES AND WHISPERS', winner of best cinematography award, 1973

'DAY FOR NIGHT', best foreign language film, 1973.

Fredric March in his Oscar winning performance in Rouben Mamoulian's
'DR. JEKYLL AND MR. HYDE', 1931/32. (Paramount Pictures)

Grace Kelly (best actress) with William Holden in 'THE COUNTRY GIRL',
1954. (Paramount Pictures)

From the MGM release 'EASTER PARADE'. © 1948 Loew's Incorporated
Copyright renewed 1975 by Metro-Goldwyn-Mayer Inc.

Walt Disney's 'DUMBO', best scoring of a musical, 1941. (Photograph: © Walt Disney Productions)
'FANTASTIC VOYAGE', best colour art direction, 1966, and special effects award. (Twentieth-Century Fox Film Company Limited)

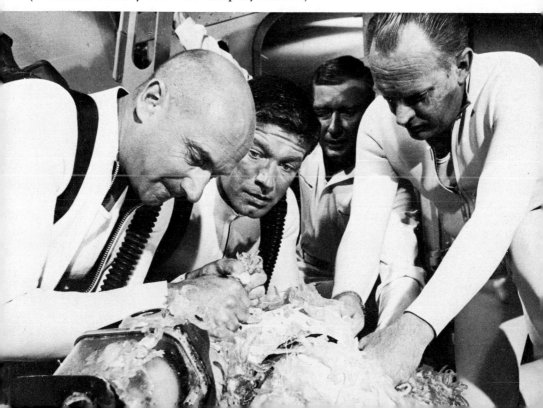

Brando's second best actor Oscar for his Don Vito Corleone in
'THE GODFATHER', 1972. (Paramount Pictures)

The Glenn Miller Story (1954)

Oscars (1) best sound recording   Leslie I. Carey

Biographical movie of the 40's bandleader Glenn Miller, an American trombonist who wanted to make music *his* way and who brought a new kind of sound to popular band music. A brilliant Harlem jam session featuring Louis Armstrong, Gene Krupa and other jazz stars is the film's highlight.

A Universal-International Picture, directed by Anthony Mann. With James Stewart, June Allyson, Henry Morgan, Charles Drake, George Tobias. Technicolor. 116 mins.

The Godfather (1972)

Oscars (3) best film   Albert S. Ruddy (producer)
            best actor   Marlon Brando
            best screenplay   Mario Puzo & Francis Ford Coppola

The gangster film of the contemporary cinema, a massive saga of honour, loyalty and brutal murder as the Corleone family of New York fights to keep its ascendancy over rival Mafia type families trying to muscle in and take over. Marlon Brando won his second Oscar for his Mafia chief Don Vito Corleone; Al Pacino (as the son who eventually succeeds to his throne), James Caan and Robert Duvall all earned supporting actor nominations. Along with its sequel, the only out and out gangster film ever to win the best picture award.

A Paramount Picture, directed by Francis Ford Coppola. With Marlon Brando, Al Pacino, James Caan, Richard Castellano, Robert Duvall, Sterling Hayden, John Marley, Richard Conte, Diane Keaton, Al Lettieri, Talia Shire, John Cazale. Technicolor. 175 mins.

The Godfather Part II (1974)

Oscars (6) best film   (Francis Ford Coppola, producer)
            best direction   Francis Ford Coppola
            best supporting actor   Robert De Niro
            best screenplay   Francis Ford Coppola &
              adaptation   Mario Puzo
            best art direction   Dean Tavoularis &
                                           Angelo Graham
                                         George R. Nelson (set
                                           decoration)
            best original dramatic   Nino Rota &
              score   Carmine Coppola

The continuing family saga with both a prelude showing how Brando's Don Vito character (played as a young man by Robert De Niro) arrived in the States from Sicily and attained his position of power, and also a sequel to Part I with Al Pacino carrying on his bloodthirsty reign. *The Godfather Part II* marks the only occasion that a sequel has won the best movie award. As in the first film, three of the year's supporting actor nominees came from the cast — De Niro, Michael V. Gazzo and Lee Strasberg.

A Paramount Picture, directed by Francis Ford Coppola. With Al Pacino, Robert Duvall, Diane Keaton, Robert De Niro, John Cazale, Talia Shire, Lee Strasberg, Michael V. Gazzo. Technicolor. 200 mins.

Going My Way (1944)

Oscars (7)	best film	(Leo McCarey, producer)
	best direction	Leo McCarey
	best actor	Bing Crosby
	best supporting actor	Barry Fitzgerald
	best screenplay	Frank Butler & Frank Cavett
	best original story	Leo McCarey
	best song	'Swinging On A Star' (James Van Heusen, music: Johnny Burke, lyrics)

Singing priest Bing Crosby turns a group of young Manhattan delinquents into a choir and tours the country with them to raise funds for the old mortgage ridden church of St. Dominics. Sentimental comedy made saltier by Barry Fitzgerald who, as a vain, stubborn little priest of a poor parish, brings out all the pathos of old age. The New York critics voted Fitzgerald best actor of the year. The Academy named Crosby best actor and Fitzgerald for the supporting award.

A Paramount Picture, directed by Leo McCarey. With Bing Crosby, Rise Stevens, Barry Fitzgerald, James Brown, Jean Heather, Eily Malyon. 130 mins.

Goldiggers of 1935 (1935)

Oscars (1)	best song	'Lullaby of Broadway' (Harry Warren, music: Al Dubin, lyrics)

The film that elevated dance director Busby Berkeley to full directorial status, a slight story of Dick Powell and Gloria Stuart finding romance in a swank New England summer hotel but made memorable by the climactic number 'Lullaby of Broadway' which is almost a film within a film, tells of the tragedy of life in a big city and which is breathtakingly performed by an army of Warner tap dancers.

A Warner Bos. Picture, directed by Busby Berkeley. With Dick Powell, Adolphe Menjou, Gloria Stuart, Alice Brady, Glenda Farrell, Frank McHugh. 95 mins.

Goldfinger (1964)

Oscars (1) best sound effects   Norman Wanstall

The third of the Bond sagas with never a let-up as Bond drives his Aston Martin special, out-judoes Honor Blackman, escapes being cut in two by a laser and fights Oddjob to the death in Fort Knox with a ticking atom bomb attached to his wrist. Gert Frobe as a criminal financier obsessed by gold is chief villain, the hat-throwing Korean Oddjob a close second.

A United Artists Picture, directed by Guy Hamilton. With Sean Connery, Gert Frobe, Honor Blackman, Shirley Eaton, Tania Mallett, Harold Sakata, Bernard Lee. Technicolor. 108 mins.

Gone with the Wind (1939)

Oscars (9) best film   (David O. Selznick, producer)
            best direction   Victor Fleming
            best actress   Vivien Leigh
            best supporting actress   Hattie McDaniel
            best screenplay   Sidney Howard
            best colour   Ernest Haller &
              cinematography   Ray Rennahan
            best art direction   Lyle Wheeler
            best editing   Hal C. Kern & James E. Newcom
        special award to William Cameron Menzies for outstanding achievement in the use of colour for the enhancement of dramatic mood in *Gone With The Wind*.

The loves of tempestuous Southern Belle Scarlett O'Hara during and after the American Civil War. At the time of the 1939 Oscar awards the most honoured film in the history of the Academy, its 9 Oscars (including the first award for colour photography and the first to a black performer, Hattie McDaniel) easily outstripping the 5 held by the previous record holder *It Happened One Night*. Vivien Leigh as Scarlett also became the first British actress to be honoured in the best actress category. Two of those who surprisingly missed out were Clark Gable for his Rhett Butler and Max Steiner for his memorable music score.

A Selznick International Picture (released through MGM), directed by Victor Fleming. With Vivien Leigh, Clark Gable, Leslie Howard, Olivia de Havilland, Hattie McDaniel, Thomas Mitchell. Technicolor. 219 mins.

The Goodbye Girl (1977)

Oscars (1)   best actor   Richard Dreyfuss

Neil Simon comedy about a former dancer, Marsha Mason, who is forced to share her Manhattan apartment when she finds that her ex-lover has sub-let their tenement home to aspiring young actor Richard Dreyfuss. Miss Mason's precocious ten-year-old daughter (Quinn Cummings) provides adolescent problems, Mr. Dreyfuss genial hostility and eventual romance.

An MGM/Warner Bros. Picture, directed by Herbert Ross. With Richard Dreyfuss, Marsha Mason, Quinn Cummings, Paul Benedict, Barbara Rhoades, Theresa Merritt, Michael Shawn. Metrocolor. 110 mins.

Goodbye Mr. Chips (1939)

Oscars (1)   best actor   Robert Donat

James Hilton's story of a public schoolmaster (Robert Donat) whose strict adherence to the rules makes him an unpopular and lonely figure with the boys but whose marriage to a young actress (Greer Garson) transforms him into a warm, understanding person. Donat aged from 25 to 83 for his Oscar winning performance — a performance incidentally that robbed Clark Gable of what seemed like a certain Oscar for Rhett Butler the same year.

An MGM Picture, directed by Sam Wood. With Robert Donat, Greer Garson, Terry Kilburn, John Mills, Paul Von Henreid, Judith Furse, Lyn Harding. 114 mins.

The Good Earth (1937)

Oscars (2)   best actress   Luise Rainer
             best cinematography   Karl Freund

Pearl Buck's moving story about Chinese farming peasants (Paul Muni and Luise Rainer) fighting for survival in pre-revolutionary China. Karl Freund's superb photography of the exterior production effects —

storm, famine, locust plague — earned him the only Oscar of his distinguished career. Rainer's acting award made her the first performer — male or female, to win two Academy Awards.

An MGM Picture, directed by Sidney Franklin. With Paul Muni, Luise Rainer, Walter Connolly, Tillie Losch, Jessie Ralph, Charley Grapewin. 138 mins.

The Graduate (1967)

Oscars (1) best direction   Mike Nichols

Satirical comedy about a young college graduate (Dustin Hoffman) who returns home a hero to his middle-class parents, finds himself protesting against the values their world represents but at the same time takes time off to have affairs with a neighbour's neurotic wife (Anne Bancroft) and her daughter (Katharine Ross). A film about the great U.S.A. dilemma — lack of communication between the generations.

A United Artists Picture, directed by Mike Nichols. With Anne Bancroft, Dustin Hoffman, Katharine Ross, William Daniels, Murray Hamilton, Elizabeth Wilson. Panavision/Technicolor. 108 mins.

Grand Hotel (1931/32)

Oscars (1) best picture   (Paul Bern, producer)

The first of Hollywood's all-star portmanteau pictures and the only one ever to win a best picture Oscar. Based on Vicki Baum's successful novel and play, it looked at life in a large luxury Berlin hotel and included just about every major star on the MGM lot — among them Garbo as a mercurial ballerina, John Barrymore as an impoverished baron, Wallace Beery as a Prussian business tycoon, Joan Crawford as his ambitious hotel stenographer and Lionel Barrymore as a dying clerk out on a final spending spree.

An MGM Picture, directed by Edmund Goulding. With Greta Garbo, John Barrymore, Joan Crawford, Wallace Beery, Lionel Barrymore, Lewis Stone, Jean Hersholt. 112 mins.

Grand Prix (1966)

Oscars (3) best editing   Frederic Steinkamp, Henry
                                    Berman, Stewart Linder &
                                    Frank Santillo
            best sound   Franklin E. Milton
            best sound effects   Gordon Daniel

Formula One motor racing looked at in depth by John Frankenheimer in a story of four drivers — Garner, Montand, Bedford, Sabato —
all out for the title of motor racing champion in a typical Grand Prix
season. Superb special effects — use of split screen and multiple images,
zooms into cars, helicopter shots, smash-ups etc.

An MGM Picture, directed by John Frankenheimer. With James
Garner, Eva Marie Saint, Yves Montand, Toshiro Mifune, Brian Bedford,
Jessica Walter, Antonio Sabato. Cinerama & Super Panavision/Metro-
color. 179 mins.

The Grapes of Wrath (1940)

Oscars (2) best direction   John Ford
            best supporting actress   Jane Darwell

John Steinbeck's odyssey of the Joads, a family of Oakies who are
driven from their homestead in the Oklahoma Dustbowl in the Depression and journey westward in a battered old ford to the promised land
of California. Henry Fonda (in his only Oscar nomination) featured as
the wanderlust son Tom Joad, Jane Darwell, in a heartbreaking performance, as his never-say-die ma.

A 20th Century-Fox Picture, directed by John Ford. With Henry
Fonda, Jane Darwell, John Carradine, Charles Grapewin, Dorris
Bowden, Russell Simpson. 127 mins.

The Great Caruso (1951)

Oscars (1) best sound recording   Douglas Shearer

MGM's Technicolor rags-to-riches musical of lowly-born Neapolitan
boy Enrico Caruso (Mario Lanza) who rises from street singer to world
famous tenor. The film made Lanza a star of the first magnitude,
earned Metro a small fortune and with its 27 songs and operatic ex-
cerpts thoroughly deserved its sound award.

An MGM Picture, directed by Richard Thorpe. With Mario Lanza,
Ann Blyth, Dorothy Kirston, Jarmila Novotna, Richard Hageman, Carl
Benton Reid, Eduard Franz. Technicolor. 109 mins.

The Greatest Show on Earth (1952)

Oscars (2) best film   (Cecil B. DeMille, producer)
            best motion picture story   Fredric M. Frank, Theodore,
                                           St. John & Frank Cavett

The only DeMille film to win the best picture award and the only time the famous producer-director was honoured with a creative Oscar although in this case it was for the former capacity as producer of the best film. Mixed in with the Ringling Bros. & Barnum and Bailey Circuses was a romantic triangle — Heston, Hutton, Wilde — a clown (James Stewart) wanted for murder and a real humdinger of a train crash which lets loose all the animals on the circus train.

A Paramount Picture, directed by Cecil B. DeMille. With James Stewart, Betty Hutton, Cornel Wilde, Charlton Heston, Gloria Grahame, Dorothy Lamour, Emmett Kelly. Technicolor. 153 mins.

Great Expectations (1947)

Oscars (2) best b/w cinematography Guy Green
            best b/w art direction   John Bryan
                  set direction   Wilfred Shingleton

Charles Dickens' novel about a young country blacksmith (John Mills) who becomes a gentleman in London society through the generosity of an unknown benefactor. Important in the history of the Awards in that together with *Black Narcissus* (see page 15) it became the first British film to scoop all four Oscars in the photography and art direction categories.

A Cineguild-Rank Picture, directed by David Lean. With John Mills, Valerie Hobson, Bernard Miles, Francis L. Sullivan, Finlay Currie, Martita Hunt, Anthony Wager, Jean Simmons, Alec Guinness. 115 mins.

The Great Gatsby (1974)

Oscars (2) best costume design   Theoni V. Aldredge
            best original song score   Nelson Riddle
                  or scoring adaptation

The third film version of Scott Fitzgerald's classic 20's novel of a mysterious racketeer, Jay Gatsby (Robert Redford) who buys a fabulous Long Island estate to be near the woman he loved and lost. Robert Redford stars as the poor little rich boy, Mia Farrow as his spoilt aristocratic ex-lover.

A Paramount Picture, directed by Jack Clayton. With Robert Redford, Mia Farrow, Bruce Dern, Karen Black, Scott Wilson, Sam Waterston, Lois Chiles. Eastman Color. 140 mins.

The Great Lie (1941)

Oscars (1) best supporting actress   Mary Astor

Unrestrained soap opera, Warners 40's style, with Bette Davis in a maternal role for a change raising George Brent's child — by fiery Mary Astor — as her own. For once Davis didn't have the acting awards all her own way and it was Astor, as Brent's spoiled first wife, who took the Oscar, albeit a supporting one.

A Warner Bros. Picture, directed by Edmund Goulding. With Bette Davis, George Brent, Mary Astor, Lucile Watson, Hattie McDaniel, Grant Mitchell, Jerome Cowan. 102 mins.

The Great McGinty (1940)

Oscars (1) best original screenplay   Preston Sturges

Brian Donlevy, down-and-out and on the skids, gains the favour of crooked political boss Akim Tamiroff by voting 37 times in one day for the same candidate thus taking the first steps towards the governor's mansion. Only when he attempts to go straight does he become less secure. Preston Sturges' first film as a writer-director.

A Paramount Picture, directed by Preston Sturges. With Brian Donlevy, Muriel Angelus, Akim Tamiroff, Allyn Joslyn, William Demarest, Louis Jean Heydt. 81 mins.

The Great Race (1965)

Oscars (1) best sound effects   Tregoweth Brown

Slapstick, comic-strip type of movie about an international car race from New York to Paris in the early 1900's. Tony Curtis as the handsome, daredevil hero, Natalie Wood as the heroine in distress and Jack Lemmon as the sneering villain in malevolent black, are the three whose paths criss-cross during the massive race.

A Warner Bros. Picture, directed by Blake Edwards. With Tony Curtis, Jack Lemmon, Natalie Wood, Peter Falk, Keenan Wynn, Arthur O'Connell, Vivian Vance. Panavision/Technicolor. 150 mins.

The Great Waltz (1938)

Oscars (1) best cinematography   Joseph Ruttenberg

Lavish MGM biography of Austrian composer Johann Strauss with Parisian Fernand Gravet as the Waltz King. Joseph Ruttenberg's swirling cameras earned him the first of his four Oscars for cinematography, a record he shares with the late Leon Shamroy.

An MGM Picture, directed by Julien Duvivier. With Luise Rainer, Fernand Gravet, Miliza Korjus, Hugh Herbert, Lionel Atwill, Minna Gombell, Herman Bing, Sig Ruman, Henry Hull. 102 mins.

The Great Ziegfeld (1936)

Oscars (3)	best film	(Hunt Stromberg, producer)
	best actress	Luise Rainer
	best dance direction	Seymour Felix for the 'A Pretty Girl Is Like A Melody' number

The story of American showman Florenz Ziegfeld (William Powell), charting his rise to fame and boasting some of the most lavish musical numbers ever put on the screen. The Oscar-winning 'A Pretty Girl Is Like A Melody' sequence is set on a massive revolving set-piece shaped like a gigantic wedding cake and carrying hundreds of men, girls, costumes and props. Luise Rainer won her Oscar for her portrayal of Ziegfeld's first wife Anna Held; Myrna Loy appeared as wife no. 2, Billie Burke.

An MGM Picture, directed by Robert Z. Leonard. With William Powell, Myrna Loy, Luise Rainer, Frank Morgan, Fanny Brice, Ray Bolger, Virginia Bruce, Nat Pendleton, Reginald Owen. 184 mins.

Green Dolphin Street (1947)

| Oscars (1) | best special effects | A. Arnold Gillespie & Warren Newcombe: visual, Douglas Shearer & Michael Steinore: audible |

Soap opera from the novel by Elizabeth Goudge with two sisters (Lana Turner and Donna Reed) after the same man (Richard Hart) in 19th century New Zealand. Native uprisings, earthquakes and tidal waves interfere with their plans to a certain extent.

An MGM Picture, directed by Victor Saville. With Lana Turner, Van Heflin, Donna Reed, Richard Hart, Frank Morgan, Edmund Gwenn, Dame May Whitty, Reginald Owen. 141 mins.

Guess Who's Coming to Dinner? (1967)

Oscars (2)   best actress   Katharine Hepburn
             best story & screenplay   William Rose

Spencer Tracy as a liberal American father and Kate Hepburn as his equally progressive wife are brought face to face with their ideals as their one and only daughter brings home black Sidney Poitier and announces her intention to marry him. The 9th and last of the movies that Tracy and Hepburn made together, Tracy dying just a few days after shooting had ended.

A Columbia Picture, directed by Stanley Kramer. With Spencer Tracy, Katharine Hepburn, Sidney Poitier, Katharine Houghton, Cecil Kellaway, Beah Richards, Roy E. Glenn Sr. Technicolor. 112 mins.

The Guns of Navarone (1961)

Oscars (1)   best special effects   Bill Warrington, visual:
                                       Vivian C. Greenham, audible

Alistair MacLean World War 2 adventure about a tough team of allied saboteurs — Peck, Niven, Quinn, etc. — who make a daring raid on a Greek island, break into the fortress of Navarone and blow up the giant German guns hidden in a cave of solid rock.

A Columbia Picture, directed by J. Lee Thompson. With Gregory Peck, David Niven, Anthony Quayle, Anthony Quinn, Stanley Baker, Irene Papas, Gia Scala, James Darren, James Robertson Justice. CinemaScope/Eastman Color. 159 mins.

Hamlet (1948)

Oscars (4) best film   (Laurence Olivier, producer)
            best actor   Laurence Olivier
            best b/w art direction   Roger K. Furse
                    set decoration   Carmen Dillon
            best b/w costume design   Roger K. Furse

Shakespeare's great tragedy transformed and reduced (from 4½ hours to 2½) by Laurence Olivier, who both directed and starred as the Prince of Denmark, who learns from a ghost that his father has been murdered and that his mother has married the murderer. The first wholly British film to be named best of the year. The b/w costume designs were also the first to be awarded an Oscar in that category; the first colour costume designs going to *Joan of Arc* (see page 82).

A Two Cities Picture, directed by Laurence Olivier. With Laurence Olivier, Eileen Herlie, Basil Sydney, Jean Simmons, Norman Wooland, Felix Aylmer 155 mins.

Harry and Tonto (1974)

Oscars (1) best actor   Art Carney

The experiences, funny and sad by turn, of elderly widower Art Carney who, after being evicted from his West Side Manhattan apartment, travels across America with his cat Tonto to start a new life in California. Carney's best actor award proved to be one of the major surprises of the 70s with the 56-year-old actor coming out ahead of such hotly fancied contenders as Albert Finney in *Murder On The Orient Express*, Dustin Hoffman in *Lenny*, Jack Nicholson in *Chinatown* and Al Pacino in *The Godfather Part II*.

A 20th Century-Fox Picture, directed by Paul Mazursky. With Art Carney, Ellen Burstyn, Chief Dan George, Geraldine Fitzgerald, Larry Hagman, Arthur Hunnicutt. De Luxe Color. 115 mins.

Harvey (1950)

Oscars (1) best supporting actress Josephine Hull

James Stewart in perhaps his most famous role as the gently eccentric Elwood P. Dowd whose amiable life in a small American town with his invisible 6ft 4in white rabbit causes considerable consternation to his sister and niece. Josephine Hull, as the sister who finishes up for a period in the mental home she had intended for her brother, won the supporting actress award. Stewart received a nomination but lost out to Jose Ferrer's *Cyrano de Bergerac*.

A Universal International Picture, directed by Henry Koster. With James Stewart, Josephine Hull, Peggy Dow, Charles Drake, Cecil Kellaway, Victoria Horne, Jesse White. 103 mins.

The Harvey Girls (1946)

Oscars (1) best song 'On The Atchison, Topeka and Santa Fe' (Harry Warren, music: Johnny Mercer, lyrics)

Boisterous Judy Garland musical about the famous Fred Harvey travelling waitresses who brought clean living, chastity and clean tablecloths to the rough-tough towns of the pioneer Southwest. Famous mainly for the Oscar winning Harry Warren/Johnny Mercer song.

An MGM Picture, directed by George Sidney. With Judy Garland, John Hodiak, Ray Bolger, Angela Lansbury, Preston Foster, Virginia O'Brien, Kenny Baker, Marjorie Main. Technicolor. 104 mins.

The Heiress (1949)

Oscars (4) best actress Olivia de Havilland
best b/w art direction Harry Horner & John Meehan
set decoration Emile Kuri
best b/w costume design Edith Head & Gile Steele
best scoring of a drama or Aaron Copland
comedy

Adaptation of Henry James' 'Washington Square' with Olivia de Havilland winning her second Oscar in four years as a plain spinster heiress who is wooed for her money by handsome fortune hunter Montgomery Clift. Ralph Richardson co-starred as the unfortunate girl's arrogant doctor father.

A Paramount Picture, directed by William Wyler. With Olivia de Havilland, Ralph Richardson, Montgomery Clift, Miriam Hopkins, Vanessa Brown, Betty Linley, Ray Collins. 115 mins.

Hello Dolly (1969)

Oscars (3) best art direction   John De Cuir, Jack Martin Smith
      & Herman Blumenthal

      set decoration   Walter M. Scott, George Hopkins, Raphael Bretton

      best scoring of a musical   Lennie Hayton & Lionel Newman

      best sound   Jack Solomon & Murray Spivak

Musical version of the Thornton Wilder play 'The Matchmaker' with Barbra Streisand as widowed Dolly Levi setting her sights on rich merchant Walter Matthau and conniving and singing her hardest until she gets him. Guest appearance of the late Louis Armstrong in the lavish title number.

A 20th Century-Fox Picture, directed by Gene Kelly. With Barbra Streisand, Walter Matthau, Michael Crawford, Louis Armstrong. Todd-AO/De Luxe Color. 148 mins.

Hello, Frisco, Hello (1943)

Oscars (1) best song   'You'll Never Know'
      (Harry Warren, music:
      Mack Gordon, lyrics)

The ups and downs of honky tonk singer Alice Faye and saloon keeper John Payne on San Francisco's Barbary coast at the turn-of-the-century. Miss Faye suffers, Mr. Payne reaches Nob Hill and then comes down again. The song 'You'll Never Know' continually links them together.

A 20th Century-Fox Picture, directed by Bruce Humberstone. With Alice Faye, John Payne, Jack Oakie, June Havoc, Lynn Bari, Laird Cregar, Ward Bond. Technicolor. 98 mins.

Here Comes Mr. Jordan (1941)

Oscars (2) best original story   Harry Segall
      best screenplay   Sidney Buchman & Seton I. Miller

Heavenly messenger Edward Everett Horton makes a dreadful error and sends prizefighter Robert Montgomery up to heaven 50 years before his time — and just as Montgomery was set to win the world's boxing championship. The problem the celestial powers have to solve? To find a new body for the boxer to occupy on his return to earth.

A Columbia Picture, directed by Alexander Hall. With Robert Montgomery, Evelyn Keyes, Claude Rains, Rita Johnson, Edward Everett Horton, James Gleason, John Emery. 93 mins.

Here Comes the Groom (1951)

Oscars (1) best song 'In The Cool, Cool, Cool Of The Evening'
(Hoagy Carmichael, music: Johnny Mercer, lyrics)

Roving reporter Bing Crosby, after sentimentally importing three French orphans to the States, finds he needs a wife to look after them and sets his sights on the highly eligible Jane Wyman even though she's already engaged to rich Bostonian Franchot Tone. Like many other movies, a film remembered primarily for a song, the Oscar-winning 'In The Cool, Cool, Cool Of The Evening'.

A Paramount Picture, directed by Frank Capra. With Bing Crosby, Jane Wyman, Alexis Smith, Franchot Tone, James Barton, Robert Keith. 113 mins.

The High and the Mighty (1954)

Oscars (1) best music score of a Dimitri Tiomkin
drama or comedy

Almost a 'Grand Hotel' of the air with the passengers and crew of a Honolulu to San Francisco airliner finding themselves looking back over their lives as the plane runs into trouble. Based on the novel by Ernest Gann and full of nervous strains and tensions even with pilots John Wayne and Robert Stack at the controls. Dimitri Tiomkin's music score was favoured over that of Leonard Bernstein's (*On The Waterfront*) which was also nominated that year.

A Warner Bros. Picture, directed by William A. Wellman. With John Wayne, Claire Trevor, Laraine Day, Robert Stack, Jan Sterling, Phil Harris, Robert Newton, David Brian, Paul Kelly, Sidney Blackmer. CinemaScope/Warner Color. 147 mins.

High Noon (1952)

Oscars (4)	best actor	Gary Cooper
	best editing	Elmo Williams & Harry Gerstad
	best music score of a drama or comedy	Dimitri Tiomkin
	best song	'High Noon' (Do Not Forsake Me, Oh My Darlin') (Dimitri Tiomkin, music: Ned Washington, lyrics)

Gary Cooper winning his second Oscar as a retiring small-town marshal who is completely abandoned by the townspeople he has defended for so long and left alone at noon to face a vengeful killer and his gang of outlaws.

A United Artists Picture, directed by Fred Zinnemann. With Gary Cooper, Katy Jurado, Thomas Mitchell, Lloyd Bridges, Grace Kelly, Otto Kruger, Lon Chaney Jr. 85 mins.

The Hindenburg (1975)

Oscars (2)	best special visual effects	Albert Whitlock & Glen Robinson
	best sound effects	Peter Berkos

The last transatlantic flight of the German airship Hindenburg before its destruction through sabotage above Lakehurst, New Jersey in April 1937. The film hinges on which of the star-studded passengers and crew is the saboteur but its real appeal lies in the brilliant photography and special effects work.

A Universal Picture, directed by Robert Wise. With George C. Scott, Anne Bancroft, William Atherton, Roy Thinnes, Gig Young, Burgess Meredith. Panavision/Technicolor. 116 mins.

A Hole in the Head (1959)

Oscars (1)	best song	'High Hopes' (James Van Heusen, music: Sammy Cahn, lyrics)

The emotional and business problems of small-time promoter-widower Frank Sinatra who operates a fleabag hotel in Miami Beach. Among his problems — his 11-year-old son, a rich widow, and an older more sensible brother (Edward G. Robinson) who bales him out from time to time. Sinatra's recording of the film's hit song 'High Hopes' earned him more fame than his performance and became one of his biggest hits.

A United Artists Picture, directed by Frank Capra. With Frank Sinatra, Edward G. Robinson, Eleanor Parker, Carolyn Jones, Thelma Ritter, Keenan Wynn. CinemaScope/De Luxe Color. 120 mins.

Holiday Inn (1942)

Oscars (1) best song   'White Christmas'
                                       (Irving Berlin: music & lyrics)

Fred Astaire and Bing Crosby in the first of the two films in which they starred together (they later appeared in *Blue Skies*) competing for the hand of blonde Marjorie Reynolds in a holiday nightclub converted from an old New England farm. Mainly a series of musical episodes, containing some of Berlin's most famous numbers as well as the Oscar-winning 'White Christmas.'

A Paramount Picture, directed by Mark Sandrich. With Bing Crosby, Fred Astaire, Marjorie Reynolds, Virginia Dale, Walter Abel, Louise Beavers, Irving Bacon. 101 mins.

The Hospital (1971)

Oscars (1) best story & screenplay   Paddy Chayefsky

George C. Scott at the top of his form as a hospital Chief of Medicine who is almost at the end of his tether both personally through the break-up of his 24-year-old marriage and professionally when he finds to his dismay that he has a mad killer loose in the wards.

A United Artists Picture, directed by Arthur Hiller. With George C. Scott, Diana Rigg, Barnard Hughes, Nancy Marchand, Stephen Elliott. De Luxe Color 102 mins.

The House on 92nd Street (1945)

Oscars (1) best original story   Charles G. Booth

Semi-documentary movie — the first of several of its kind in the post-war period — showing how the FBI smashed an American based spy ring which in 1941 was gaining access to the secrets of Process 97, code name for the Atomic Bomb.

A 20th Century-Fox Picture, directed by Henry Hathaway. With William Eythe, Lloyd Nolan, Signe Hasso, Gene Lockhart, Leo G. Carroll. 88 mins.

How Green Was My Valley (1941)

Oscars (5)	best film	Darryl F. Zanuck (producer)
	best direction	John Ford
	best supporting actor	Donald Crisp
	best b/w cinematography	Arthur Miller
	best b/w art direction	Richard Day & Nathan Juran
	int. decoration	Thomas A. Little

Novelist Richard Llewellyn's remembrance of things past, about the life and slow disintegration of a coal mining family living in a Welsh valley at the end of the last century. Donald Crisp's portrait of the head of the Morgan family earned him a supporting Oscar; art directors Richard Day and Nathan Juran earned theirs mainly for their magnificent set of the Welsh village with its cobbled streets, stone houses and colliery. The film won the best picture Oscar in a year when *Citizen Kane, The Maltese Falcon* and *The Little Foxes* were all up for the award.

A 20th Century-Fox Picture, directed by John Ford. With Walter Pidgeon, Maureen O'Hara, Donald Crisp, Anna Lee, Roddy McDowall, John Loder, Sara Allgood, Barry Fitzgerald. 118 mins.

How the West Was Won (1963)

Oscars (3)	best story & screenplay	James R. Webb
	best editing	Harold F. Kress
	best sound	Franklin E. Milton

Super-western in Cinerama tracing, through the lives of a single family, fifty years in the growth of the West from the early days of the pioneers of the Ohio River Valley through the days of the wagon trains, the gold rush and the building of the railroads, to the outlaws and the final winning of the West.

An MGM Picture, directed by John Ford, Henry Hathaway and George Marshall. With Gregory Peck, James Stewart, Henry Fonda, Richard Widmark, Debbie Reynolds, Karl Malden, Carroll Baker, George Peppard, Robert Preston, Lee J. Cobb, Eli Wallach, John Wayne. Cinerama/Technicolor. 165 mins.

Hud (1963)

Oscars (3)	best actress	Patricia Neal
	best supporting actor	Melvyn Douglas
	best b/w cinematography	James Wong Howe

Drama of modern Texas contrasting the enduring values of veteran rancher Melvyn Douglas with those of his rootless amoral son (Paul Newman) whose idea of the new breed of cowboy is to make a buck as quick as he can and own a pink cadillac convertible. Newman's swaggering contemporary rebel was perhaps unlucky not to gain an Oscar; Melvyn Douglas and Patricia Neal as the rancher's sexy housekeeper were more fortunate.

A Paramount Picture, directed by Martin Ritt. With Paul Newman, Melvyn Douglas, Patricia Neal, Brandon de Wilde, Whit Bissell, John Ashley. 112 mins.

The Human Comedy (1943)

Oscars (1) best original story   William Saroyan

The lives of ordinary people living in a small Californian town in World War II and of the joys and sorrows they experience during the bitterness of the war years. Micky Rooney stars as the Western Union delivery boy who has the unenviable task of delivering telegrams during a time when a telegram can only mean that someone has been killed or wounded overseas.

An MGM Picture, directed by Clarence Brown. With Mickey Rooney, James Craig, Frank Morgan, Fay Bainter, Marsha Hunt, Van Johnson, Donna Reed. 118 mins.

The Hurricane (1937)

Oscars (1) best sound recording   Thomas T. Moulton

Jon Hall and Dorothy Lamour as two South Seas Islanders whose idyllic way of life is almost destroyed by the vindictive French governor of the islands. The hurricane of the title was the work of James Basevi who would almost certainly have won an Oscar if the special effects awards had then been in existance (they didn't begin until 1939). As it was it was the sound rather than the sight of the terrifying hurricane that brought an award to UA's sound dept.

A Sam Goldwyn Production (released through United Artists), directed by John Ford. With Dorothy Lamour, Jon Hall, Mary Astor, C. Aubrey Smith, Thomas Mitchell, Raymond Massey, John Carradine. 110 mins.

The Hustler (1961)

Oscars (2) best b/w cinematography   Eugene Shuftan
            best b/w art direction   Harry Horner
                 set decoration   Gene Callahan

Paul Newman as a young pool shark who cons a living in cheap pool rooms whilst waiting to take on (and over from) reigning pool champ Minnesotta Fats (Jackie Gleason). Nominated for as many as 9 Oscars, the film was unlucky in being released the same year as the musical *West Side Story* and subsequently finished up with only camerawork and design awards.

A 20th Century-Fox Picture, directed by Robert Rossen. With Paul Newman, Piper Laurie, George C. Scott, Jackie Gleason, Myron McCormick, Murray Hamilton. CinemaScope. 135 mins.

I Want to Live (1958)

Oscars (1) best actress   Susan Hayward

Robert Wise's powerful indictment of capital punishment with Susan Hayward at last winning her Oscar (she had 4 previous nominations) as the habitual petty criminal Barbara Graham who went to the gas chamber in San Quentin on a charge of murder but who protested her innocence right to the end.

A United Artists Picture, directed by Robert Wise. With Susan Hayward, Simon Oakland, Virginia Vincent, Theodore Bikel, Wesley Lau, Philip Coolidge. 120 mins.

I Wanted Wings (1941)

Oscars (1) best special effects   Farciot Edouart & Gordon
                                        Jennings (photographic),
                                        Louis Mesenkop (sound)

Wartime propaganda piece about three very different young men — Long Island playboy Ray Milland, garage mechanic William Holden and college athlete Wayne Morris — undergoing rigorous training for the Army Air Corps. A class 'B' story given excitement in its time by special effects wizardry and aerial shots of planes flashing across the sky.

A Paramount Picture, directed by Mitchell Leisen. With Ray Milland, William Holden, Wayne Morris, Brian Donlevy, Constance Moore, Veronica Lake, Harry Davenport. 131 mins.

I'll Cry Tomorrow (1955)

Oscars (1) best b/w costume design   Helen Rose

Susan Hayward suffering almost as much as she did three years later in *I Want To Live* as singer Lillian Roth who slips from the top to skid row because of chronic alcoholism. Hayward, who sang her own songs, was recognised as best actress at the Cannes Film Festival; Hollywood gave her only a nomination preferring Anna Magnani in *The Rose Tattoo* as the year's best.

An MGM Picture, directed by Daniel Mann. With Susan Hayward, Richard Conte, Eddie Albert, Jo Van Fleet, Don Taylor, Ray Danton, Margo. 117 mins.

The Informer (1935)

Oscars (4) best direction   John Ford
            best actor   Victor McLaglen
            best screenplay   Dudley Nichols
            best music score   Max Steiner

Liam O'Flaherty's novel of Dublin during the troubles centering around a slow-witted Irish giant (McLaglen) who turns traitor and betrays a comrade to the police because he needs the money to go to America. A monumental performance from McLaglen as Gypo Nolan and very atmospheric direction from John Ford who here won the first of his four Academy Awards.

An RKO Picture, directed by John Ford. With Victor McLaglen, Heather Angel, Preston Foster, Margot Grahame, Wallace Ford, Una O'Connor. 91 mins.

Interrupted Melody (1955)

Oscars (1) best story & screenplay   William Ludwig & Sonya Levien

Another MGM movie of '55 which dealt with the comeback of a famous entertainer, this time Australian opera singer Marjorie Lawrence who was stricken with polio at the height of her fame but who courageously overcame her disability and made a triumphant return to the stage. Eileen Farrell dubbed 8 arias for Eleanor Parker who was nominated for an Academy Award for her performance but remained one of those actresses who was frequently on the verge of winning but never won an Oscar.

An MGM Picture, directed by Curtis Bernhardt. With Glenn Ford, Eleanor Parker, Roger Moore, Cecil Kellaway, Peter Leeds, Evelyn Ellis. CinemaScope/Eastman Color 106 mins.

In Old Arizona (1928/29)

Oscars (1) best actor   Warner Baxter

Warner Baxter as the caballero The Cisco Kid (a character played later by several other actors) but here in Academy Award winning style by Baxter as he robs Wells Fargo, keeps one step ahead of the law and comes dangerously near to death as he becomes infatuated with double-dealing Mexican girl, Dorothy Burgess.

A Fox Picture, directed by Raoul Walsh and Irving Cummings. With Edmund Lowe, Warner Baxter, Dorothy Burgess, J. Farrell MacDonald, Ivan Linow. 95 mins.

In Old Chicago (1937)

Oscars (2) best supporting actress   Alice Brady
            best assistant direction   Robert Webb

Melodrama built around the great Chicago fire of 1871 with the special effects men winning the honours for their recreation of the fire — said to have burned on the Fox lot for fully three days. The Oscar, however, went to Alice Brady for her portrayal of Mrs. O'Leary whose three sons, Tyrone Power, Don Ameche and Tom Brown find adventure and political opportunity in the city. Alice Faye co-starred as the girl who loves Power taking over the role from Jean Harlow who had been cast for the film just prior to her death.

A 20th Century-Fox Picture, directed by Henry King. With Tyrone Power, Alice Faye, Don Ameche, Alice Brady, Andy Devine, Brian Donlevy, Phyllis Brooks, Tom Brown. 110 mins.

In the Heat of the Night (1967)

Oscars (5) best film   Walter Mirisch (producer)
            best actor   Rod Steiger
            best screenplay   Stirling Silliphant
            best editing   Hal Ashby
            best sound   Walter Goss

Quiet little movie which, like *Crossfire* some twenty years before, explored an important social problem — racial prejudice in the Deep South — through the form of a crime thriller. Rod Steiger stars as the thick-witted, small town police chief who has to investigate a murder, Sidney Poitier is the black homicide expert from Philadelphia who is ordered to help the grudging Steiger find the suspect. The film won the best picture award over the more hotly fancied *Bonnie and Clyde* and *The Graduate* — and in retrospect deservedly so.

A United Artists Picture, directed by Norman Jewison. With Rod Steiger, Sidney Poitier, Warren Oates, Lee Grant, James Patterson, Quentin Dean, Larry Gates. De Luxe Color. 109 mins.

The Invaders (1942)

(Original U.K. title: Forty Ninth Parallel)

Oscars (1) best original story   Emeric Pressburger

War drama, heavily laced with propaganda, about the adventures of a group of Nazis when their submarine is sunk and they try to make it to safety across Canada. Chief Nazi is Eric Portman, assorted democrats, Leslie Howard, Laurence Olivier, Anton Walbrook. The story by Pressburger won the film its Oscar; more deserving would have been Vaughan Williams beautiful music which was not even among the best music score nominees.

An Ortus Film, directed by Michael Powell. With Leslie Howard, Raymond Massey, Laurence Olivier, Anton Walbrook, Eric Portman, Glynis Johns, Niall MacGinnis. 123 mins.

Investigation of a Citizen Above Suspicion (1970)

Oscars (1) best foreign language film Italy

Drama about a powerful Rome police chief who meddles in the investigation of a murder he has himself committed, perfectly sure in his own mind that, since he has been promoted to a high office in political intelligence, he is above the law.

A Vera Film, directed by Elio Petri. With Gian Maria Volonte, Florinda Bolkan, Salvo Randone, Gianni Santuccio, Arturo Dominici. Technicolor. 115 mins.

Irma La Douce (1963)

Oscars (1) best scoring: adaptation   Andre Previn
              or treatment

Billy Wilder's straight comedy of the Broadway musical hit, omitting the 16 numbers and concentrating solely on the relationship between a Parisian prostitute (Shirley MacLaine) and a gendarme (Jack Lemmon) who is so jealous of his love for her that he disguises himself as an English nobleman in order to keep her for himself.

A United Artists Picture, directed by Billy Wilder. With Jack Lemmon, Shirley MacLaine, Lou Jacobi, Bruce Yarnell, Herschel Bernardi, Hope Holiday, Joan Shawlee. Panavision/Technicolor. 147 mins.

It Happened One Night (1934)

Oscars (5)	best film	Harry Cohn (producer)
	best direction	Frank Capra
	best actor	Clark Gable
	best actress	Claudette Colbert
	best writing adaptation	Robert Riskin

The first, and until *One Flew Over The Cuckoo's Nest*, only film to win all five major Academy Awards — a sleeper from Columbia (who had never won a best picture award before) about a runaway heiress (Colbert) and a wandering journalist (Gable) who form a lasting relationship in their journey across country together. The movie earned Frank Capra the first of the three directorial awards he won in the thirties. Note: Capra still holds the record of being the only director to win 3 Oscars within a five year span of film-making. See also *Mr. Deeds Goes To Town* and *You Can't Take It With You*.

A Columbia Picture, directed by Frank Capra. With Claudette Colbert, Clark Gable, Walter Connolly, Roscoe Karns, Jameson Thomas, Alan Hale, Ward Bond. 105 mins.

It's a Mad, Mad, Mad, Mad World (1963)

Oscars (1)	best sound effects	Walter G. Elliott

Retiring police captain Spencer Tracy, determined to go out with a last big 'cop', chases a group of people towards a dead gangster's hidden treasure — and then makes off with the loot himself. Massive slapstick comedy full of wild chases, car and plane crashes, etc.

A United Artists Picture, directed by Stanley Kramer. With Spencer Tracy, Milton Berle, Sid Caesar, Buddy Hackett. Ethel Merman, Mickey Rooney, Phil Silvers, Terry Thomas. Ultra Panavision/Technicolor. 190 mins.

Jaws (1975)

Oscars (3) best editing   Verna Fields
              best sound   Robert Hoyt, Roger Heman,
                                              Earl Madery & John Carter
              best original score   John Williams

A trio of shark hunters put out to sea in a ramshackle boat to track down the massive shark that has terrorised and killed along the beaches of a Long Island holiday resort. For a short period the number one box-office attraction of all time, but a long way from an Oscar record holder, coming out way behind 75's top winner *One Flew Over The Cuckoo's Nest.*

A Universal Picture, directed by Steven Spielberg. With Roy Scheider, Robert Shaw, Richard Dreyfuss, Lorraine Gary, Murray Hamilton, Carl Gottlieb. Panavision/Technicolor. 125 mins.

Jezebel (1938)

Oscars (2) best actress   Bette Davis
              best supporting actress   Fay Bainter

Romantic melodrama of New Orleans in the 1850s with spoiled wealthy Southern belle (Davis) finding through bitter experience that life is not all sweetness and light and hers for the taking. Handsome young banker Henry Fonda and George Brent are the rivals for her affections, Fay Bainter her sympathetic aunt.

A Warner Bros. Picture, directed by William Wyler. With Bette Davis, Henry Fonda, George Brent, Donald Crisp, Fay Bainter, Margaret Lindsay, Henry O'Neill, John Litel. 100 mins.

Joan of Arc (1948)

Oscars (2) best colour cinematography Joseph Valentine, William V.
Skall & Winton C. Hoch
best colour costume design Dorothy Jeakins & Karinska

Account of the life of the young French farm girl (Ingrid Bergman) who, in 15th century France, had religious visions when she was 13, went on to lead the French armies against the English and was eventually tried for sorcery and burned at the stake. The first film to win an Award in the colour costume category.

An RKO Picture, directed by Victor Fleming. With Ingrid Bergman, Jose Ferrer, Francis L. Sullivan, J. Carrol Naish, Ward Bond, Gene Lockhart. Technicolor. 145 mins.

Johnny Belinda (1948)

Oscars (1) best actress Jane Wyman

Deaf-mute farm girl Jane Wyman, living in a remote Nova Scotia fishing community, is befriended and educated by kindly local doctor Lew Ayres after being raped by drunken seaman Stephen McNally. Wyman's Oscar was the film's only award despite the fact that it was nominated in 12 categories.

A Warner Bros. Picture, directed by Jean Negulesco. With Jane Wyman, Lew Ayres, Charles Bickford, Agnes Moorehead, Stephen McNally, Jan Sterling, Rosalind Ivan. 102 mins.

Johnny Eager (1942)

Oscars (1) best supporting actor Van Heflin

Robert Taylor, vicious for once as a paroled convict who runs a host of criminal activities on the side, gets together with good girl Lana Turner, stepdaughter of the D.A. who put Taylor away in the first place. Advertised as TNT ('Taylor 'n Turner') the film's most memorable performance came from Van Heflin as Taylor's drunken, cynical pal, a many-shaded portrayal that won Heflin an Oscar and made him a star in his own right.

An MGM Picture, directed by Mervyn LeRoy. With Robert Taylor, Lana Turner, Edward Arnold, Van Heflin, Robert Sterling, Patricia Dane, Glenda Farrell. 107 mins.

The Joker is Wild (1957)

Oscars (1)   best song   'All The Way'
                                          (James Van Heusen, music:
                                          Sammy Cahn, lyrics)

Frank Sinatra as Joe E. Lewis, an entertainer who started out as a pro-
mising young nightclub singer of the roaring 20s, had his vocal chords
slashed when he fell foul of the mobsters and then made an unlikely
comeback as a humourist. Downbeat drama, with alcoholism and
several women, among them Mitzi Gaynor and Jeanne Crain, adding
further complications to Lewis' life.

A Paramount Picture, directed by Charles Vidor. With Frank Sinatra,
Jeanne Crain, Mitzi Gaynor, Eddie Albert, Beverly Garland, Jackie
Coogan, Barry Kelley, Ted de Corsia. Vista Vision. 126 mins.

The Jolson Story (1946)

Oscars (2)   best sound recording   John Livadary
             best scoring of a musical   Morris Stoloff
                picture

Columbia biography of the legendary vaudeville entertainer from his
boyhood to his success on stage and in the early talkies. Jolson, who
wanted to play himself in the movie, sang the songs and actor Larry
Parks mimed all-time hits like 'Swanee', 'April Showers', 'Mammy.'
Evelyn Keyes featured as Jolson's first wife, Ruby Keeler.

A Columbia Picture, directed by Alfred E. Green. With Larry Parks,
Evelyn Keyes, William Demarest, Bill Goodwin, Ludwig Donath,
Tamara Shayne, John Alexander. Technicolor. 128 mins.

Judgment at Nuremberg (1961)

Oscars (2)   best actor   Maximilian Schell
             best screenplay   Abby Mann

Just how guilty and responsible were the German people for Hitler's
Third Reich? This gigantic movie attempts to answer the unanswerable
as it follows the trial of four former Hitler judges in a Nuremberg court
presided over by small town American judge Spencer Tracy. Maximilian
Schell won an Oscar for his fiercely nationalistic defence counsel, Tracy
a best actor nomination, and Judy Garland and Montgomery Clift
supporting nominations for their Nazi victims of torture.

A United Artists Picture, directed by Stanley Kramer. With Spencer
Tracy, Burt Lancaster, Richard Widmark, Marlene Dietrich, Maximilian
Schell, Judy Garland, Montgomery Clift. 178 mins.

Julia (1977)

Oscars (3) best supporting actor   Jason Robards
              best supporting actress   Vanessa Redgrave
              best screenplay   Alvin Sargent

The awakening in the thirties of playwright Lillian Hellman (Jane Fonda) to the threat of Nazism through the persecution and final execution of her beloved childhood friend Julia (Vanessa Redgrave). A sensitive Fred Zinnemann film made with taste, style and elegance. Jason Robards as Hellman's lover, author Dashiell Hammett, won his second successive supporting Oscar, the only supporting performer to do so in the history of the Academy.

    A 20th Century-Fox Picture, directed by Fred Zinnemann. With Jane Fonda, Vanessa Redgrave, Jason Robards, Maximilian Schell, Hal Holbrook, Rosemary Murphy. Technicolor; prints by Deluxe. 117 mins.

Julius Caesar (1953)

Oscars (1) best b/w art direction   Cedric Gibbons &
                                    Edward Carfagno
             set decoration   Edwin B. Willis &
                                      Hugh Hunt

Shakespeare's 'political thriller' about the assassination of Julius Caesar in 44 B.C. Straight Shakespeare, acted with great power by Brando as Marc Antony and with intelligence and subtlety by James Mason as Brutus. The actual assassination was filmed twice by director Joe Mankiewicz, firstly in this film when Louis Calhern featured as the doomed emperor and a decade later when Rex Harrison played the role in *Cleopatra*.

    An MGM Picture, directed by Joseph L. Mankiewicz. With James Mason, Marlon Brando, Louis Calhern, John Gielgud, Edmond O'Brien, Greer Garson, Deborah Kerr, George Macready. 121 mins.

Kentucky (1938)

Oscars (1) best supporting actor   Walter Brennan

A story of rival horsebreeding families in the blue grass country with Loretta Young as the heroine of the hour paying her family's debts by winning the Kentucky Derby. Walter Brennan collected his second supporting Oscar in three years as Loretta's uncle.

A 20th Century-Fox Picture, directed by David Butler. With Loretta Young, Richard Greene, Walter Brennan, Douglas Dumbrille, Karen Morley, Moroni Olsen. Technicolor. 95 mins.

Key Largo (1948)

Oscars (1) best supporting actress   Claire Trevor

Gangster thriller with ex-bootlegger Edward G. Robinson and his hoods holding Bogie, Bacall and Lionel Barrymore hostage in a resort hotel on the stormy Florida Keys. The film's highspot is Claire Trevor's performance as a faded torch singer, a portrait in jaded alcoholism that deservedly won her the year's best supporting actress award.

A Warner Bros. Picture, directed by John Huston. With Humphrey Bogart, Edward G. Robinson, Lauren Bacall, Lionel Barrymore, Claire Trevor, Thomas Gomez. 101 mins.

The King and I (1956)

Oscars (5) best actor   Yul Brynner
best colour art direction   Lyle R. Wheeler & John De Cuir
set decoration Walter M. Scott & Paul S. Fox
best colour costume design Irene Sharaff
best sound recording   Carl Faulkner
best scoring of a musical   Alfred Newman & Ken Darby

The musical remake of *Anna And The King Of Siam* (see page 7) with Yul Brynner as the stubborn Siamese King and Deborah Kerr as his children's spirited tutor. Music by Rodgers & Hammerstein. Oscars – Brynner's apart, mainly for the film's sumptuous production values.

A 20th Century-Fox Picture, directed by Walter Lang. With Deborah Kerr, Yul Brynner, Rita Moreno, Martin Benson, Terry Saunders, Rex Thompson, Carlos Rivas. CinemaScope/De Luxe Color. 133 mins.

King Kong (1976)

Oscars (1) best special visual effects   Carlo Rimbaldi, Glen Robinson
and Frank Van Der Veer

Remake of the 1933 monster classic with the 40ft Kong once again being discovered on Skull Island and transported to civilization to be humiliated. Part of the film's 'special effects' were performed by actor Rick Baker including some of the close-ups in ape costume. The 1933 movie – incredibly – didn't win a single award or nomination.

A Dino De Laurentiis Corporation Picture, directed by John Guillermin. With Jeff Bridges, Charles Grodin, Jessica Lange, John Randolph, Rene Auberjonois, Julius Harris. Panavision/Metrocolor. 135 mins.

King of Jazz (1929/30)

Oscars (1) best art direction   Herman Rosse

Universal's contribution to the musical revue type of movie produced by several of the top Hollywood studios at the advent of sound. Paul Whiteman and his band playing from atop a gigantic piano headlined the film which boasted huge production numbers, two-colour Technicolor sequences, and somewhere in the huge cast, The Rhythm Boys – a singing threesome one of which was Bing Crosby.

A Universal Picture, directed by John Murray Anderson. With Paul Whiteman and His Orchestra, Jeanette Loff, Stanley Smith, The Rhythm Boys (Bing Crosby, Harry Barris, Al Rinker), The Brox Sisters, John Boles. Two-Colour Technicolor sequences. 105 mins.

King Solomon's Mines (1950)

Oscars (2) best colour cinematography Robert Surtees
         best editing   Ralph E. Winters &
                                     Conrad A. Nervig

H. Rider Haggard's adventure story about the search by great white hunter Allan Quartermain (Stewart Granger) for a woman's missing explorer husband and the famed diamond mines of darkest Africa guarded by the 7ft Watusi tribe. Photographed on location by Robert Surtees who caught all the different forms of African animal life, including a stampede, in his great camerawork.

An MGM Picture, directed by Compton Bennet and Andrew Marton. With Deborah Kerr, Stewart Granger, Richard Carlson, Hugo Haas, Lowell Gilmore. Technicolor. 102 mins.

Kitty Foyle (1940)

Oscars (1) best actress   Ginger Rogers

Ginger Rogers proving that she was more than just Fred Astaire's dancing partner by winning a tear-stained Oscar as a girl from the wrong side of the tracks who falls in love with a handsome socialite but eventually finds true happiness with a man from her own level of society. Adapted by Dalton Trumbo from the novel by Christopher Morley.

An RKO Picture, directed by Sam Wood. With Ginger Rogers, Dennis Morgan, James Craig, Eduardo Ciannelli, Ernest Cossart, Gladys Cooper. 108 mins.

Klute (1971)

Oscars (1) best actress   Jane Fonda

Kafka-type thriller with Donald Sutherland as a private eye searching for a suburban husband last seen in New York City. Fonda is the call girl who once numbered the husband among her clients.

A Warner Bros. Picture, directed by Alan J. Pakula. With Jane Fonda, Donald Sutherland, Charles Cioffi, Roy Scheider, Dorothy Tristan, Rita Gam. Panavision/Technicolor. 114 mins.

Lady Be Good (1941)

Oscars (1) best song

'The Last Time I Saw Paris'
(Jerome Kern, music:
Oscar Hammerstein II, lyrics)

The ups and downs of married songwriters Ann Sothern and Robert Young in America's Tin Pan Alley. A slender plot, superb Gershwin numbers (including the Oscar-winning 'The Last Time I Saw Paris') and a lavish, Busby Berkeley staged 'Fascinating Rhythm' number with Eleanor Powell and a massive chorus line.

An MGM Picture, directed by Norman Z. McLeod. With Eleanor Powell, Ann Sothern, Robert Young, Lionel Barrymore, John Carroll, Red Skelton, Virginia O'Brien. 111 mins.

The Last Command (1927/28)

Oscars (1) best actor   Emil Jannings

Emil Jannings as a one-time White Russian General who flees the revolution and ends up as an extra in Hollywood. The film was based on an idea by Ernst Lubitsch and allowed a European performer to win the first best actor Oscar ever awarded, Jannings also being named for his performance in *The Way Of All Flesh* (see page 176). Jannings' competition in that historic first year came from Richard Barthelmess (*The Noose* & *The Patent Leather Kid*) and Charles Chaplin (*The Circus*).

A Paramount Picture, directed by Josef Von Sternberg. With Emil Jannings, Evelyn Brent, William Powell, Nicholas Soussanin, Michael Visaroff. 95 mins.

The Last Picture Show (1971)

Oscars (2) best supporting actor   Ben Johnson
            best supporting actress   Cloris Leachman

Study of the day-to-day life in a bleak little Texas town in the early 50's. From a cast filled mainly with young American unknowns, the two older members of the cast — Ben Johnson as the owner of the pool hall and the local fleapit cinema (the only entertainment in town) and Cloris Leachman as a neglected wife — emerged as the film's Oscar winners.

A Columbia Picture, directed by Peter Bogdanovich. With Timothy Bottoms, Jeff Bridges, Cybill Shepherd, Ben Johnson, Cloris Leachman, Ellen Burstyn, Eileen Brennan, Clu Gulager, Sam Bottoms. 118 mins.

Laugh, Clown, Laugh (1927/28)

Oscars (1) best title writing   Joseph Farnham

One of the three films to be awarded a title writing Oscar (see also *The Fair Co-Ed* and *Telling The World* written by Farnham the same year) before sound finally took over in the late 20s — the near tragic story of a clown (Lon Chaney) and his love for a young woman he adopted as a child who, in turn, is desired by wealthy nobleman Nils Asther.

An MGM Picture, directed by Herbert Brenon. With Lon Chaney, Bernard Siegel, Loretta Young, Cissy Fitzgerald, Nils Asther, Gwen Lee. 8 reels.

Laura (1944)

Oscars (1) best b/w cinematography Joseph LaShelle

Mystery thriller about a detective's obsession with the portrait of a beautiful woman (Gene Tierney) whose violent death he is investigating. High among the suspects: Vincent Price, Judith Anderson and Clifton Webb as the cynical, acid-tongued New York columnist Waldo Lydecker. The latter was pipped on the post for the supporting award by Barry Fitzgerald who won for his priest in *Going My Way*.

A 20th Century-Fox Picture, directed by Otto Preminger. With Gene Tierney, Dana Andrews, Clifton Webb, Vincent Price, Judith Anderson. 88 mins.

The Lavender Hill Mob (1952)

Oscars (1) best story & screenplay   T. E. B. Clarke

Meek little bank clerk Alec Guinness, sculptor associate Stanley Holloway and small-time crooks Sid James and Alfie Bass steal a million pounds worth of gold bullion, melt it down and smuggle it out of the country in the form of miniature Eiffel Towers. The only Ealing comedy ever to be honoured by the Academy. Those Ealing films that were nominated in their respective years were: *Saraband For Dead Lovers* (art direction), *Passport To Pimlico* (story and screenplay) — both 49, *The Lavender Hill Mob* (again, this time for best actor, Alec Guinness), *The Cruel Sea* (screenplay) — 53, and *The Ladykillers* (story and screenplay) — 56.

An Ealing Picture, directed by Charles Crichton. With Alec Guinness, Stanley Holloway, Sidney James, Alfie Bass, Marjorie Fielding, John Gregson, Clive Morton. 78 mins.

Lawrence of Arabia (1962)

Oscars (7)	best film	Sam Spiegel (producer)
	best direction	David Lean
	best colour cinematography	Freddie A. Young
	best colour art direction	John Box & John Stoll
	set decoration	Dario Simoni
	best editing	Anne Coates
	best sound recording	John Cox
	best original music score	Maurice Jarre

The film that many called the first truly satisfying epic, combining on the one hand a spectacular look at two years of Lawrence's Arabian campaigns and on the other a deeper investigation into the complexities of Lawrence's character. Freddie Young's enormous desert vistas remain among the most beautiful ever put on the screen.

A Columbia Picture, directed by David Lean. With Peter O'Toole, Alec Guinness, Anthony Quinn, Jack Hawkins, Omar Sharif, Anthony Quayle, Claude Rains, Arthur Kennedy, Jose Ferrer, Donald Wolfit, Super Panavision 70/Technicolor. 221 mins.

Leave Her to Heaven (1945)

Oscars (1) best colour cinematography Leon Shamroy

Gene Tierney in her element — and in one of her best roles of the 40's — as a femme fatale of the most demented kind, a murderously possessive wife who allows her husband's crippled brother to drown before her eyes, deliberately kills her own unborn child and finally takes poison in order to incriminate her half-sister Jeanne Crain for the crime. Lurid but handsomely photographed.

A 20th Century-Fox Picture, directed by John M. Stahl. With Gene Tierney, Cornel Wilde, Jeanne Crain, Vincent Price, Mary Philips, Ray Collins, Gene Lockhart. Technicolor. 111 mins.

Les Girls (1957)

Oscars (1) best costume design   Orry-Kelly

Until Kelly's reappearance in the *That's Entertainment* films his last
musical picture at MGM, a smart sophisticated film about an American
hoofer (Kelly) who tours with his dancing act through Europe falling
in love with each of his dancing partners in turn — American Mitzi
Gaynor, scatterbrained British dancer Kay Kendall and French beauty
Taina Elg.
   An MGM Picture, directed by George Cukor. With Gene Kelly, Mitzi
Gaynor, Kay Kendall, Taina Elg, Jacques Bergerac, Leslie Phillips, Henry
Daniels. CinemaScope/Metrocolor. 114 mins.

Let it Be (1970)

Oscars (1) best original song score   (music & lyrics by The Beatles)

Beatles documentary providing an intimate view of the group as musical
creators and performers, showing them at rehearsing, recording and off-
set sessions.
   A United Artists Picture, directed by Michael Lindsay-Hogg. With
Paul McCartney, John Lennon, George Harrison, Ringo Starr. Technicolor. 81 mins.

A Letter to Three Wives (1949)

Oscars (2) best direction   Joseph L. Mankiewicz
            best screenplay   Joseph L. Mankiewicz

Three small-town wives receive a joint message from their best friend
telling them that she has run off with one of their husbands only she
doesn't say which one. During the course of the film each wife
examines her marriage in flashback wondering if her husband is the
guilty party. An intriguing aspect of the film is that the lady who sent the
letter is never seen, only heard. Her voice belonged to that of Celeste
Holm.
   A 20th Century-Fox Picture, directed by Joseph L. Mankiewicz.
With Jeanne Crain, Linda Darnell, Ann Sothern, Kirk Douglas, Paul
Douglas, Barbara Lawrence, Jeffrey Lynn, Connie Gilchrist, Florence
Bates, Thelma Ritter. 103 mins.

The Life of Emile Zola (1937)

Oscars (3)	best film	Jack L. Warner (producer)
	best supporting actor	Joseph Schildkraut
	best screenplay	Norman Reilly Raine
		Heinz Herald & Geza Herczeg

Not really a life story, more a reconstruction of the notorius Dreyfus affair when the famed novelist (Paul Muni) dared all the powers of France — the army, the law, the government — to stop him in his crusade to free the wrongly imprisoned Dreyfus, a French captain condemned to Devil's Isand because of the anti-semitism in the hierarchy of the French army. The first Warner Bros. picture to be named best of the year since the awards were started ten years earlier: Previous Warner nominees which missed out — *Disraeli, 42nd Street, I Am A Fugitive From A Chain Gang, Here Comes The Navy, Captain Blood, A Midsummer Night's Dream, Anthony Adverse* and *The Story Of Louis Pasteur.*

A Warner Bros. Picture, directed by William Dieterle. With Paul Muni, Gale Sondergaard, Joseph Schildkraut, (Dreyfus) Gloria Holden, Donald Crisp, Erin O'Brien-Moore, John Litel, Henry O'Neill. 116 mins.

Lili (1953)

| Oscars (1) | best music score of a drama or comedy | Bronislau Kaper |

Lonely little orphan girl Leslie Caron attaches herself to a travelling French carnival and is adored by a crippled puppeteer (Mel Ferrer) who can only bring himself to speak to her through the mouths of his marionettes. The song 'Hi Lili, Hi Lo' was not among the best five song nominees but composer Bronislau Kaper received consolation for his admirable music score which won him his only Oscar.

An MGM Picture, directed by Charles Walters. With Leslie Caron, Mel Ferrer, Jean-Pierre Aumont, Zsa Zsa Gabor, Kurt Kasznar. Technicolor. 81 mins.

Lilies of the Field (1963)

| Oscars (1) | best actor | Sidney Poitier |

24 years after Hattie McDaniel had become the first black performer to win a supporting Academy Award, Sidney Poitier won the main acting Oscar for his portrait of the footloose, light-hearted handyman Homer Smith who, against his better judgment, agrees to help some

refugee nuns build a chapel in the middle of the Arizona desert. McDaniel and Poitier remain the only two black performers to have won Oscars.

A United Artists Picture, directed by Ralph Nelson. With Sidney Poitier, Lilia Skala, Lisa Mann, Isa Crino. 94 mins.

Limelight (1952)

| Oscars (1) | best original dramatic score of 1972 | Charles Chaplin, Raymond Rasch & Larry Russell |

An ageing, once famous music hall comedian (Charles Chaplin) saves a young dancer (Claire Bloom) from suicide, restores her self-confidence as he nurses her back to health and finally makes a successful ballerina out of her. The film's music award is unique in that it was awarded 20 years after the picture's first release in Europe, the film being banned in the USA until 1972.

A United Artists Picture, directed by Charles Chaplin. With Charles Chaplin, Claire Bloom, Sydney Chaplin, Nigel Bruce, Norman Lloyd, Buster Keaton, Marjorie Bennett. 143 mins.

The Lion in Winter (1968)

Oscars (3)	best actress	Katharine Hepburn
	best screenplay	James Goldman
	best original music score	John Barry

Power politics in the twelfth century depicting the ruthless skirmishing among England's royal family — Henry II (Peter O'Toole), his wife Eleanor of Aquitaine (Katharine Hepburn) and their three scheming sons — in choosing a successor to the crown. Based on the play by Goldman and boasting the only shared best actress award in Academy history (see Barbra Streisand in *Funny Girl* for the year's other best actress winner).

An Avco-Embassy Picture, directed by Anthony Harvey. With Peter O'Toole, Katharine Hepburn, Jane Merrow, John Castle, Anthony Hopkins, Nigel Terry, Timothy Dalton. Panavision/Eastman Color. 134 mins.

A Little Night Music (1977)

| Oscars (1) | best adaptation music score | Jonathan Tunick |

Elegant period comedy of manners set in Vienna and adapted from the Stephen Sondheim Broadway musical which, in turn, was inspired by the Ingmar Bergman film, *Smiles Of A Summer Night*. Elizabeth Taylor as the immoral actress-mother Desiree, Diana Rigg a tart officer's wife and Lesley-Ann Down an enchanting tease are the women who engage in the love charades; Len Cariou, Laurence Guittard and Christopher Guard are the men who accompany the frolics.

A Sascha Wien Film Production/Elliott Kastner New World Pictures Release, directed by Hal Prince. With Elizabeth Taylor, Diana Rigg, Len Cariou, Hermione Gingold, Lesley-Ann Down, Laurence Guittard, Christopher Guard. Eastmancolor. 124 mins.

Little Women (1932/33)

Oscars (1) best writing: adaptation   Sarah Y. Mason &
Victor Heerman

Louisa M. Alcott's gentle classic about four sisters growing up to womanhood during the Civil War in the small Massachusetts town of Concord. A notable adaptation by Mason and Heerman won the Academy Award; George Cukor and the picture itself were both among the nominees. Miss Hepburn played Jo, Joan Bennett Amy, Frances Dee Meg and Jean Parker featured as Beth.

An RKO Picture, directed by George Cukor. With Katharine Hepburn, Joan Bennett, Paul Lukas, Edna May Oliver, Jean Parker, Frances Dee, Henry Stephenson, Douglass Montgomery. 107 mins.

Little Women (1949)

Oscars (1) best colour art direction   Cedric Gibbons & Paul Groesse
set decoration Edwin B. Willis & Jack D. Moore

The same story, retold less imaginatively but more lushly in colour by MGM. June Allyson this time was the tomboyish Jo, Elizabeth Taylor was Amy, Janet Leigh Meg and Margaret O'Brien the young Beth.

An MGM Picture, directed by Mervyn LeRoy. With June Allyson, Peter Lawford, Margaret O'Brien, Elizabeth Taylor, Janet Leigh, Rossano Brazzi, Mary Astor, Lucile Watson, C. Aubrey Smith. Technicolor. 121 mins.

Lives of a Bengal Lancer (1935)

Oscars (1) best assistant direction   Clem Beauchamp & Paul Wing

High adventure on the North West Frontier in India with Gary Cooper,

Franchot Tone and Richard Cromwell as three British officers performing heroic feats of valour against treacherous border tribes on the
Khyber Pass. From the novel by Francis Yeats Brown.

A Paramount Picture, directed by Henry Hathaway. With Gary
Cooper, Franchot Tone, Richard Cromwell, Sir Guy Standing, C.
Aubrey Smith, Monte Blue. 111 mins.

Logan's Run (1976)

Oscars (1) best special visual effects   L. B. Abbott, Glen Robinson &
                                          Matthew Yuricich

Life in the 23rd century where life ends at thirty unless you become a
'runner' and escape the sealed off existence in a huge domed city where
everything is pleasurable until the deadly age of no return. Michael York
and Jenny Agutter feature as the two who try to escape the super
mechanisation.

An MGM Picture, directed by Michael Anderson. With Michael York,
Richard Jordan, Jenny Agutter, Rosco Lee Browne, Farrah Fawcett-
Majors, Michael Anderson Jr, Peter Ustinov. Todd-AO 35/Metrocolor.
118 mins.

The Longest Day (1962)

Oscars (2) best b/w cinematography Jean Bourgoin & Walter Wottitz
             best special effects   Robert MacDonald (visual)
                                        Jacques Maumont (audible)

The Allied landings in Normandy on June 6, 1944, retold by Darryl F.
Zanuck on a grand scale and with an international all-star cast. Finan-
cially one of the most successful war movies ever made, it was high up
in the Oscar nomination stakes but lost out in the major categories to
the year's multi-award winner *Lawrence of Arabia*.

A 20th Century-Fox Picture, directed by Ken Annakin, Andrew
Marton, Bernard Wicki. With John Wayne, Robert Mitchum, Richard
Todd, Red Buttons, Richard Beymer and all-star cast. CinemaScope.
180 mins.

Lost Horizon (1937)

Oscars (2) best art direction   Stephen Goosson
             best editing   Gene Milford & Gene Havlick

James Hilton fantasy with Ronald Colman as a young English diplomat who, along with a group of other passengers, survives a 'plane crash and stumbles across an idyllic Utopian community hidden away in the Himalayas in Tibet. Art director Goosson won his Oscar for his ingenious Shangri La set designs.

A Columbia Picture, directed by Frank Capra. With Ronald Colman, Jane Wyatt, Joan Howard, Edward Everett Horton, Isabel Jewell, H. B. Warner, Sam Jaffe. 125 mins.

The Lost Weekend (1945)

Oscars (4)	best film	Charles Brackett (producer)
	best direction	Billy Wilder
	best actor	Ray Milland
	best screenplay	Billy Wilder & Charles Brackett

Three harrowing days in the life of a failed novelist (Ray Milland) driven to the verge of suicide by his addiction to drink. A history making picture in two ways, both as the first film to treat alcoholism with any seriousness and as the first so-called message picture to win the top award.

A Paramount Picture, directed by Billy Wilder. With Ray Milland, Jane Wyman, Philip Terry, Howard da Silva, Doris Dowling, Frank Faylen. 102 mins.

Lovers and Other Strangers (1970)

Oscars (1)	best song	'For All We Know'
		(Fred Karlin, music:
		Robb Wilson &
		Arthur James, lyrics)

Comedy about a young couple who decide to take the plunge and get married after 18 months of living together and the subsequent repercussions among the friends and relatives who find at the reception that they have plenty of problems of their own to deal with.

A Cinerama Distribution-ABC Picture, directed by Cy Howard. With Gig Young, Bonnie Bedelia, Beatrice Arthur, Michael Brandon, Richard Castellano. Metrocolor. 104 mins.

Love is a Many Splendoured Thing (1955)

Oscars (3) best colour costume design Charles LeMaire
            best music score of a   Alfred Newman
               drama or comedy
            best song   'Love Is A Many Splendoured
                                            Thing'
                                         (Sammy Fain, music:
                                            Paul Francis Webster, lyrics)

Tragic love affair between an unhappily married foreign correspondent (William Holden) and a beautiful Eurasian doctor (Jennifer Jones) working in a Hong Kong hospital at the time of the Korean War. Lush backgrounds in CinemaScope and a title love song helped earn the film millions.

A 20th Century-Fox Picture, directed by Henry King. With William Holden, Jennifer Jones, Torin Thatcher, Isobel Elsom, Murray Matheson, Virginia Gregg. CinemaScope. De Luxe Color. 102 mins.

Love Me or Leave Me (1955)

Oscars (1) best motion picture story   Daniel Fuchs

Real-life drama of the prohibition days covering the stormy marriage between 20's torch singer Ruth Etting (Doris Day) and tough little racketeer Martin Snyder (James Cagney). Vintage numbers from Miss Day and a crackerjack performance from Cagney who here earned the last of his three Oscar nominations for best actor. Previously he had won for *Yankee Doodle Dandy* (42) and been nominated for *Angels With Dirty Faces* (38).

An MGM Picture, directed by Charles Vidor. With Doris Day, James Cagney, Cameron Mitchell, Robert Keith, Tom Tully, Harry Bellaver. CinemaScope/Eastman Color. 122 mins.

Love Story (1970)

Oscars (1) best original music score   Francis Lai

Simple love story between two college students, Harvard boy Ryan O'Neal and Radcliffe girl Ali MacGraw, which ends in tragedy with the girl's sudden death and which somehow caught the public mood of the early 70's by earning 50 million dollars at the box office. At Oscar time only Francis Lai's lush music score was recognised.

A Paramount Picture, directed by Arthur Hiller. With Ali MacGraw, Ryan O'Neal, John Marley, Ray Milland, Russell Nype, Katherine Balfour, Movielab Color. 100 mins.

Lust for Life (1956)

Oscars (1) best supporting actor   Anthony Quinn

The turbulent life of tormented artist Vincent Van Gogh (Kirk Douglas), from his early manhood and his endeavours to do religious work to his final anguished years as a painter of genius. Anthony Quinn's Gauguin was recognised by the Academy but the year's best actor award went to Yul Brynner for a repeat of his Broadway performance in *The King And I*. Douglas had to be content with a nomination and the award of the New York critics who at least recognised the quality of his extraordinary performance.

An MGM Picture, directed by Vincente Minnelli. With Kirk Douglas, Anthony Quinn, James Donald, Pamela Brown, Everett Sloane, Niall MacGinnis. Noel Purcell, Henry Daniell. CinemaScope/Metrocolor. 122 mins.

Madame Rosa (1977)

Oscars (1) best foreign language   France
                  film

The moving relationship between an ageing, ailing Jewish woman who cares for the children of prostitutes, and one of her charges, a young Arab boy. Set mainly in the milieu of prostitutes and pimps in the Arab and Jewish worker section of Paris and starring Simone Signoret as Madame Rosa, herself a former whore and concentration camp victim.

   A Lira Films Production, directed by Moshe Mizrahi. With Simone Signoret, Claude Dauphin, Samy Ben Youb, Gabriel Jabbour, Michal Bat Adam, Costa Gavras, Stella Anicette. Eastmancolor. 105 mins.

A Man and a Woman (1966)

Oscars (2) best foreign language film France
                  best story & screenplay   Claude Lelouch, story:
                                                       Pierre Uytterhoeven & Claude
                                                       Lelouch, screenplay

Romantic and very lush treatment of a simple love affair between two glamorous getaway people — he a racing driver, she a script girl — who have both lost their partners in death and who first meet while visiting their respective children at a school in Deauville. The famous Francis Lai music score was not even among the year's five top nominees.

   A Les Films 13 Production, directed by Claude Lelouch. With Anouk Aimee, Jean-Louis Trintignant, Pierre Barouh, Valerie Lagrange, Simone Paris. Eastman Color. 102 mins.

A Man for All Seasons (1966)

Oscars (6) best film   Fred Zinnemann (producer)
            best direction   Fred Zinnemann
            best actor   Paul Scofield
            best screenplay   Robert Bolt
            best colour cinematography Ted Moore
            best colour costume design Elizabeth Haffenden &
                                               Joan Bridge

The battle of wills between Sir Thomas More (Paul Scofield), Chancellor of England and one of the most widely respected catholics in Europe and the ebullient Henry VIII (Robert Shaw) who, in 1528 was seeking a divorce from Catherine of Aragon in order that he might marry Anne Boleyn. Adapted by Robert Bolt from his own stage play.

A Columbia Picture, directed by Fred Zinnemann. With Paul Scofield, Wendy Hiller, Leo McKern, Robert Shaw, Orson Welles, Susannah York, Nigel Davenport, John Hurt. Technicolor. 120 mins.

Manhattan Melodrama (1934)

Oscars (1) best original story   Arthur Caesar

Crime melodrama most famous for being the last film Public Enemy Number 1, John Dillinger, saw just prior to his death outside a Chicago movie house. William Powell features as a D.A. who has to prosecute his boyhood friend, gangster Clark Gable. Myrna Loy is the latter's mistress.

An MGM Picture, directed by W. S. Van Dyke. With Clark Gable, William Powell, Myrna Loy, Leo Carrillo, Nat Pendleton. 93 mins.

The Man Who Knew Too Much (1956)

Oscars (1) best song   'Que Sera, Sera'
                                         (Ray Evans & Jay Livingston,
                                             music and lyrics)

Hitchcock's remake of his British classic of 20 years earlier with James Stewart and Doris Day as two American tourists who have their son kidnapped while holidaying in Morocco and become involved in a plot to assassinate a foreign political leader in London. Despite Hitch's genius it is for the song 'Que Sera, Sera' that the film stands firmly in the Oscar record books.

A Paramount Picture, directed by Alfred Hitchcock. With James Stewart, Doris Day, Daniel Gelin, Bernard Miles, Brenda de Banzie. Technicolor/Vista Vision. 119 mins.

Marie-Louise (1945)

Oscars (1) best original screenplay   Richard Schweizer

Simply told story from Switzerland about a group of French children, and one girl in particular, who seek refuge for a few months from the bombs of war-torn France in the peace of neutral Switzerland. The first European movie to win an award in one of the major Oscar categories.

Praesens — Films Ltd, Zurich, directed by Leopold Lindtberg. With Josiane, Heinrich Gretler, Margrit Winter, Anne-Marie Blane, Armin Schweizer. 93 mins.

Marooned (1969)

Oscars (1) best special visual effects   Robbie Robinson

Modern science-fact drama about three American astronauts — Richard Crenna, James Franciscus, Gene Hackman — who are launched into space to link up with an orbiting space laboratory and then find, through technical malfunctions, that the ground crew are unable to bring them back to earth.

A Columbia Picture, directed by John Sturges. With Gregory Peck, Richard Crenna, David Janssen, James Franciscus, Gene Hackman, Lee Grant. Panavision 70/Technicolor. 133 mins.

Marty (1955)

Oscars (4) best film   Harold Hecht (producer)
            best direction   Delbert Mann
            best actor   Ernest Borgnine
            best screenplay   Paddy Chayefsky

The 'sleeper' best picture winner of the 1950's, an adaptation of Paddy Chayefsky's TV drama about a fat ugly butcher (Ernest Borgnine) from the Bronx who, after despairing of ever getting married, at last finds romance with a plain schoolteacher (Betsy Blair) who has been stood up at a dance. Also the Grand Prize winner at Cannes, it defeated such heavyweight best picture contenders as *Picnic, The Rose Tattoo* and *Mister Roberts*.

A United Artists Picture, directed by Delbert Mann. With Ernest Borgnine, Betsy Blair, Esther Minciotti, Augusta Ciolli, Joe Mantell, Karen Steele, Jerry Paris. 99 mins.

Mary Poppins (1964)

Oscars (5)	best actress	Julie Andrews
	best editing	Cotton Warburton
	best visual effects	Peter Ellenshaw, Hamilton Luske, Eustace Lycett
	best original music score	Richard M. & Robert B. Sherman
	best song	'Chim Chim Cher-ee' Richard M. & Robert B. Sherman, (music & lyrics)

Julie Andrews 'descending' to movie stardom with umbrella and carpet bag as P. L. Travers' magical nanny and providing two London children with a whole series of magical adventures. The irony of Julie Andrews' award was that the same year Warners had turned her down for the part of Eliza Doolittle in *My Fair Lady* (which she had played on the stage) and plumped instead for Audrey Hepburn who didn't even figure in 64's list of nominees. *Mary Poppins* remains the only Disney film ever to be nominated for best picture.

A Walt Disney Picture, directed by Robert Stevenson. With Julie Andrews, Dick Van Dyke, David Tomlinson, Glynis Johns, Hermione Baddeley, Karen Dotrice, Matthew Garber, Elsa Lanchester, Ed Wynn, Jane Darwell. Technicolor. 140 mins.

M.A.S.H. (1970)

Oscars (1)	best screenplay	Ring Lardner, Jr.

Black comedy, set in a mobile hospital unit during the Korean War, and exposing through humour and not bloody action sequences, the brutalising effects of war itself. Elliott Gould and Donald Sutherland feature as the two irreverent young soldier surgeons with a liking for Martinis and nurses and who don't give a damn for red tape or authority.

A 20th Century-Fox Picture, directed by Robert Altman. With Donald Sutherland, Elliott Gould, Tom Skerritt, Sally Kellerman, Robert Duvall, Jo Ann Pflug. Panavision/De Luxe Color. 116 mins.

The Merry Widow (1934)

Oscars (1)	best art direction	Cedric Gibbons & Frederic Hope

Lubitsch version of the Lehar operetta, set in romantic Paris, with Chevalier as the roguish Prince Danilo and Jeanette MacDonald as the beautiful rich widow of the title. Also around: Geroge Barbier as the cuckolded King Achmed, Una Merkel as his wife and Edward Everett Horton as the hapless ambassador.

An MGM Picture, directed by Ernst Lubitsch. With Maurice Chevalier, Jeanette MacDonald, Edward Everett Horton, Una Merkel. 110 mins.

Midnight Cowboy (1969)

Oscars (3)   best film   Jerome Hellman (producer)
             best direction   John Schlesinger
             best screenplay   Waldo Salt

Two young drifters — John Voight as a would-be stud in leather cowboy gear and Dustin Hoffman as a tubercular down-and-outer — come gradually to depend on each other as they struggle to exist in the seamy, unfriendly backstreets of New York. The best film winner of its particular year, although *Butch Cassidy* with four wins against *Cowboy's* three was the year's biggest overall winner in terms of Oscars won.

A United Artists Picture, directed by John Schlesinger. With Jon Voight, Dustin Hoffman, Sylvia Miles, Brenda Vaccaro, John McGiver, Barnard Hughes, Ruth White. De Luxe Color. 113 mins.

A Midsummer Night's Dream (1935)

Oscars (2)   best cinematography   Hal Mohr
             best editing   Ralph Dawson

Shakespeare's woodland comedy-fantasy, cut to ribbons text-wise, but retaining as compensations, handsome sets and costumes as well as music by Mendelssohn. James Cagney is Bottom, Dick Powell Lysander, Victor Jory a majestic Oberon, the 11-year-old Mickey Rooney a mischievous Puck and Olivia de Havilland, in her first film, a lovely Hermia.

A Warner Bros. Picture, directed by William Dieterle and Max Reinhardt. With James Cagney, Dick Powell, Joe E. Brown, Jean Muir, Hugh Herbert, Ian Hunter, Frank McHugh, Victor Jory, Olivia de Havilland, Mickey Rooney. 132 mins.

Mighty Joe Young (1949)

Oscars (1)   best special effects   Willis O'Brien

A sort of post-war *King Kong*, about a 10ft gorilla named Joe who is found in Africa and taken to Hollywood to appear in a night club act. The special effects award to Willis O'Brien compensated somewhat for him not receiving anything for his brilliant efforts on *King Kong*, the special effects category not being in existence at the time of that film's release in 1933.

An RKO Picture, directed by Ernest B. Schoedsack. With Terry Moore, Ben Johnson, Robert Armstrong, Frank McHugh, Douglas Fowley 93 mins.

Mildred Pierce (1945)

Oscars (1) best actress   Joan Crawford

The story of a self sacrificing mother (Crawford) who determines to give her selfish little monster of a daughter all the opportunities and luxuries she never had herself. Zachary Scott features as a wealthy playboy, Jack Carson as an unscrupulous estate agent and Eve Arden as a wise-cracking pal. Crawford's edgy, tear-stained performance won her her only Academy Award; Ann Blyth's as the daughter her only nomination.

A Warner Bros. Picture, directed by Michael Curtiz. With Joan Crawford, Jack Carson, Zachary Scott, Eve Arden, Ann Blyth, Bruce Bennett, George Tobias, Lee Patrick, Moroni Olsen. 113 mins.

Min and Bill (1930/31)

Oscars (1) best actress   Marie Dressler

61-year-old Marie Dressler as a hard-boiled proprietress of a waterfront hotel who brings up a young girl deserted by her mother in infancy and is then forced to kill the dissolute mother when, years later, she tries to reclaim the child. The film proved the biggest box-office hit of the year and the peak of Dressler's career. She died just four years later.

An MGM Picture, directed by George Hill. With Marie Dressler, Wallace Beery, Dorothy Jordan, Marjorie Rambeau, Donald Dillaway, DeWitt Jennings. 69 mins.

Miracle on 34th Street (1947)

Oscars (3) best supporting actor   Edmund Gwenn
            best screenplay   George Seaton
            best original story   Valentine Davies

Gentle department store Father Christmas (Edmund Gwenn), employed by Macy's in New York for the Christmas season, encounters among his young visitors, an unbelieving child (Natalie Wood) and finds that he has to prove that he really is Santa Claus. The first of George

Seaton's two writing Oscars, the second being earned for his script of *The Country Girl.*

A 20th Century-Fox Picture, directed by George Seaton. With Maureen O'Hara, John Payne, Edmund Gwenn, Gene Lockhart, Natalie Wood, Porter Hall, William Frawley, Jerome Cowan. 96 mins.

The Miracle Worker (1962)

Oscars (2) best actress   Anne Bancroft
            best supporting actress Patty Duke

The childhood of blind, deaf mute Helen Keller (Patty Duke) when she was little more than a savage animal and when she was gradually turned into a young woman of intelligence and intellect by Annie Sullivan (Anne Bancroft), a dedicated young teacher from Boston. A *tour-de-force* of power acting by both Bancroft and Duke. From the play by William Gibson.

A United Artists Picture, directed by Arthur Penn. With Anne Bancroft, Patty Duke, Victor Jory, Inga Swenson, Andrew Prince, Kathleen Comegys. 106 mins.

Mister Roberts (1955)

Oscars (1) best supporting actor   Jack Lemmon

Henry Fonda repeating his famous stage role as the restless Lieutenant Roberts who finds himself stuck aboard a World War II 'cargo bucket' and longs to be transferred to the fighting zone. James Cagney stars as his eccentric captain, William Powell as the philosophical ship's doctor and the young Oscar winning Jack Lemmon as the opportunistic Ensign Pulver.

A Warner Bros. Picture, directed by John Ford and Mervyn LeRoy. With Henry Fonda, James Cagney, William Powell, Jack Lemmon, Betsy Palmer, Ward Bond, Phil Carey, Martin Milner. CinemaScope/Warner Color. 123 mins.

Mon Oncle (1958)

Oscars (1) best foreign language film France/Italy

The second of Jacques Tati's Monsieur Hulot films with the accident-prone humanitarian at constant odds with the mechanized society of today, particularly with his sister's ultra-modern house with all its numerous gadgets, electronic garage, fully mechanized kitchen.

A Specta Films/Gray Film/Alter Film (Paris) and Film del Centauro (Rome) Production, directed by Jacques Tati. With Jacques Tati, Jean-Pierre Zola, Alain Becourt, Lucien Fregis, Dominique Marie. Eastman Color. 116 mins.

The More the Merrier (1943)

Oscars (1) best supporting actor   Charles Coburn

George Stevens' comedy about the housing shortage in wartime Washington with Jean Arthur as a government employee letting half of her flat to elderly industrialist Charles Coburn who, in turn, lets half of his half to homeless aircraft technician Joel McCrea. Smart, civilised, consistently funny movie.

A Columbia Picture, directed by George Stevens. With Jean Arthur, Joel McCrea, Charles Coburn, Richard Gaines, Bruce Bennett, Clyde Fillmore. 104 mins.

Morning Glory (1932/33)

Oscars (1) best actress   Katharine Hepburn

Adaptation of Zoe Akins' play about a stage-struck girl (Hepburn) from Vermont who struggles to become a great Broadway actress and eventually makes it to the top when temperamental star Mary Duncan walks out on opening night. Douglas Fairbanks Jr. as a young playwright, Adolphe Menjou as a theatrical manager and C. Aubrey Smith as a veteran actor co-star. This was the first of Katharine Hepburn's three Oscar wins. She was 26 when she won the award. Her subsequent Oscars were won more than thirty years later for *Guess Who's Coming To Dinner* (67) and *The Lion In Winter* (68).

An RKO Picture, directed by Lowell Sherman. With Katharine Hepburn, Douglas Fairbanks Jr., Adolphe Menjou, Mary Duncan, C. Aubrey Smith, Don Alvarado. 74 mins.

Mother Wore Tights (1947)

Oscars (1) best scoring of a musical   Alfred Newman

Archetypical Fox movie of the late 40's with vaudeville couple Betty Grable and Dan Dailey suddenly running into family trouble when the eldest of their two daughters (Mona Freeman) realises she lacks social standing at finishing school.

A 20th Century-Fox Picture, directed by Walter Lang. With Betty

Grable, Dan Dailey, Mona Freeman, Connie Marshall, Vanessa Brown, Robert Arthur, Sara Allgood, William Frawley. Technicolor. 107 mins.

Moulin Rouge (1952)

Oscars (2) best colour art direction   Paul Sheriff
                          set decoration Marcel Vertes
            best colour costume design Marcel Vertes

Biography of the crippled French painter Toulouse Lautrec (JoseFerrer) whose stunted growth as a child led to his living a life of despair and loneliness among the whores and entertainers of old Montmartre. The brilliant use of colour and design led to two Oscar awards although cameraman Oswald Morris was undeservedly not among the winning names. Top colour photographers of 1952 were Winton C. Hoch and Archie Stout for *The Quiet Man*.

A Romulus Films Production, directed by John Huston. With Jose Ferrer, Colette Marchand, Suzanne Flon, Zsa Zsa Gabor, Katherine Kath, Claude Nollier, Muriel Smith. Technicolor. 123 mins.

Mr. Deeds Goes to Town (1936)

Oscars (1) best direction   Frank Capra

Gary Cooper as Longfellow Deeds, a tuba-playing country boy who suddenly inherits a million dollars and then gives it all away when he discovers that his so-called big city associates are crooks and swindlers. Capra won the direction award for the second time in three years but the film, although nominated, lost out somewhat surprisingly to *The Great Ziegfeld* as best of the year.

A Columbia Picture, directed by Frank Capra. With Gary Cooper, Jean Arthur, George Bancroft, Lionel Stander, Douglas Dumbrille, Raymond Walburn, H. B. Warner. 115 mins.

Mr. Smith Goes to Washington (1939)

Oscars (1) best original story   Lewis R. Foster

Not quite the same story as *Mr. Deeds* but with the same theme – the people against big business and politics – as naive Wisconsin senator James Stewart, determined to do his best for his State, comes face to face with Washington graft and corruption and eventually exposes it in an idealistic speech to the Senate. A surefire winner of top awards in most years, it was unlucky enough to be released the same year as *Gone With The Wind* and had to be content with a solitary best story Oscar.

A Columbia Picture, directed by Frank Capra. With James Stewart, Jean Arthur, Claude Rains, Edward Arnold, Guy Kibbee, Thomas Mitchell, Eugene Pallette. 126 mins.

Mrs. Miniver (1942)

Oscars (6)	best film	Sidney Franklin (producer)
	best direction	William Wyler
	best actress	Greer Garson
	best supporting actress	Teresa Wright
	best screenplay	Arthur Wimperis, George Froeschel, James Hilton & Claudine West
	best b/w cinematography	Joseph Ruttenberg

Greer Garson and Walter Pidgeon as the mother and father of a supposedly typical English family struggling against the Blitz and surviving through Dunkirk in the darkest days of World War II. Teresa Wright co-starred as the Miniver's daughter-in-law, Dame May Whitty as the lady of the manor. A propaganda piece of its time that took six Oscars, its nearest contender *Yankee Doodle Dandy* winning three awards. Other best picture nominees of that year included *The Magnificent Ambersons, Wake Island, King's Row, Random Harvest* and *Talk Of The Town*.

An MGM Picture, directed by William Wyler. With Greer Garson, Walter Pidgeon, Teresa Wright, Dame May Whitty, Henry Travers, Reginald Owen, Henry Wilcoxon, Richard Ney. 134 mins.

Murder on the Orient Express (1974)

Oscars (1) best supporting actress   Ingrid Bergman

Who killed nasty American millionaire Richard Widmark on the train journey between Istanbul and Paris? English army officer Sean Connery, the dead man's personal assistant Anthony Perkins, aged countess Wendy Hiller, or any one of a dozen passengers including timid little Swedish spinster Ingrid Bergman? Private detective Hercule Poirot (Albert Finney) duly finds out. From the classic thriller by Agatha Christie. Note: For her role in this film Miss Bergman became the second actress to win both a major acting Oscar (see *Gaslight*) and a supporting award. Helen Hayes (for *The Sin of Madelon Claudet* and *Airport*) was the first.

An EMI Picture, directed by Sidney Lumet. With Albert Finney, Lauren Bacall, Martin Balsam, Ingrid Bergman, Jacqueline Bisset, Jean-Pierre Cassel, Sean Connery, John Gielgud, Wendy Hiller, Anthony Perkins, Vanessa Redgrave, Rachel Roberts, Richard Widmark, Michael York. Technicolor. 131 mins.

The Music Man (1962)

Oscars (1) best score: adaptation or   Ray Heindorf
                treatment

Breezy stage musical, set in the early 1900's, with Robert Preston repeating his Broadway role as the dynamic Professor Harold Hill, a travelling salesman of musical instruments who tries to organise a boy's band in the small town of River City, Iowa. Preston was not as lucky as Yul Brynner (*The King And I*) and Rex Harrison (*My Fair Lady*) who both won Oscars for repeating their Broadway successes, and was not even among the year's five best actor nominees. 1962's best actor was Gregory Peck for *To Kill A Mockingbird*.

A Warner Bros. Picture, directed by Morton Da Costa. With Robert Preston, Shirley Jones, Paul Ford, Buddy Hackett, Hermione Gingold. Technirama/Technicolor. 151 mins.

Mutiny on the Bounty (1935)

Oscars (1) best film   Frank Lloyd (producer)

The story of the famous mutiny on HMS Bounty which under the command of the ruthless Captain Bligh set sail for Tahiti on a scientific expedition in 1787. The best picture winner of 1935 and the only film in the history of the Academy to boast three best actor nominees — Clark Gable (as Fletcher Christian), Charles Laughton (as Bligh) and Franchot Tone — out of the four actors nominated. But none of them won. The award went to the fourth nominee, Victor McLaglen for *The Informer*.

An MGM Picture, directed by Frank Lloyd. With Charles Laughton, Clark Gable, Franchot Tone, Herbert Mundin, Eddie Quillan, Dudley Digges, Donald Crisp, Henry Stephenson. 131 mins.

My Fair Lady (1964)

Oscars (8)	best film	Jack L. Warner (producer)
	best direction	George Cukor
	best actor	Rex Harrison
	best colour cinematography	Harry Stradling
	best colour art direction	Gene Allen & Cecil Beaton
	set decoration	George James Hopkins
	best colour costume design	Cecil Beaton
	best sound	George R. Groves
	best music score: adaptation or treatment	Andre Previn

Broadway's musical version of Shaw's *Pygmalion* filmed completely straight and taking eight Oscars with ease including one to Rex Harrison for his arrogant Professor Higgins and two to Cecil Beaton for his costumes and designs. The only surprise was that Audrey Hepburn's cockney flower girl Eliza Doolittle was not among the winners nor even among the nominees.

A Warner Bros. Picture, directed by George Cukor. With Rex Harrison, Audrey Hepburn, Stanley Holloway, Wilfrid Hyde-White, Gladys Cooper, Jeremy Brett, Theodore Bikel. Super Panavision 70/ Technicolor. 170 mins.

My Gal Sal (1942)

Oscars (1)	best colour art direction	Richard Day & Joseph C. Wright
	int. dec.	Thomas Little

90's songwriter Victor Mature falls in love with beautiful musical queen Rita Hayworth and after innumerable ups and downs finally manages to settle down with her to a life of happiness. Formula Fox musical for the period, richly designed and with songs like 'On The Banks Of The Wabash' and 'Blue And Grey'.

A 20th Century-Fox Picture, directed by Irving Cummings. With Rita Hayworth, Victor Mature, John Sutton, Carole Landis, James Gleason, Phil Silvers. Technicolor. 103 mins.

The Naked City (1948)

Oscars (2) best b/w cinematography William Daniels
           best editing Paul Weatherwax

Realistic crime story of New York — the murder of a beautiful model and the tracking down of her killer — filmed almost entirely on location when the streets and buildings of the great city were sweltering in a heat wave. The last picture of producer Mark Hellinger, it also marked the only time that Garbo's favourite cameraman of the 30's, William Daniels, was honoured by the Academy.

A Universal-International Picture, directed by Jules Dassin. With Barry Fitzgerald, Howard Duff, Dorothy Hart, Don Taylor, Ted De Corsia, Jean Adair. 96 mins.

Nashville (1975)

Oscars (1) best song 'I'm Easy'
                                   (Keith Carradine, music & lyrics)

Robert Altman parody of the music metropolis of Nashville, a town significant in the history of popular music since the late 50's. Almost plotless, the film presents a cross-section of Nashville society during the preparation and performance of a gigantic concert being held in the city to aid the campaign of a leading presidential candidate.

A Paramount Picture, directed by Robert Altman. With David Arkin, Barbara Baxley, Ned Beatty, Karen Black, Ronee Blakley, Timothy Brown, Keith Carradine, Geraldine Chaplin, Robert Doqui, Shelley Duvall, Allen Garfield, Henry Gibson, Scott Glenn, Jeff Goldblum, Barbara Harris, David Hayward, Michael Murphy, Allan Nicholls, Dave Peel, Christina Raines, Bert Remsen, Lily Tomlin, Gwen Welles, Keenan Wynn. Panavision/Colour by MGM Film Laboratories. 161 mins.

National Velvet (1945)

Oscars (2) best supporting actress   Anne Revere
          best editing   Robert J. Kern

Enid Bagnold's famous story about a little girl's love for her horse and her subsequent ride to victory (disguised as a boy) in the Grand National. 12-year-old Elizabeth Taylor plays the girl, Mickey Rooney the ex-jockey who helps her train her horse and Oscar winner Anne Revere Liz's quiet, understanding ma.

    An MGM Picture, directed by Clarence Brown. With Mickey Rooney, Donald Crisp, Elizabeth Taylor, Anne Revere, Angela Lansbury. Technicolor. 125 mins.

Naughty Marietta (1935)

Oscars (1) best sound recording   Douglas Shearer

The first teaming of Jeanette MacDonald and Nelson Eddy, a version of the operetta by Victor Herbert with Jeanette as a French princess who runs away to America and Nelson as her loving Indian scout. Songs include 'Tramp, Tramp, Tramp' and 'Ah, Sweet Mystery Of Life'.

    An MGM Picture, directed by W. S. Van Dyke. With Jeanette MacDonald, Nelson Eddy, Frank Morgan, Elsa Lanchester, Douglas Dumbrille. 106 mins.

Neptune's Daughter (1949)

Oscars (1) best song   'Baby, It's Cold Outside'
                                    (Frank Loesser, music & lyrics)

Swimming star Esther Williams as a bathing suit designer, Ricardo Montalban as a handsome polo player, Red Skelton as a comic masquerader, South American settings but best of all the catchy song 'Baby, It's Cold Outside' which became a big hit the world over and won 49's best song award.

    An MGM Picture, directed by Edward Buzzell. With Esther Williams, Red Skelton, Ricardo Montalban, Betty Garrett, Keenan Wynn, Xavier Cugat and His Orchestra, Ted De Corsia, Mike Mazurki. Technicolor. 93 mins.

Network (1976)

Oscars (4)	best actor	Peter Finch
	best actress	Faye Dunaway
	best supporting actress	Beatrice Straight
	best original screenplay	Paddy Chayefsky

Savage satire on contemporary TV with Peter Finch as a deranged news commentator who threatens to kill himself on the air, thus increasing his 'ratings' overnight. Faye Dunaway features as a ruthlessly ambitious TV executive determined to climb to the top at any cost and William Holden co-stars as a director of the TV news division. Finch's Oscar made him the first posthumous best actor winner in the history of the Academy; Beatrice Straight won her supporting award for her one sequence as Holden's neglected wife.

An MGM-United Artists Picture, directed by Sidney Lumet. With Faye Dunaway, William Holden, Peter Finch, Robert Duvall, Wesley Addy, Ned Beatty, Beatrice Straight. Panavision/Metrocolor. 121 mins.

Never on Sunday (1960)

Oscars (1)	best song	'Never On Sunday' (Manos Hadjidakis, music & lyrics)

Jules Dassin shoestring comedy about an American writer (played by Dassin himself) who tries to persuade happy-go-lucky prostitute Melina Mercouri from parading her ample wares on the waterfront of Piraeus in the Port of Athens to concentrating on the high-minded ideals of Aristotle. Needless to say, he fails. The happy, infectious theme song became one of the biggest hits of the early 60's.

A Lopert Pictures-Melina Film (distributed through United Artists), directed by Jules Dassin. With Melina Mercouri, Jules Dassin, George Foundas, Tito Vandis, Mitsos Liguisos, Despo Diamantidou. 91 mins.

Nicholas and Alexandra (1971)

Oscars (2)	best art direction	John Box, Ernest Archer, Jack A. Maxsted & Gil Parrondo
	set decoration	Vernon Dixon
	best costume design	Yvonne Blake & Antonio Castillo

The last turbulent years of Tsar Nicholas II (Michael Jayston) and his German-born wife Alexandra (Janet Suzman) before the 1917 Revolution caused the upheaval of the Russian social order and led to the deaths of the Russian rulers and their families. As in most films of its type, the settings and costumes dazzled the eye far more than the performances, all Oscar recipients thoroughly deserving their awards for their recreation of the Russian Imperial scene.

A Columbia Picture, directed by Franklin J. Schaffner. With Michael Jayston, Janet Suzman, Roderic Noble, Harry Andrews, Tom Baker, Timothy West, Jack Hawkins, Laurence Olivier. Panavision/Eastman Color. 189 mins.

The Night of the Iguana (1964)

Oscars (1) best b/w costume design   Dorothy Jeakins

Richard Burton as a defrocked priest turned tourist-coach driver, set firmly down in Tennessee Williams country at a seedy Mexican resort hotel where he becomes involved with proprietress Ava Gardner, rapacious teenager Sue Lyon and anguished spinster Deborah Kerr. Symbolic writing, brilliant black-and-white photography.

An MGM Picture, directed by John Huston. With Richard Burton, Ava Gardner, Deborah Kerr, Sue Lyon, James Ward, Grayson Hall. 125 mins.

The Nights of Cabiria (1957)

Oscars (1) best foreign language film Italy/France

The hopes, fears and sorrows of waifish Italian prostitute Giulietta Masina, always dreaming of a wonderful life just around the corner but always finishing up penniless and with just another unhappy experience to remember. The second of Fellini's best foreign film awards (see also *La Strada, 8½* and *Amarcord*) and the basis for the subsequent stage and film musical *Sweet Charity*.

Dino De Laurentiis/Films Marceau Production, directed by Federico Fellini. With Giulietta Masina, Francois Perier, Amadeo Nazzari, Franca Marzi, Dorian Gray, Aldo Silvana. 110 mins.

None But The Lonely Heart (1944)

Oscars (1) best supporting actress   Ethel Barrymore

Version of Richard Llewellyn's novel about a cockney drifter (Cary Grant) who, embittered by the death of his father in the First World War and his mother's subsequent struggle against poverty, tries to find some kind of spiritual fulfillment in the days leading up to World War II. Set in London's pre-war slums, it provided Grant with a rare dramatic acting role which earned him a best actor Academy nomination; Ethel Barrymore's Oscar was for her performance as Grant's mother.

An RKO Picture, directed by Clifford Odets. With Cary Grant, Ethel Barrymore, Barry Fitzgerald, June Duprez, Jane Wyatt, George Coulouris. 113 mins.

North West Mounted Police (1940)

Oscars (1) best editing   Anne Bauchens

DeMille's first all-colour picture, an adventure of 3 men (Texas Ranger Gary Cooper, Canadian mounties Preston Foster and Robert Preston) and 2 women (frontier nurse Madeleine Carroll and half-breed Paulette Goddard) all caught up in Canada's 'Civil War', an abortive little frontier rebellion led by Louis Riel in 1885. Anne Bauchens who won the year's editing award cut all of DeMille's pictures between *We Can't Have Everything* in 1918 and *The Ten Commandments* in 1956.

A Paramount Picture, directed by Cecil B. DeMille. With Gary Cooper, Madeleine Carroll, Paulette Goddard, Preston Foster, Robert Preston, George Bancroft, Lynne Overman, Akim Tamiroff. Technicolor. 125 mins.

Now Voyager (1942)

Oscars (1) best music score of a   Max Steiner
                    drama or comedy

The story of a plain, neurotic young spinster (Bette Davis) who eventually escapes her mother's petty tyranny through a course in Claude Rains psychiatry and Paul Henreid love-making. Chiefly remembered for Max Steiner's famous music score, one of the lushest that famous composer ever wrote, and for Henreid's famous trick of lighting two cigarettes in his mouth at the same time.

A Warner Bros. Picture, directed by Irving Rapper. With Bette Davis, Paul Henreid, Claude Rains, Gladys Cooper, Bonita Granville, John Loder, Ilka Chase, Lee Patrick. 117 mins.

Oklahoma (1955)

Oscars (2) best scoring of a musical   Robert Russell Bennett, Jay
                                          Blackton & Adolph Deutsch
          best sound recording   Fred Hynes

Trendsetting Rodgers and Hammerstein musical about the rivalry between the farmers and the cowmen in Old Oklahoma. Gordon Macrae and Shirley Jones feature as the romantic leads, Gloria Grahame as Ado Annie, Rod Steiger as the psycopathic Jud Fry. Hit songs include 'Oh What A Beautiful Morning', 'The Surrey With A Fringe On Top' and 'People Will Say We're In Love.'
    A Magna Picture (released by RKO), directed by Fred Zinnemann. With Gordon Macrae, Shirley Jones, Gloria Grahame, Gene Nelson, Rod Steiger, Charlotte Greenwood, Eddie Albert, James Whitmore. Todd-AO/Eastman Color. 145 mins.

The Old Man and The Sea (1958)

Oscars (1) best music score of a   Dimitri Tiomkin
            drama or comedy

Hemingway's simple parable of an old Cuban fisherman (Spencer Tracy) who battles to hold on to the giant marlin he has hooked at sea — his first fish in three months — and then has to watch it gradually eaten away by attacking sharks. Felipe Pazes features as the small boy who alone still has faith in the old man.
    A Warner Bros. Picture, directed by John Sturges. With Spencer Tracy, Felipe Pazes, Harry Bellaver, Donald Diamond, Don Blackman, Joey Ray, Richard Alameda. Warner Color. 86 mins.

Oliver (1968)

Oscars (5)	best film	John Woolf (producer)
	best direction	Carol Reed
	best art direction	John Box & Terence Marsh
	set decoration	Vernon Dixon & Ken Muggleston
	best sound	Shepperton Studios Sound Dept.
	best music score adaptation	John Green

Lionel Bart's musical version of Dickens' *Oliver Twist* with Mark Lester as the orphan boy who falls into the clutches of a gang of thieves in 19th century London. Ron Moody is a merry Fagin, Oliver Reed a surly Bill Sikes and Shani Wallis the pathetic street girl Nancy. The first and only Oscar won by Carol Reed — his only other nominations coming for *The Fallen Idol* in '49 and *The Third Man* in '50 — and the only British born and bred musical to win the best film award. Note: A special Oscar was also awarded to Onna White for her choreography.

A Columbia Picture, directed by Carol Reed. With Ron Moody, Shani Wallis, Oliver Reed, Harry Secombe, Hugh Griffith, Jack Wild. Panavision 70/Technicolor. 146 mins.

The Omen (1976)

Oscars (1) best original music score   Jerry Goldsmith

The commercial 'sleeper' of '76, a horror drama with U.S. Ambassador Gregory Peck and wife Lee Remick adopting a baby in a Rome hospital only to find as he grows to boyhood that he is the child of the Devil who destroys everyone he comes in contact with.

A 20th Century-Fox Picture, directed by Richard Donner. With Gregory Peck, Lee Remick, David Warner, Billie Whitelaw, Harvey Stephens, Leo McKern, Patrick Troughton. Panavision/De Luxe Color. 111 mins.

On the Town (1949)

Oscars (1) best scoring of a musical   Roger Edens & Lennie Hayton

Three sailors (Kelly, Sinatra, Munshin) dance and sing their way glee-fully around New York on a 24-hour shore leave in the big city. Slim beauty Vera-Ellen, wisecracking taxi driver Betty Garrett and hoofer Ann Miller are the girls they meet on the way. An exhilarating, history-making piece of perpetual motion, adapted from the Leonard Bernstein stage ballet 'Fancy Free'.

An MGM Picture, directed by Gene Kelly and Stanley Donen. With Gene Kelly, Frank Sinatra, Betty Garrett, Ann Miller, Jules Munshin, Vera-Ellen. Technicolor. 97 mins.

On the Waterfront (1954)

Oscars (8)	best film	Sam Spiegel (producer)
	best direction	Elia Kazan
	best actor	Marlon Brando
	best supporting actress	Eva Marie Saint
	best story & screenplay	Budd Schulberg
	best b/w cinematography	Boris Kaufman
	best b/w art direction	Richard Day
	best editing	Gene Milford

Angry indictment of the corruption and tyranny existing in a New York longshoreman's union in the early 50's with Marlon Brando giving arguably the finest performance of his career as a broken-down ex-boxer in the pay of the racketeers. Eva Marie Saint's Oscar, for her portrayal of a murdered longshoreman's sister, was for her first screen role, while the film itself was the first to have three members of its male cast — Lee J. Cobb's gang boss, Karl Malden's tough, dockland priest and Rod Steiger as Brando's older brother — nominated in the supporting actor category. (see also *Godfather* Parts I and II).

A Columbia Picture, directed by Elia Kazan. With Marlon Brando, Eva Marie Saint, Karl Malden, Lee J. Cobb, Rod Steiger, Pat Henning. 108 mins.

One Flew Over the Cuckoo's Nest (1975)

Oscars (5)	best film	Mike Douglas & Saul Zaentz (producers)
	best direction	Milos Forman
	best actor	Jack Nicholson
	best actress	Louise Fletcher
	best screenplay	Lawrence Hauben & Bo Goldman

The staff of a State Mental Hospital — symbolised by stern disciplinarian Louise Fletcher — against the normally apathetic patients who suddenly find a hero in their midst in the character of effervescent Jack Nicholson, a criminal transferred from a penal work-farm for clinical observation. In short, man against the system. The first movie in 41 years to win all five major awards and very different in subject matter to the film that won all five previously — *It Happened One Night*.

A United Artists Picture, directed by Milos Forman. With Jack Nicholson, Louise Fletcher, Brad Dourif, Sydney Lassick, William Redfield, Dean R. Brooks. De Luxe Color. 134 mins.

One Hundred Men and a Girl (1937)

Oscars (1) best music score   Charles Previn

Golden voiced Deanna Durbin, daughter of a poor, unemployed violinist, reaches the pinnacle of her dreams by singing at a great concert conducted by the celebrated Leopold Stokowski. Typical, fluffy Durbin vehicle but the only one that ever figured in the Oscar Awards.

A Universal Picture, directed by Henry Koster. With Deanna Durbin, Leopold Stokowski, Adolphe Menjou, Alice Brady, Eugene Pallette, Mischa Auer, Billy Gilbert. 84 mins.

One Night of Love (1934)

Oscars (2) best sound recording   Paul Neal
            best music score   Louis Silvers

Grace Moore as an American girl soprano who studies opera in Italy under demanding teacher Tullio Carminati and finally makes it to the top at the Metropolitan. On the way up she renders six famous operatic arias. Moore was nominated for best actress but lost to Claudette Colbert in *It Happened One Night*. The film was the first to win in the best music score category.

A Columbia Picture, directed by Victor Schertzinger. With Grace Moore, Tullio Carminati, Lyle Talbot, Mona Barrie, Nydia Westman, Jessie Ralph, Luis Alberni. 82 mins.

One Way Passage (1932/33)

Oscars (1) best original story   Robert Lord

Old fashioned weepie romance, set on board an ocean liner, between con-man William Powell and fatally ill Kay Francis — doomed to an early death by an incurable heart disease. Also on board and accompanying the action, two other con-artists — lightfingered Frank McHugh and fake countess Aline MacMahon.

A Warner Bros. Picture, directed by Tay Garnett. With William Powell, Kay Francis, Frank McHugh, Aline MacMahon, Warren Hymer, Frederick Burton. 69 mins.

The Paleface (1948)

Oscars (1) best song   'Buttons And Bows'
(Jay Livingston & Ray Evans,
music & lyrics)

Bob Hope as travelling dentist 'Painless' Peter Potter involved with Jane Russell's Calamity Jane in the Wild West of the 1870's. More satire than usual in a Hope comedy and also the hit song 'Buttons And Bows.'

A Paramount Picture, directed by Norman Z. McLeod. With Bob Hope, Jane Russell, Robert Armstrong, Iris Adrian, Robert Watson, Jack Searl. Technicolor. 91 mins.

Panic in the Streets (1950)

Oscars (1) best motion picture story Edna & Edward Anhalt

Documentary style thriller by Elia Kazan with medical health officer Richard Widmark and weary cop Paul Douglas tracking down Jack Palance an on-the-run criminal carrying a deadly plague germ through the city streets. The film won for its story although Joe MacDonald's lensing of the back alleys, low bars and wharfs of New Orleans deserved, but did not receive, mention.

A 20th Century-Fox Picture, directed by Elia Kazan. With Richard Widmark, Paul Douglas, Barbara Bel Geddes, Walter Jack Palance, Zero Mostel. 96 mins.

Papa's Delicate Condition (1963)

Oscars (1) best song   'Call Me Irresponsible'
(James Van Heusen, music:
Sammy Cahn, lyrics)

Another movie remembered more for its song — 'Call Me Irresponsible'

Robert Redford and Mia Farrow in 'THE GREAT GATSBY', winner of best costume design and best song score, 1974. (Paramount Pictures)

From the MGM release 'THE GREAT ZIEGFELD'. © 1936 Metro-Goldwyn-Mayer Corporation. Copyright renewed 1963 by Metro-Goldwyn-Mayer Inc.

From the MGM release 'GIGI'. © 1958 Loew's Incorporated and Arthur Freed Productions, Inc.

From the MGM release 'GOODBYE MR. CHIPS'. © 1939 Loew's Incorporated

'THE GUNS OF NAVARONE', best special effects winner 1961. (Columbia Pictures Corporation Limited)

From the MGM release 'GRAND HOTEL'. © 1932 Metro-Goldwyn-Mayer
Distributing Corporation. Copyright renewed 1959 by Loew's Incorporated

Olivier's 'HAMLET', best film, 1948

Patricia Neal, best actress in 'HUD', 1963. (Paramount Pictures)

Josephine Hull, left, best supporting actress for her portrayal as James Stewart's sister in 'HARVEY', 1950. (Universal Pictures)

Walter Matthau and Barbra Streisand in 'HELLO DOLLY', triple Oscar winner of 1969. (Twentieth-Century Fox Limited)

From the MGM release 'LILI'. © 1953 Loew's Incorporated

Yul Brynner, best actor in 'THE KING AND I', 1956.
(Twentieth-Century Fox Film Company Limited)

From the MGM release 'JULIUS CEASAR'. © 1953 Loew's Incorporated

'ON THE WATERFRONT', winner of eight Oscars, 1954.
(Columbia Pictures Corporation Limited)

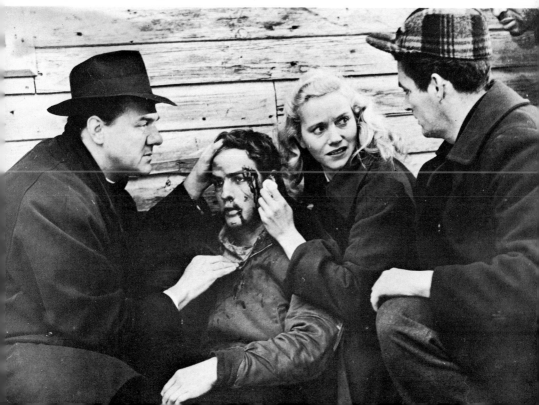

Ryan O'Neal and Ali MacGraw in 'LOVE STORY', best music score, 1970. (Paramount Pictures)

Cloris Leachman, supporting Oscar winner for 'THE LAST PICTURE SHOW', 1971. (Columbia Pictures Corporation Limited)

John Huston's 'MOULIN ROUGE', best colour art direction and costume design, 1952. (Romulus Films)

Alfie Bass, Alec Guinness and Sid James in 'THE LAVENDER HILL MOB', best story and screenplay, 1952. (Ealing Films)

From the MGM release 'LOVE ME OR LEAVE ME'. © 1955 Loew's
Incorporated

Keith Carradine, composer of best song 'I'm Easy', in 'NASHVILLE', 1975. (Paramount Pictures)

— than for its story about the family life of silent film actress Corinne Griffith when she was a child back in the 1900's. Jackie Gleason features as Griffith's semi-drunk railroad inspector father, Glynis Johns as his elegant wife but the song still comes out tops.

A Paramount Picture, directed by George Marshall. With Jackie Gleason, Glynis Johns, Linda Bruhl, Charles Ruggles, Laurel Goodwin, Ned Glass. Technicolor. 98 mins.

The Paper Chase (1973)

Oscars (1) best supporting actor   John Houseman

The pressures on a young University graduate (Timothy Bottoms) when he arrives at Harvard Law School determined to do his best in obtaining good grades but finding his best is appreciated elsewhere by the daughter (Lindsay Wagner) of his tyrannical class professor. For this last-named role the then 71-year-old John Houseman won a supporting Oscar after a lifetime of quality work as a producer, both on stage and in films.

A 20th Century-Fox Picture, directed by James Bridges. With Timothy Bottoms, Lindsay Wagner, John Houseman, Graham Beckel, James Naughton, Edward Herrmann. Panavision/De Luxe Color. 111 mins.

Paper Moon (1973)

Oscars (1) best supporting actress   Tatum O'Neal

Con-man Ryan O'Neal, pressurised into delivering the nine-year-old daughter (Tatum O'Neal) of an old flame to an aunt in Missouri, finds that instead of becoming a burden his artful little companion becomes a valuable asset in the con game. Tatum O'Neal is the youngest ever supporting actress winner; Madeline Kahn was also nominated in the supporting category for her fading floozie Trixie Delight.

A Paramount Picture, directed by Peter Bogdanovich. With Ryan O'Neal, Tatum O'Neal, Madeline Kahn, John Hillerman, P. J. Johnson, Jessie Lee Fulton. 103 mins.

A Patch of Blue (1965)

Oscars (1) best supporting actress   Shelley Winters

Blind white girl Elizabeth Hartman falls in love with black man Sidney Poitier, not realising during their affair that her compassionate friend is coloured. For her blowsy, over-bearing mother of the blind Hartman,

Shelley Winters won her second supporting actress Oscar having received her first six years earlier for her portrayal of another mother — Mrs. Van Daan in *The Diary of Anne Frank*.

An MGM Picture, directed by Guy Green. With Sidney Poitier, Shelley Winters, Elizabeth Hartman, Wallace Ford, Ivan Dixon, Elisabeth Fraser, John Qualen. 105 mins.

The Patriot (1928/29)

Oscars (1) best writing achievement   Hans Kraly

Emil Jannings as Czar Paul the 1st of 18th century Russia who finally meets his death after being surrounded on all sides by murderous plots to remove him from the throne.

A Paramount Picture, directed by Ernst Lubitsch. With Emil Jannings, Florence Vidor, Lewis Stone, Vera Voronina, Neil Hamilton, Harry Cording. 12 reels.

Patton (1970)

Oscars (7)	best film	Frank McCarthy (producer)
	best direction	Franklin J. Schaffner
	best actor	George C. Scott
	best story & screenplay	Francis Ford Coppola & Edmund H. North
	best art direction	Urie McCleary & Gil Parrondo
	set decoration	Antonio Mateos & Pierre-Louis Thevenet
	best editing	Hugh S. Fowler
	best sound	Douglas Williams & Don Bassman

The wartime career of one of the most controversial American commanders of World War II, 'Blood and Guts' Patton (George C. Scott) who forfeited command of the 7th army in Sicily after he had struck a soldier suffering from battle fatigue. Scott created history by becoming the first actor to refuse his Oscar, contending that he wasn't in a race for awards. "Life isn't a race," he said. "And because it is not a race I don't consider myself in competition with my fellow actors for awards or recognition. That is why I have rejected the nomination and Oscar for playing Patton."

A 20th Century-Fox Picture, directed by Franklin J. Schaffner. With George C. Scott, Karl Malden, Michael Bates, Stephen Young, Michael Strong, Cary Loftin. Dimension 150/De Luxe Color. 173 mins.

The Phantom of the Opera (1943)

Oscars (2)   best colour cinematography Hal Mohr & W. Howard Greene
             best colour art direction   Alexander Golitzen &
                                           John B. Goodman
                          int. dec.   R. A. Gausman & Ira Webb

Gaston LeRoux's tale of a demented violinist whose face has been hideously disfigured by acid and who is forced to haunt the innermost depths of the Paris Opera House. Claude Rains stars as the masked phantom but the colour and sets, dominated by the huge chandelier hanging high above the opera audience, impress the most as the Academy rightly appreciated at the Awards presentations.

A Universal Picture, directed by Arthur Lubin. With Nelson Eddy, Susanna Foster, Claude Rains, Edgar Barrier, Leo Carrillo, Jane Farrar, J. Edward Bromberg. Technicolor. 92 mins.

The Philadelphia Story (1940)

Oscars (2)   best actor   James Stewart
             best screenplay   Donald Ogden Stewart

Philip Barry's play about a spoiled society girl (Katharine Hepburn) whose impending second marriage is disrupted suddenly by the appearance of ex-husband Cary Grant and two gossip columnists (James Stewart and Ruth Hussey) covering the marriage for their magazine.

An MGM Picture, directed by George Cukor. With Cary Grant, Katharine Hepburn, James Stewart, Ruth Hussey, John Howard, Roland Young, John Halliday. 112 mins.

Picnic (1955)

Oscars (2)   best colour art direction William Flannery & Jo Mielziner
                       set decoration   Robert Priestly
             best editing   Charles Nelson & William A. Lyon

William Holden as a wandering young hobo who arrives in a small Kansas town on Labour Day and during his brief stay there changes the lives of a number of its inhabitants. Rosalind Russell as a frustrated schoolmistress on the brink of spinsterhood, Arthur O'Connell as a lonely bachelor and Kim Novak as a small-town beauty co-star.

A Columbia Picture, directed by Joshua Logan. With William Holden, Rosalind Russell, Kim Novak, Betty Field, Susan Strasberg, Cliff Robertson, Arthur O'Connell. CinemaScope/Technicolor. 113 mins.

The Picture of Dorian Gray (1945)

Oscars (1) best b/w cinematography Harry Stradling

Oscar Wilde's frightening fantasy of a handsome young man (Hurd Hatfield) who gets the gift of eternal youth from the gods and remains young while his portrait — the only part of the film to be photographed in Technicolor — shows the horrific marks of age, vice and corruption. Set in gaslit London and starring George Sanders as Wilde's evil genius Lord Henry Wooton who appropriately delivers the author's witty dialogue and epigrams.

An MGM Picture, directed by Albert Lewin. With George Sanders, Hurd Hatfield, Donna Reed, Angela Lansbury, Peter Lawford, Lowell Gilmore. 110 mins.

Pillow Talk (1959)

Oscars (1) best story & screenplay   Russell Rouse, Clarence Greene,
                                            story: Stanley Shapiro,
                                            Maurice Richlin, screenplay

Pert interior decorator Doris Day and song writing wolf Rock Hudson get together — after many squabbles — via the good old-fashioned device of a telephone party line. Thelma Ritter as Day's inebriated maid won the fifth of her six supporting Oscar nominations, a record that still stands in that category. For all her nominations she never came out a winner.

A Universal-International Picture, directed by Michael Gordon. With Rock Hudson, Doris Day, Tony Randall, Thelma Ritter. CinemaScope/ Eastman Color. 110 mins.

Pinocchio (1940)

Oscars (2) best original music score   Leigh Harline, Paul J. Smith &
                                            Ned Washington
            best song   'When You Wish Upon A Star'
                                            (Leigh Harline, music:
                                            Ned Washington, lyrics)

Disney's second full-length feature cartoon based on the Carlo Coleddi fairy tale of a wooden puppet who is turned into a real boy. Contains some of the early Disney's most memorable creations i.e. Pinocchio's 'conscience' Jiminy Cricket, puppet master Stromboli and the roguish fox J. Worthington Foulfellow as well as some of his best songs — the

Oscar winning 'When You Wish Upon A Star', 'Hi-Diddle-Dee-Dee' and 'Give A Little Whistle.' The first Disney full-length feature to be honoured by the Academy.

A Walt Disney Picture, released by RKO. Supervising directors — Ben Sharpsteen and Hamilton Luske. With the voices of Dickie Jones, Christian Rub, Cliff Edwards, Evelyn Venable, Walter Catlett, Frankie Darro, Charles Judels. Technicolor. 88 mins.

A Place in the Sun (1951)

Oscars (6)	best direction	George Stevens
	best screenplay	Michael Wilson & Harry Brown
	best b/w cinematography	William C. Mellor
	best b/w costume design	Edith Head
	best editing	William Hornbeck
	best music score of a drama or comedy	Franz Waxman

The tragic story of a poor factory worker (Montgomery Clift) who becomes hopelessly involved with two women in different stratams of society — one a plain working girl (Shelley Winters), the other an alluring society beauty (Elizabeth Taylor) — and finds that murder is the only way out of his dilemma. A favourite, like *A Streetcar Named Desire*, for the best film award of '51, it lost surprisingly to the musical *An American In Paris*. Of the principal performers both Clift and Winters were nominated.

A Paramount Picture, directed by George Stevens. With Montgomery Clift, Elizabeth Taylor, Shelley Winters, Anne Revere, Raymond Burr, Herbert Heyes, Keefe Brasselle, Shepperd Strudwick. 122 mins.

Plymouth Adventure (1952)

Oscars (1)	best special effects	A. Arnold Gillespie

A retelling of the voyage of the Mayflower to the New World in the 17th century with Spencer Tracy as the down-to-earth ship's captain and Gene Tierney — wife of staunch Pilgrim leader Leo Genn — the woman he yearns for.

An MGM Picture, directed by Clarence Brown. With Spencer Tracy, Gene Tierney, Van Johnson, Leo Genn, Lloyd Bridges, Dawn Addams, Barry Jones. Technicolor. 105 mins.

Porgy and Bess (1959)

Oscars (1) best scoring of a musical   Andre Previn & Ken Darby

Gershwin's classic Negro folk opera about life in the South Carolina slums of Catfish Row. Sidney Poitier is the crippled beggar Porgy, Dorothy Dandridge the beautiful reckless girl who loves and eventually leaves him, and Sammy Davis is 'Sportin' Life.'
   A Columbia Picture, directed by Otto Preminger. With Sidney Poitier, Dorothy Dandridge, Sammy Davis Jr., Pearl Bailey, Brock Peters, Leslie Scott, Diahann Carroll. Todd-AO/Technicolor. 138 mins.

Portrait of Jennie (1948)

Oscars (1) best special effects   Paul Eagler, J. McMillan Johnson,
                                        Russell Shearman, Clarence
                                        Slifer (visual): Charles Freeman,
                                        James G. Stewart (audible)

Fantasy about a struggling artist (Joseph Cotten) who becomes infatuated with a young woman (Jennifer Jones) he meets in Central Park, then finds that she is no more than the spirit of a girl who died several years before. An imaginative use of colour (in an otherwise black-and-white film) in the climactic storm sequence helped earn the special effects men their Oscar.
   A David O. Selznick Production (released through the Selznick Releasing Organisation) directed by William Dieterle. With Joseph Cotten, Jennifer Jones, Ethel Barrymore, Lillian Gish, Cecil Kellaway, David Wayne, Albert Sharpe, Henry Hull. 86 mins.

The Poseidon Adventure (1972)

Oscars (1) best song   'The Morning After'
                                    (Al Kasha & Joel Hirschhorn,
                                    music & lyrics)

Two hours of 'will they, won't they make it' suspense as a small band of passengers struggle to the top (i.e. the bottom) of a luxury ocean liner when it capsizes after being struck by a tidal wave in the Mediterranean. Gene Hackman, Ernest Borgnine, Shelley Winters, Jack Albertson and Carol Lynley feature among those fighting for survival. Note: The film was also awarded a special Board of Governor's Oscar for its visual effects. L. B. Abbott, A. D. Flowers.
   A 20th Century-Fox Picture, directed by Ronald Neame. With Gene Hackman, Ernest Borgnine, Red Buttons, Carol Lynley, Roddy McDowall, Stella Stevens, Shelley Winters, Jack Albertson. Panavision/ De Luxe Color. 117 mins.

Pride and Prejudice (1940)

Oscars (1) best b/w art direction   Cedric Gibbons & Paul Groesse

Adaptation of Helen Jerome's play (based on Jane Austen's classic novel) about the mode of life, manners and customs in a 19th century English village when family pride and position were considered to be all that mattered in life. Laurence Olivier features as the dashing Mr. Darcy seeking the hand of Greer Garson and Edmund Gwenn cameos as the harrassed father with five unwedded daughters on his hands.

An MGM Picture, directed by Robert Z. Leonard. With Laurence Olivier, Greer Garson, Mary Boland, Edna May Oliver, Maureen O'Sullivan, Ann Rutherford, Frieda Inescort, Edmund Gwenn. 118 mins.

Pride of the Yankees (1942)

Oscars (1) best editing   Daniel Mandell

Biography of the famous American baseball star Lou Gehrig (Gary Cooper), the Yankee first baseman who played more than 2,000 consecutive games for the Yankees before falling victim to a rare neurological disease similar to multiple sclerosis — a disease that resulted in his early death at the age of 37 in June of 1941.

A Sam Goldwyn Production (released through RKO), directed by Sam Wood. With Gary Cooper, Teresa Wright, Walter Brennan, Dan Duryea, Babe Ruth, Elsa Janssen, Ludwig Stossel, Virginia Gilmore. 128 mins.

The Prime of Miss Jean Brodie (1969)

Oscars (1) best actress   Maggie Smith

Maggie Smith as Muriel Spark's eccentric Scottish schoolmistress who ignores the prescribed school curriculum and teaches her own individual concepts of life — which include supporting Fascism — to the children in her care. Pamela Franklin is the pupil who rebels against her insidious influence and destroys her, Celia Johnson the headmistress. Set in Edinburgh in the 1930's.

A 20th Century-Fox Picture, directed by Ronald Neame. With Maggie Smith, Robert Stephens, Pamela Franklin, Gordon Jackson, Celia Johnson. De Luxe Color. 116 mins.

Princess O'Rourke (1943)

Oscars (1) best original screenplay   Norman Krasna

Norman Krasna comedy-romance about an all-American pilot (Robert Cummings, who finds that his fiancee (Olivia de Havilland) is a bona-fide exiled princess. Directed by Krasna, one of the few occasions he directed from one of his own screenplays.

A Warner Bros. Picture, directed by Norman Krasna. With Olivia de Havilland, Robert Cummings, Charles Coburn, Jack Carson, Jane Wyman, Harry Davenport, Gladys Cooper. 94 mins.

The Private Life of Henry VIII (1932/33)

Oscars (1) best actor   Charles Laughton

The matrimonial misadventures of one of Britain's most tyrannical kings with Charles Laughton giving a virtuoso performance as the restless Henry and becoming the first Englishman to win an Oscar in a British-made film. Elsa Lanchester features as Anne of Cleves, Binnie Barnes as Katherine Howard, Wendy Barrie as Jane Seymour, Merle Oberon as Anne Boleyn, Everley Gregg as Catherine Parr.

A London Films Picture, directed by Alexander Korda. With Charles Laughton, Robert Donat, Merle Oberon, Binnie Barnes, Lady Tree, Elsa Lanchester, Franklin Dyall, Miles Mander. 97 mins.

The Producers (1968)

Oscars (1) best story & screenplay   Mel Brooks

Brash Mel Brooks comedy with Zero Mostel as a down-and-out ham producer conning meek accountant Gene Wilder into a fraudulent scheme to get rich quick by producing a flop Broadway show called 'Springtime For Hitler.' The plot backfires, however, and the show comes out a hit.

An Avco-Embassy Picture, directed by Mel Brooks. With Zero Mostel, Gene Wilder, Dick Shawn, Kenneth Mars, Estelle Winwood. Pathe Color. 88 mins.

Pygmalion (1938)

Oscars (2) best writing adaptation   W. P. Lipscomb, Cecil Lewis &
                                          Ian Dalrymple
          best screenplay   George Bernard Shaw

The straight version of *My Fair Lady* with Leslie Howard as Professor Higgins and Wendy Hiller as the cockney guttersnipe he turns into a lady. Not the multiple Oscar winner the musical later turned out to be, but the first British movie to win any writing awards, one of the four recipients being Shaw himself.

A Gabriel Pascal Production (released through GFD), directed by Anthony Asquith and Leslie Howard. With Leslie Howard, Wendy Hiller, Wilfrid Lawson, Marie Lohr, Scott Sunderland, Jean Cadell, David Tree. 96 mins.

The Quiet Man (1952)

Oscars (2) best direction   John Ford
                best colour cinematography Winton C. Hoch & Archie Stout

The film for which John Ford won his fourth directorial Oscar (a record) and cameraman Winton Hoch his third in four years — a fairy tale set in never-never Ireland with ex-boxer John Wayne returning to his native Galway to court fiery Irish colleen Maureen O'Hara.

A Republic Picture, directed by John Ford. With John Wayne, Maureen O'Hara, Barry Fitzgerald, Ward Bond, Victor McLaglen, Mildred Natwick, Francis Ford. Technicolor. 129 mins.

The Rains Came (1939)

Oscars (1) best special effects   E. H. Hansen & Fred Sersen

The first film to win a special effects award, an adaptation of Louis Bromfield's novel about the love affair between an English socialite wife (Myrna Loy) and a handsome young Indian doctor (Tyrone Power). Full of brilliantly staged monsoon floods, earthquakes, toppling temples, etc.

A 20th Century-Fox Picture, directed by Clarence Brown. With Myrna Loy, Tyrone Power, George Brent, Brenda Joyce, Nigel Bruce, Maria Ouspenskaya, Joseph Schildkraut, Mary Nash, Jane Darwell. 103 mins.

The Razor's Edge (1946)

Oscars (1) best supporting actress   Anne Baxter

Somerset Maugham's philosophical novel about an idealistic young man (Tyrone Power) who sheds his rich background to search for faith and spiritual fulfilment in his life. Gene Tierney co-stars as a deceitful old flame, Clifton Webb as an aristocratic snob and Anne Baxter (the film's only Oscar winner) as a tragic young woman who becomes a dipsomaniac after the death of her husband and child in a car crash.

A 20th Century-Fox Picture, directed by Edmund Goulding. With Tyrone Power, Gene Tierney, John Payne, Anne Baxter, Clifton Webb, Herbert Marshall, Lucile Watson, Frank Latimore, Elsa Lanchester. 146 mins.

Reap the Wild Wind (1942)

Oscars (1) best special effects   Gordon Jennings, Farciot Edouart
      & William L. Pereira (photo):
      Louis Mesenkop (sound)

DeMille spectacular — set in the 1840's — about America's fight to crush the pirate wreckers who ransacked the ships that went to pieces on the treacherous Florida reefs. John Wayne, Paulette Goddard and Ray Milland provide a three-way romance, the special effects men a giant squid which in a thrilling fight to the death conveniently gets rid of one of the lovers so that Miss Goddard is left free to marry the other.

A Paramount Picture, directed by Cecil B. DeMille. With Ray Milland, John Wayne, Paulette Goddard, Raymond Massey, Robert Preston, Lynne Overman, Susan Hayward, Charles Bickford. Technicolor. 124 mins.

Rebecca (1940)

Oscars (2) best film   David O. Selznick (producer)
            best b/w cinematography George Barnes

Daphne du Maurier's romantic novel about a timid, newly-wed young girl (Joan Fontaine) who finds that her aristocratic husband (Laurence Olivier) is still dominated by the memory of his mysteriously deceased first wife. Set for the most part in the sombre Cornish mansion of Manderley, the film was Hitchcock's first in the US and proved an Oscar winner first time out although Hitch himself — nominated for this one and four other films — has never won. Hitchcock's nominations: *Rebecca* (40), *Lifeboat* (44), *Spellbound* (45), *Rear Window* (54) and *Psycho* (60).

A Selznick International Picture (released through United Artists), directed by Alfred Hitchcock. With Laurence Olivier, Joan Fontaine, George Sanders, Judith Anderson, Nigel Bruce, C. Aubrey Smith, Reginald Denny, Gladys Cooper. 130 mins.

The Red Balloon (1956)

Oscars (1) best original screenplay   Albert Lamorisse

Half-hour fantasy about the adventures of a little boy and a big red balloon he rescues from a Paris lamp post. Photographed entirely in the picturesque backstreets and alleys of Old Montmartre and starring the director's own 6-year-old son Pascal.

A Films Montsouris Production, directed by Albert Lamorisse. With Pascal Lamorisse, the children of Menilmontant and all the balloons of Paris. Technicolor. 35 mins.

The Red Shoes (1948)

Oscars (2)   best colour art direction   Hein Heckroth
                       set decoration Arthur Lawson
               best scoring of a   Brian Easdale
                   drama or comedy

The only truly successful box-office ballet film, hampered by its trite story — young ballerina torn between her love for her composer husband and her love for dancing — but almost completely redeemed by Brian Easdale's exciting music and the brilliant colour of cameraman Jack Cardiff. The final 20 minute ballet is based on the Hans Christian Andersen story about the magic red shoes that dance a little girl to death.

An Archers Film, directed by Michael Powell and Emeric Pressburger. With Moira Shearer, Leonide Massine, Robert Helpmann, Anton Walbrook, Marius Goring. Technicolor. 133 mins.

The Robe (1953)

Oscars (2)   best colour art direction   Lyle Wheeler & George W. Davis
                       set decoration Walter M. Scott & Paul S. Fox
               best colour costume design Charles LeMaire & Emile Santiago

Lloyd C. Douglas' story of the conversion to Christianity of the Roman tribune (Richard Burton) in charge of Christ's Crucifixion on Calvary. Jean Simmons featured as the innocent maid, Jay Robinson as the screaming Emperor Caligula but, not surprisingly it was CinemaScope that received the biggest notices, this being the first film to be shot in the then revolutionary process.

A 20th Century-Fox Picture, directed by Henry Koster. With Richard Burton, Jean Simmons, Victor Mature, Michael Rennie, Jay Robinson, Dean Jagger. CinemaScope/Technicolor. 135 mins.

Rocky (1976)

Oscars (3)   best film   Irwin Winkler &
                                    Robert Chartoff (producers)
               best direction   John G. Avildsen
               best editing   Richard Halsey & Scott Conrad

Cinderella story of a young punch-drunk bum boxer (Sylvester Stallone) who, by a freak of fate, gets his chance to have a crack at the heavyweight title and in doing so wins for himself the self-respect he has been missing all his life. Co-starring Talia Shire as his shy young girl friend, the film is the only 'sport movie' ever to be named best picture of the year.

A United Artists Picture, directed by John G. Avildsen. With Sylvester Stallone, Talia Shire, Burt Young, Carl Weathers, Burgess Meredith, Thayer David. De Luxe Color. 119 mins.

Roman Holiday (1953)

Oscars (3) best actress   Audrey Hepburn
           best motion picture story   Ian McLellan Hunter
           best b/w costume design   Edith Head

Romantic comedy which made Audrey Hepburn a star and earned her an Oscar in her first major role — that of a young princess who escapes from the pomp and ceremony of her surroundings for 24 hours and enjoys a brief romance with American journalist Gregory Peck. Shot entirely in Rome.

A Paramount Picture, directed by William Wyler. With Gregory Peck, Audrey Hepburn, Eddie Albert, Hartley Power, Laura Solari, Harcourt Williams, Margaret Rawlings. 119 mins.

Romeo and Juliet (1968)

Oscars (2) best cinematography   Pasqualino De Santis
           best costume design   Danilo Donati

Shakespeare's immortal tragedy of two young lovers whose families — the Montagues and the Capulets — try to keep them apart but succeed only in being responsible for their suicides. Leonard Whiting and Olivia Hussey feature as the star-crossed lovers, Michael York as Tybalt, John McEnery as Mercutio.

A Paramount Release, directed by Franco Zeffirelli. With Leonard Whiting, Olivia Hussey, Milo O'Shea, Michael York, John McEnery. Technicolor. 152 mins.

Room at the Top (1959)

Oscars (2) best actress   Simone Signoret
           best screenplay   Neil Paterson

One of the very few British movies to deal openly with the subject of class, the tale of a young working class accountant (Laurence Harvey) who ruthlessly makes it to the top in one bounce by the simple expedient of putting the daughter of a rich industrialist in the family way. Based on the novel by John Braine. Top performance in the movie came from Simone Signoret who, as Harvey's tragic fading mistress, became the first French actress to win the best actress award.

A Remus Picture, directed by Jack Clayton. With Simone Signoret, Laurence Harvey, Heather Sears, Donald Wolfit, Donald Houston, Hermione Baddeley. 117 mins.

Rosemary's Baby (1968)

Oscars (1) best supporting actress   Ruth Gordon

Thriller about witchcraft and satanism in contemporary New York with Mia Farrow as the luckless girl chosen to bear the child (unseen) of the Devil. Co-starring John Cassavetes as her husband, Sidney Blackmer as the leader of the coven and Ruth Gordon as the flamboyant witch, Minnie Castevet who 'looks after' Miss Farrow during her pregnancy.

A Paramount Picture, directed by Roman Polanski. With Mia Farrow, John Cassavetes, Ruth Gordon, Sidney Blackmer, Maurice Evans, Ralph Bellamy, Angela Dorian, Patsy Kelly. Technicolor. 136 mins.

The Rose Tattoo (1955)

Oscars (3) best actress   Anna Magnani
            best b/w cinematography James Wong Howe
            best b/w art direction   Hal Pereira & Tambi Larsen
                set decoration   Sam Comer & Arthur Krams

Anna Magnani as Tennessee Williams' tempestuous, Sicilian born peasant Serafina who mourns deeply for her dead truck driver husband and settles in the end for a great sweating oaf of a man (Burt Lancaster) whose body alone reminds her of her former partner. Set in the Italian quarter of a steamy town on the gulf coast of America.

A Paramount Picture, directed by Daniel Mann. With Anna Magnani, Burt Lancaster, Marisa Pavan, Ben Cooper, Jo Van Fleet. Vista Vision. 117 mins.

Ryan's Daughter (1970)

Oscars (2) best supporting actor   John Mills
            best cinematography   Freddie Young

David Lean's simple love story of Ireland in 1916 centering around a romantic and excitable young Irish girl (Sarah Miles) who marries the simple, plodding schoolteacher (Robert Mitchum) of the village — a man twice her age — and has an affair with a shell-shocked young British officer (Christopher Jones) stationed in a nearby garrison. Mills' Oscar was for his portrayal of the misshapen village idiot, Michael; Freddie Young's was his third for his work in a Lean film. (see also *Lawrence of Arabia* and *Doctor Zhivago*).

An MGM Picture, directed by David Lean. With Sarah Miles, Robert Mitchum, Trevor Howard, Christopher Jones, John Mills, Leo McKern, Barry Foster. Super Panavision 70/Metrocolor. 206 mins.

Sabrina (1954)

Oscars (1) best b/w costume design   Edith Head

Lubitsch-type sophisticated comedy with chauffeur's daughter Audrey Hepburn being romanced by the two sons of a wealthy Long Island family — ageing business tycoon Humphrey Bogart and his wealthy playboy brother William Holden. From the Broadway play by Samuel Taylor.

A Paramount Picture, directed by Billy Wilder. With Humphrey Bogart, Audrey Hepburn, William Holden, Walter Hampden, John Williams, Martha Hyer. 113 mins.

Samson and Delilah (1950)

Oscars (2) best colour art direction   Hans Dreier & Walter Tyler
                        set decoration Sam Comer & Ray Moyer
        best colour costume design Edith Head, Dorothy Jeakins,
                            Eloise Jenssen, Gile Steele &
                            Gwen Wakeling

DeMille's first post-war Biblical spectacular, the story of mighty Danite strong man Samson (Victor Mature) who destroys an entire army with a jawbone of an ass but who falls victim to the wiles of Philistine temptress Hedy Lamarr. Hokum, although the final destruction of the temple of Gaza is impressive.

A Paramount Picture, directed by Cecil B. DeMille. With Hedy Lamarr, Victor Mature, George Sanders, Angela Lansbury, Henry Wilcoxon. Technicolor. 128 mins.

The Sandpiper (1965)

Oscars (1) best song   'The Shadow Of Your Smile'
                            (John Mandel, music:
                            Paul Francis Webster, lyrics)

The adulterous love affair between free-thinking beatnik mother, Elizabeth Taylor and Episcopal clergyman Richard Burton. Big-star soap-opera photographed on California's Big Sur coast and scored to romantic perfection by John Mandel whose song 'The Shadow Of Your Smile' came out easily as the year's best.

An MGM Picture, directed by Vincente Minnelli. With Elizabeth Taylor, Richard Burton, Eva Marie Saint, Charles Bronson, Robert Webber, James Edwards, Torin Thatcher. Panavision/Metrocolor. 116 mins.

San Francisco (1936)

Oscars (1) best sound recording   Douglas Shearer

Robust melodrama of love and adventure on the notorious Barbary Coast following the intertwined lives of saloon owner/gambler Clark Gable, opera singer Jeanette MacDonald and two-fisted priest Spencer Tracy. Climaxed, of course, by the historic earthquake of 1906.

An MGM Picture, directed by W. S. Van Dyke. With Clark Gable, Jeanette MacDonald, Spencer Tracy, Jack Holt, Jessie Ralph. 115 mins.

Save the Tiger (1973)

Oscars (1) best actor   Jack Lemmon

A day in the life of American businessman Jack Lemmon (forced by his partner to consider arson as a way out of financial trouble) who has become disenchanted by the degradation he submits himself to in his working life and bemused by the collapse of a lifetime's values. For his portrayal of Harry Stoner, Lemmon became the first, and to date only actor to win both a supporting Oscar (for *Mister Roberts* 18 years earlier) and a major acting Oscar in his career.

A Paramount Picture, directed by John G. Avildsen. With Jack Lemmon, Jack Gilford, Laurie Heineman, Norman Burton, Patricia Smith, Thayer David. Movielab Color. 100 mins.

Sayonara (1957)

Oscars (4)	best supporting actor	Red Buttons
	best supporting actress	Miyoshi Umeki
	best art direction	Ted Haworth
	set decoration	Robert Priestly
	best sound recording	George R. Groves

U.S. Korean war ace Marlon Brando, sent to Japan for rest and rehabilitation, falls in love with Japanese actress Miiko Taka and finds himself coming up against the brutal racial policies practiced by the American military authorities. The movie's main Oscars went to Red Buttons as an American flier and Miyoshi Umeki as a Japanese girl who play out a delicate, ultimately doomed love affair.

A Warner Bros. Picture, directed by Joshua Logan. With Marlon Brando, Patricia Owen, James Garner, Martha Scott, Miyoshi Umeki, Miiko Taka, Red Buttons. Technirama/Technicolor. 147 mins.

The Scoundrel (1935)

Oscars (1) best original story   Ben Hecht & Charles MacArthur

Ruthless and hated New York publisher Noel Coward, killed suddenly in a plane crash, finds his path into eternity blocked by a divine voice which gives him exactly one month in which to return to life and find someone who will mourn for him. A modern miracle play wittily scripted by Hecht and MacArthur.

A Paramount Picture, directed by Ben Hecht and Charles MacArthur. With Noel Coward, Julie Haydon, Stanley Ridges, Martha Sleeper, Ernest Cossart, Alexander Woollcott. 68 mins.

The Search (1948)

Oscars (1) best motion picture story Richard Schweizer &
                                       David Wechsler

Deeply moving account of a Czech mother who wanders aimlessly through post-war Germany searching for the child who was taken from her in a German concentration camp. Jarmila Novotna plays the mother, Ivan Jandl the boy, and Montgomery Clift the sympathetic American soldier who befriends him. Made by Zinnemann in Switzerland and the American Zone of Germany.

An MGM Picture, directed by Fred Zinnemann. With Montgomery Clift, Aline MacMahon, Jarmila Novotna, Wendell Corey, Ivan Jandl. 105 mins.

Separate Tables (1958)

Oscars (2) best actor   David Niven
            best supporting actress   Wendy Hiller

Terence Rattigan's two one-act plays about the individual personal dramas of a group of guests at a British seaside resort hotel. Niven won his Oscar for his ex-colonel who is really a fraud, Hiller won hers for portraying the proprietress of the establishment.

A United Artists Picture, directed by Delbert Mann. With Rita Hayworth, Deborah Kerr, David Niven, Wendy Hiller, Burt Lancaster, Gladys Cooper, Cathleen Nesbitt, Felix Aylmer, Rod Taylor, Audrey Dalton. 98 mins.

Sergeant York (1941)

Oscars (2) best actor   Gary Cooper
             best editing   William Holmes

Gary Cooper's first Oscar — as Sergeant Alvin York, a Tennessee hillbilly with pacifist convictions, who is drafted during World War I and becomes America's greatest hero of the conflict, destroying or capturing an entire German battalion single-handed.

A Warner Bros. Picture, directed by Howard Hawks. With Gary Cooper, Walter Brennan, Joan Leslie, George Tobias, Stanley Ridges, Margaret Wycherly. 134 mins.

Seven Brides for Seven Brothers (1954)

Oscars (1) best scoring of a musical   Adolph Deutsch & Saul Chaplin

The last of the great original musicals from MGM, a story of seven Oregon backwoods boys who, influenced by the story of the Rape of the Sabine Women, kidnap several girls from the local township and make them their brides. The extraordinary acrobatic dancing of Messrs. Tamblyn, Rall and Co. earned Michael Kidd a special award for choreography.

An MGM Picture, directed by Stanley Donen. With Jane Powell, Howard Keel, Jeff Richards, Russ Tamblyn, Tommy Rall, Howard Petrie, Virginia Gibson. CinemaScope/Ansco Color. 102 mins.

Seven Days to Noon (1951)

Oscars (1) best motion picture story Paul Dehn & James Bernard

Inventive, and for its period, topical tale of an atom scientist (Barry Jones) who has a nervous breakdown and makes off with an atom bomb, threatening to destroy London unless the British government agrees to make a public announcement that it will cease production of all nuclear weapons.

A London Films Production, directed by Roy Boulting. With Barry Jones, Andre Morell, Olive Sloane, Sheila Manahan, Hugh Cross, Joan Hickson. 94 mins.

Seventh Heaven (1927/28)

Oscars (3)   best direction   Frank Borzage
             best actress   Janet Gaynor
             best writing adaptation   Benjamin Glazer

Among the most famous screen romances of all time, set prior to and during World War I, with Janet Gaynor in one of the three roles that won her the first best actress Oscar (see also *Street Angel* and *Sunrise*). As Diane, a mistreated Parisian waif, she is victimised by her unscrupulous lover, but redeemed by the love of honest sewer worker Chico. Gaynor's competitors in the first best actress race were Gloria Swanson in *Sadie Thompson* and Louise Dresser in *A Ship Comes In*. Borzage's direction award was also the first in the history of the Academy although the same year Lewis Milestone was voted best comedy director for his *Two Arabian Knights*, an award which was not continued in subsequent years.

   A Fox Picture, directed by Frank Borzage. With Janet Gaynor, Charles Farrell, Ben Bard, David Butler, Marie Mosquini, Albert Gran. 12 reels.

The Seventh Veil (1946)

Oscars (1) best original screenplay   Muriel & Sydney Box

Famous British tearjerker about a young woman (Ann Todd) who runs away from home to become a famous concert pianist and finds that her personal life with several different men is distinctly less successful. James Mason, in one of his most famous roles, co-stars as Todd's brutal guardian.

   A Theatrecraft/Sydney Box/Ortus Production, directed by Compton Bennett. With James Mason, Ann Todd, Herbert Lom, Hugh McDermott, Albert Lieven. 94 mins.

Shaft (1971)

Oscars (1) best song   'Theme From Shaft'
                                        (Isaac Hayes, music & lyrics)

Black private eye John Shaft (Richard Roundtree) is hired to find the kidnapped daughter of a wealthy Harlem racketeer. Workmanlike all-black thriller which won the year's best song award defeating, among other competitors, the Sherman Bros. song 'The Age Of Not Believing' from *Bedknobs And Broomsticks*.

An MGM Picture, directed by Gordon Parks. With Richard Roundtree, Moses Gunn, Charles Cioffi, Christopher St. John, Gwenn Mitchell, Lawrence Pressman. Metrocolor. 100 mins.

Shampoo (1975)

Oscars (1) best supporting actress   Lee Grant

The complex and amorous adventures of a young hairdresser (Warren Beatty) in Beverly Hills at the time of the 1968 Presidential elections. A brilliantly written social comedy that, through the exploits of its main character, looks at the moral and political atmosphere of America in the late 60's. Lee Grant's Oscar was for her portrayal of the frustrated wife of businessman Jack Warden.

A Columbia Picture, directed by Hal Ashby. With Warren Beatty, Julie Christie, Goldie Hawn, Lee Grant, Jack Warden, Tony Bill, Carrie Fisher, Jay Robinson. Technicolor. 110 mins.

Shane (1953)

Oscars (1) best colour cinematography Loyal Griggs

Classic western about a mysterious gunfighter (Alan Ladd) who rides into a Wyoming valley and helps the homesteaders in their fight against the cattlemen. Van Heflin and Jean Arthur feature as the farming Starrett family, Jack Palance as a hired killer. A certain best picture winner in any normal year (it took 6 nominations) it won only in the colour photography category being up against *From Here To Eternity* which swept all before it at the '53 awards.

A Paramount Picture, directed by George Stevens. With Alan Ladd, Jean Arthur, Van Heflin, Brandon De Wilde, Jack Palance, Ben Johnson, Edgar Buchanan, Emile Meyer, Elisha Cook Jr. Technicolor. 118 mins.

Shanghai Express (1931/32)

Oscars (1) best cinematography   Lee Garmes

Sternberg and Dietrich's greatest commercial success (three million dollars gross), an oriental extravaganza set on board a train journey from Peking to Shanghai, with Dietrich as the notorious white prostitute Shanghai Lily saving the life of former lover Clive Brook when he is held hostage by revolutionaries.

A Paramount Picture, directed by Josef von Sternberg. With Marlene Dietrich, Clive Brook, Anna May Wong, Warner Oland, Eugene Pallette, Lawrence Grant. 80 mins.

She Wore a Yellow Ribbon (1949)

Oscars (1)   best colour cinematography   Winton C. Hoch

Retiring captain Nathan Brittles (John Wayne) and the U.S. Cavalry successfully put down a large-scale Indian uprising just after the Civil War. John Ford's first western in colour and a deserved winner in the colour photography category, full of glowing sunsets, red mountain peaks and men riding silhouetted against the skyline.

An RKO Picture, directed by John Ford. With John Wayne, Joanne Dru, John Agar, Ben Johnson, Harry Carey Jr., Victor McLaglen, Mildred Natwick. Technicolor. 103 mins.

Ship of Fools (1965)

Oscars (2)   best b/w cinematography   Ernest Laszlo
            best b/w art direction   Robert Clatworthy
                set decoration   Joseph Kish

Katherine Anne Porter's symbolic, floating 'Grand Hotel' about a shipful of assorted passengers going back to Germany from South America in the early Nazi days of 1933. Vivien Leigh as a disillusioned divorcee, Oskar Werner and Simone Signoret as two doomed illicit lovers and Lee Marvin as a punchy baseball player head an all-star cast.

A Columbia Picture, directed by Stanley Kramer. With Vivien Leigh, Simone Signoret, Jose Ferrer, Lee Marvin, Oskar Werner, Elizabeth Ashley, George Segal, Jose Greco, Michael Dunn, Charles Korvin. 149 mins.

The Shop on Main Street (1965)

Oscars (1)   best foreign language film   Czechoslovakia

World War II story, set in a small provincial town in occupied Czechoslovakia, about a henpecked carpenter who becomes the Aryan controller of a button shop, kept going by the Jewish community so that its widow proprietress will think she is earning her own living from the proceeds.

A Czechoslovakian Picture, directed by Jan Kadar and Elmar Klos. With Josef Kroner, Ida Kaminska, Hans Slivkova, Frantisek Zvarik, Helen Zvarikova, Martin Holly. 128 mins.

Since You Went Away (1944)

Oscars (1)   best scoring of a   Max Steiner
             drama or comedy

Selznick's companion piece to MGM's *Mrs. Miniver*, a supreme tear-jerker about a middle-class American family — its hopes, sacrifices, tragedies — as it goes about its normal everyday life while its menfolk are overseas fighting the war. Set throughout the year 1943, it featured Claudette Colbert as the mother of the family, Shirley Temple and Jennifer Jones as her two daughters and Hattie McDaniel as their maid. Composer Max Steiner won his third (see also *The Informer* and *Now Voyager*) and final Oscar for his music score.

   A David O. Selznick Production (released through United Artists), directed by John Cromwell. With Claudette Colbert, Jennifer Jones, Joseph Cotten, Shirley Temple, Monty Woolley, Lionel Barrymore, Robert Walker, Hattie McDaniel, Agnes Moorehead. 172 mins.

The Sin of Madelon Claudet (1931/32)

Oscars (1)   best actress   Helen Hayes

Helen Hayes' first Oscar-winning role as a tragic mother who makes all manner of sacrifices so that her illegitimate son can be educated and become a physician. Almost a remake of *Madame X* and Hayes' first try at the talkies. See *Airport* for her supporting Oscar won nearly forty years later.

   An MGM Picture, directed by Edgar Selwyn. With Helen Hayes, Lewis Stone, Neil Hamilton, Robert Young, Cliff Edwards, Jean Hersholt, Marie Prevost. 74 mins.

Skippy (1930/31)

Oscars (1)   best direction   Norman Taurog

Film version of the adventures of Percy Crosby's comic-strip boy character Skippy Skinner and his child friends — Eloise, the tell-tale Sidney and Sooky of Shanty Town. For his direction of the predominantly all-child cast, Norman Taurog (perhaps the most forgotten best director winner in Oscar history) scooped such star names as Josef von Sternberg (*Morocco*) and Lewis Milestone (*The Front Page*).

   A Paramount Picture, directed by Norman Taurog. With Jackie Cooper, Robert Coogan, Mitzi Green, Jackie Searl, Willard Robertson, Enid Bennett. 88 mins.

The Snake Pit (1948)

Oscars (1) best sound recording   Thomas Moulton

Grippingly effective film about the horrors of over-crowding in an understaffed American mental hospital. Olivia de Havilland challenged Jane Wyman (the year's best actress winner for *Johnny Belinda*) with her portrait of a young woman writer who has a mental breakdown and undergoes treatment in a squalid mental institution.

A 20th Century-Fox Picture, directed by Anatole Litvak. With Olivia de Havilland, Mark Stevens, Leo Genn, Celeste Holm, Glenn Langan, Helen Craig, Leif Erickson, Beulah Bondi, Lee Patrick. 108 mins.

The Solid Gold Cadillac (1956)

Oscars (1) best b/w costume design   Jean Louis

Judy Holliday in one of her most delightful roles as an unemployed actress who owns just ten shares in a vast business corporation and sets about proving that the board of directors is riddled with corruption. A Wall Street fairy story, helped along considerably by actors of the quality of Fred Clark and John Williams.

A Columbia Picture, directed by Richard Quine. With Judy Holliday, Paul Douglas, Fred Clark, John Williams, Hiram Sherman, Neva Patterson, Ralph Dumke, Ray Collins, Arthur O'Connell. 99 mins.

Somebody Up There Likes Me (1956)

Oscars (2) best b/w cinematography Joseph Ruttenberg
           best b/w art direction   Cedric Gibbons &
                                       Malcolm F. Brown
           set decoration   Edwin B. Willis & F. Keogh Gleason

Screen biography of rebellious East Side delinquent Rocky Graziano (Paul Newman) who rises above reform school, jail and army detention barracks to become middleweight boxing champion of the world. Newman starred in the role originally intended for James Dean and cameraman Joseph Ruttenberg earned the third of his four Academy Awards. Others: *The Great Waltz* (38), *Mrs. Miniver* (42), *Gigi* (58).

An MGM Picture, directed by Robert Wise. With Paul Newman, Pier Angeli, Everett Sloane, Eileen Heckart, Sal Mineo, Harold J. Stone. 112 mins.

Some Like it Hot (1959)

Oscars (1) best b/w costume design   Orry-Kelly

One of the funniest American comedies of all time with jazz musicians Jack Lemmon and Tony Curtis fleeing gangsters after witnessing a gangland massacre in Chicago and disguising themselves as members of an all-girl dance band travelling by train to Florida. Like other top films of 1959 the picture was trampled on by *Ben-Hur* and finished up with only a costume award to its name.

A United Artists Picture, directed by Billy Wilder. With Marilyn Monroe, Tony Curtis, Jack Lemmon, George Raft, Pat O'Brien, Joe E. Brown, Nehemiah Persoff, Joan Shawlee. 120 mins.

The Song of Bernadette (1943)

Oscars (4) best actress   Jennifer Jones
            best b/w cinematography   Arthur Miller
            best b/w art direction   James Basevi & William Darling
                 int. decoration   Thomas Little
            best score of a   Alfred Newman
              drama or comedy

Jennifer Jones as Bernadette Soubirous, the French peasant girl who, in 1858, saw visions of the Virgin Mary and discovered a miraculous healing spring at Lourdes. The most predigious American film of 1943 and the biggest winner of its year although *Casablanca*, the surprise hit of the period, took the best picture award.

A 20th Century-Fox Picture, directed by Henry King. With Jennifer Jones, William Eythe, Charles Bickford, Vincent Price, Lee J. Cobb, Gladys Cooper. 156 mins.

Song of the South (1947)

Oscars (1) best song   'Zip-A-Dee-Doo-Dah'
                                     Allie Wrubel, music:
                                     Ray Gilbert, lyrics

Disney version of the Tales of Uncle Remus by Joel Chandler Harris. The Oscar-winning song 'Zip-A-Dee-Doo-Dah' was sung by James Baskett against a cartoon background with animated birds perched on his shoulder — one of the earliest uses of the combined live-action/ animation process.

A Walt Disney Picture (released through RKO), directed by Harve Foster; cartoons directed by Wilfred Jackson. With Ruth Warrick, James Baskett, Bobby Driscoll, Luana Patten, Lucile Watson, Hattie McDaniel. Technicolor. 94 mins.

Song Without End (1960)

Oscars (1) best scoring of a musical   Morris Stoloff & Harry Sukman

Hollywood version of the life of Franz Liszt (Dirk Bogarde) and in particular of his romantic interlude with Princess Carolyne of Russia (Capucine).
   A Columbia Picture, directed by Charles Vidor and George Cukor. With Dirk Bogarde, Capucine, Genevieve Page, Patricia Morison, Ivan Desny, Martita Hunt, Lou Jacobi. CinemaScope/Technicolor. 130 mins.

Sons and Lovers (1960)

Oscars (1) best b/w cinematography Freddie Francis

The story of a young boy's growth to manhood in pre-World War I England with Dean Stockwell as D. H. Lawrence's sensitive Nottingham youth torn between his love for two women (Mary Ure and Heather Sears) and his desire to break away from the drab coal town in which he lives. Trevor Howard as the boy's drunken miner father was nominated for a best actor Academy Award.
   A 20th Century-Fox Picture, directed by Jack Cardiff. With Trevor Howard, Dean Stockwell, Wendy Hiller, Mary Ure, Heather Sears, William Lucas. CinemaScope. 100 mins.

The Sound of Music (1965)

Oscars (5) best film   Robert Wise (producer)
            best direction   Robert Wise
            best editing   William Reynolds
            best sound   James P. Corcoran & Fred Hynes
            best music score: Irwin Kostal
               adaptation

Just a year after winning her Oscar for *Mary Poppins* Julie Andrews was again up for the award for her performance in this picture — as the singing governess of the Von Trapp family in pre-war Austria. This time, however, she failed to win losing to Julie Christie's much more down-to-earth 60's gal in John Schlesinger's *Darling*. The Oscar Hammerstein-Richard Rodgers musical did, on the other hand capture the best picture award plus 4 others.

A 20th Century-Fox Picture, directed by Robert Wise. With Julie Andrews, Christopher Plummer, Eleanor Parker, Richard Haydn, Peggy Wood. Todd-AO/De Luxe Color. 171 mins.

South Pacific (1958)

Oscars (1) best sound recording   Fred Hynes

Another famous Rodgers/Hammerstein musical, not by any means the big winner *Music* turned out to be, but in its day very nearly as big a financial success. Rossano Brazzi, Mitzi Gaynor, John Kerr and France Nuyen featured among those suffering emotional problems on a Pacific Island in World War II. Adapted from stories by James A. Michener.

A Magna Theatre Corp Picture (released by 20th Century-Fox), directed by Joshua Logan. With Rossano Brazzi, Mitzi Gaynor, John Kerr, Ray Walston, Juanita Hall, France Nuyen. Todd-AO/Technicolor. 171 mins.

Spartacus (1960)

Oscars (4)	best supporting actor	Peter Ustinov
	best colour cinematography	Russell Metty
	best colour art direction	Alexander Golitzen & Eric Orbom
	set decoration	Russell A. Gausman & Julia Heron
	best colour costume design	Valles & Bill Thomas

Howard Fast's epic tale of the slaves' revolt (under the leadership of Spartacus) against their Roman masters in 73 B.C. One of the most unusual of Hollywood epics in that it did not boast of the coming of Christianity as its major theme. Peter Ustinov won his supporting Oscar for his master of a school of gladiators; Russell Metty, Universal's top cameraman for many years won his for his magnificent colour lensing.

A Universal Picture, directed by Stanley Kubrick. With Kirk Douglas, Laurence Olivier, Tony Curtis, Jean Simmons, Charles Laughton, Peter Ustinov, John Gavin, Nina Foch. Super Technirama 70/Technicolor 196 mins.

Spellbound (1945)

Oscars (1) best scoring of a   Miklos Rozsa
                drama or comedy

The first picture about psycho-analysis, an engaging Hitchcock thriller revolving round an amnesiac doctor (Gregory Peck) who subconsciously believes himself to be a murderer and the woman psychiatrist (Ingrid Bergman) who tries to prove his innocence. Full of trick effects including a Salvador Dali dream sequence, and a lush romantic Rozsa score which even today is still world famous and instantly recognisable.

   A David O. Selznick Production (released through United Artists), directed by Alfred Hitchcock. With Ingrid Bergman, Gregory Peck, Jean Acker, Donald Curtis, Rhonda Fleming, John Emery, Leo G. Carroll. 111 mins.

Splendour in the Grass (1961)

Oscars (1) best story & screenplay   William Inge

A William Inge original about adolescent love and frustration in a puritanical Kansas town in the 20's just prior to the Wall Street Crash. Warren Beatty (debut) and Natalie Wood star as the tormented couple. A Warner Bros. Picture, directed by Elia Kazan. With Natalie Wood, Warren Beatty, Pat Hingle, Audrey Christie, Barbara Loden. Technicolor. 124 mins.

Stagecoach (1939)

Oscars (2) best supporting actor   Thomas Mitchell
                best music score   Richard Hageman, Franke
                                           Harling, John Leipold &
                                           Leo Shuken

John Ford's famous western about a stagecoach journey across the plains of Arizona in the 1870's. John Wayne, in the Ringo Kid role that made him famous, remains the best remembered of the passengers although it was Thomas Mitchell as the drunken Doc Boone who has to be forcibly sobered up *en-route* to deliver a baby, who deservedly won the acting honours.

   A United Artists Picture, directed by John Ford. With John Wayne, Claire Trevor, Thomas Mitchell, George Bancroft, Andy Devine, John Carradine, Louise Platt, Donald Meek, Berton Churchill, Tim Holt. 96 mins.

Stalag 17 (1953)

Oscars (1) best actor   William Holden

Comedy-drama by Billy Wilder about the life of American airmen in a bleak German P.O.W. camp in World War II. A film of many moods — humorous, suspenseful, disturbing — dominated by an Oscar-winning performance by William Holden as the scrounging camp opportunist, a cynical heel who, among other things, arranges horse races with mice, builds a gin distillery and rigs a telescope for peeping into the Russian womens' barracks.

A Paramount Picture, directed by Billy Wilder. With William Holden, Don Taylor, Otto Preminger, Robert Strauss, Harvey Lembeck, Richard Erdman, Peter Graves, Neville Brand, Sig Ruman. 120 mins.

A Star is Born (1937)

Oscars (1) best original story   Robert Carson &
                                          William A. Wellman

Fredric March as a famous film actor on the way down because of drink, discovers talented farm girl Janet Gaynor in Hollywood and turns her into a star. Director Wellman's Oscar for his story of this famous film was the only Academy Award he ever won even though he was also nominated for his direction and for his handling of such subsequent films as *Battleground* and *The High And The Mighty*. Note: W. Howard Greene was awarded a special Oscar for his colour cinematography.

A United Artists Picture, directed by William A. Wellman. With Janet Gaynor, Fredric March, Adolphe Menjou, Andy Devine, May Robson, Lionel Stander. Technicolor. 111 mins.

A Star is Born (1976)

Oscars (1) best song   'Evergreen'
                                          (Barbra Streisand, music,
                                          Paul Williams, lyrics)

Third time out for this famous story of a star on the skids helping a young one on the rise, transferred this time to the rock scene with Kris Kristofferson as the rock star on the downward path and Barbra Streisand as the young hopeful. Streisand's second Oscar, her first coming nine years earlier as best actress in *Funny Girl*.

A Warner Bros. Picture, directed by Frank Pierson. With Barbra Streisand, Kris Kristofferson, Paul Mazursky, Gary Busey, Oliver Clark. Metrocolor. 140 mins.

Star Wars (1977)

Oscars (7)	best art direction	John Barry, Norman Reynolds & Leslie Dilley
	set decoration	Roger Christian
	best costume design	John Mollo
	best sound	Don MacDougall, Ray West, Bob Minkler & Derek Ball
	best editing	Paul Hirsch, Marcia Lucas & Richard Chew
	best music score	John Williams
	best visual effects	John Stears, John Dykstra, Richard Edlund, Grant McCune & Robert Blalack

Special award to Benjamin Burtt, Jr. for creating the alien, creature and robot voices featured in the picture

Vigorous space spectacular out of *Flash Gordon,* but with all the advantages of modern special effects and sound techniques. Peter Cushing is an advanced megalomaniac with plans not just to rule the world but the universe; young adventurers Mark Hamill and Harrison Ford and princess Carrie Fisher are out to stop him. Also on the side of right: Alec Guinness who provides the spiritual guidance, and androids See Threepio and Artoo-Detoo who provide mechanical chitter-chatter and mini-beeps. The biggest Oscar winner of its year.

A 20th Century-Fox Picture, directed by George Lucas. With Mark Hamill, Harrison Ford, Carrie Fisher, Peter Cushing, Alec Guinness, Anthony Daniels, Kenny Baker, Peter Mayhew, David Prowse. Panavision/Technicolor; prints by DeLuxe. 121 mins.

State Fair (1945)

| Oscars (1) | best song | 'It Might As Well Be Spring' Richard Rodgers, music: Oscar Hammerstein II, lyrics |

The second of the three versions of Philip Stong's perennial tale about a country farm family and their disappointments, romances and minor triumphs during their annual visit to the Iowa State Fair. The Oscar-winning 'It Might As Well Be Spring' was sung by Louanne Hogan who dubbed for Jeanne Crain.

A 20th Century-Fox Picture, directed by Walter Lang. With Jeanne Crain, Dana Andrews, Dick Haymes, Vivian Blaine, Charles Winninger, Fay Bainter, Donald Meek. Technicolor. 101 mins.

The Sting (1973)

Oscars (7)	best film	Tony Bill, Michael & Julia Phillips (producers)
	best direction	George Roy Hill
	best story & screenplay	David S. Ward
	best art direction	Henry Bumstead
	set decoration	James Payne
	best costume design	Edith Head
	best editing	William Reynolds
	best music score: adaptation	Marvin Hamlisch

Two confidence tricksters, Paul Newman and Robert Redford, set out to 'take' big time racketeer Robert Shaw for a vast sum of money after he has been responsible for the murder of Redford's elderly black partner. Set in Chicago in the thirties, the film cleaned up at the 73 awards pushing the other hot contender, *The Exorcist*, right out of contention for the major honours. Not the least of its merits was its unique use of piano rags by Scott Joplin for its major music themes.

A Universal Picture, directed by George Roy Hill. With Paul Newman, Robert Redford, Robert Shaw, Charles Durning, Ray Walston, Eileen Brennan, Harold Gould. Technicolor. 129 mins.

The Story of Louis Pasteur (1936)

Oscars (3)	best actor	Paul Muni
	best written screenplay	Pierre Collings & Sheridan Gibney
	best original story	Pierre Collings & Sheridan Gibney

The career of French chemist Louis Pasteur (Muni) who almost single handed battled with and defeated the diseases of anthrax and chicken cholera in 19th century France. The first of William Dieterle's distinguished Warner biographies of the 30's. Later additions included *The Life Of Emile Zola, Juarez, Dr. Ehrlich's Magic Bullet*.

A Warner Bros. Picture, directed by William Dieterle. With Paul Muni, Josephine Hutchinson, Anita Louise, Donald Woods, Fritz Leiber, Henry O'Neill. 85 mins.

La Strada (1956)

Oscars (1)   best foreign language film Italy

Fellini's first great film and the first *official* foreign language winner, all the previous awards to overseas movies being in the 'special award'

'OLIVER', 1968, the first British musical ever to win the best film award.
(Columbia Pictures Corporation Limited)

Gregory Peck in 'THE OMEN', best original music score, 1976.
(Twentieth-Century Fox Limited)

'A MAN FOR ALL SEASONS', winner of six Oscars, 1966.
(Columbia Pictures Corporation Limited)

'ONE FLEW OVER THE CUCKOO'S NEST', best film, 1975.
(United Artists)

'ROMEO AND JULIET', best costume design and cinematography, 1968.
(Paramount Pictures)

Miss Brodie (Maggie Smith), cycling to school and winning her best actress
Oscar in 'THE PRIME OF MISS JEAN BRODIE', 1969.
(Twentieth-Century Fox Limited)

Sylvester Stallone in triple Oscar winning film, 'ROCKY', 1976.
(United Artists)

From the MGM release 'SHAFT'. © 1971 Metro-Goldwyn-Mayer Inc.

Anna Magnani, best actress, for her performance in Tennessee Williams'
'THE ROSE TATTOO', 1955. (Paramount Pictures)

From the MGM release 'RYAN'S DAUGHTER'. © 1970
Metro-Goldwyn-Mayer Inc.

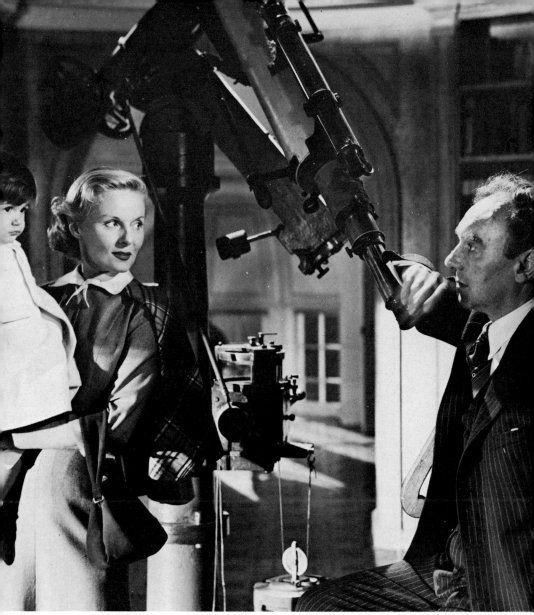

David Lean's 'BREAKING THE SOUND BARRIER', best sound recording, 1952

George Roy Hill, winner of best director award for 'THE STING', 1973.
(Universal Pictures)

George Burns receiving his Oscar for his performance in the MGM release
'THE SUNSHINE BOYS'. © 1975 Metro-Goldwyn-Mayer Inc.

John Wayne in his Oscar winning role as Marshal Rooster Cogburn in 'TRUE GRIT', 1969. (Paramount Pictures)

From the MGM release 'SEVEN BRIDES FOR SEVEN BROTHERS'.
© 1954 Loew's Incorporated
'THE SOUND OF MUSIC', winner of five Oscars, 1965.
(Twentieth-Century Fox Limited)

From the MGM release 'THE V.I.P's'. © 1963 Metro-Goldwyn-Mayer Inc.
and Taylor Productions, Inc.

Joseph Cotten in Carol Reed's 'THE THIRD MAN', 1950. (London Films)

Lee Grant, supporting actress winner in 'SHAMPOO', 1975.
(Columbia Pictures Corporation Limited)

Glenda Jackson, best actress for 'WOMEN IN LOVE', 1970. (United Artists)

From the MGM release '2001: A SPACE ODYSSEY'.
© 1968 Metro-Goldwyn-Mayer Inc.

'WAR AND PEACE', winner of best foreign language film, U.S.S.R., 1968

category. The film concentrates on the tragic relationship between a brutish strong man (Anthony Quinn) and his simple-minded waif-like assistant (Giulietta Masina) as they travel round Italy entertaining in bleak desolate towns. The hit song 'Stars Shine In Your Eyes' was not among the five best song nominees even though it later swept to success all round the world.

A Ponti-De Laurentiis Production, directed by Federico Fellini. With Giulietta Masina, Anthony Quinn, Richard Basehart, Aldo Silvani, Marcella Rovena, Lidia Venturini. 115 mins.

The Stratton Story (1949)

Oscars (1) best motion picture story Douglas Morrow

Biography of baseball pitcher Monty Stratton (James Stewart) who lost his leg in a hunting accident but still managed to make a comeback to the professional game with an artificial limb.

An MGM Picture, directed by Sam Wood. With James Stewart, June Allyson, Frank Morgan, Agnes Moorehead, Bill Williams, Bruce Cowling. 106 mins.

Street Angel (1927/28)

Oscars (1) best actress   Janet Gaynor

Janet Gaynor suffering for the third time in the first Oscar year (see also *Seventh Heaven* and *Sunrise*) as a poor Neapolitan girl who falls in love with an itinerant artist but who is arrested and separated from him on the eve of their marriage. It was said later that actresses had to suffer to win Oscars. Gaynor proved it first time out!

A Fox Film, directed by Frank Borzage. With Janet Gaynor, Charles Farrell, Alberto Rabagliati, Gino Conti, Guido Trento, Henry Armetta. 10 reels.

A Streetcar Named Desire (1951)

Oscars (4) best actress   Vivien Leigh
            best supporting actor   Karl Malden
            best supporting actress   Kim Hunter
            best b/w art direction   Richard Day
                set decoration   George James Hopkins

High voltage Tennesse Williams drama about the sordid fate of faded Southern belle Blanche du Bois (Leigh) who brings her lady-like manners and sad tale of a marriage that went wrong to the sleazy slum apartment of her sister (Hunter) in New Orleans. A feast of method acting with Leigh, Hunter and Karl Malden (as Blanche's middle-aged beau) all winning awards. Only Marlon Brando as Hunter's brutal Polak husband, a brilliant performance in every way, missed out. Bogart in *The African Queen* was the year's best actor winner.

A Warner Bros. Picture, directed by Elia Kazan. With Vivien Leigh, Marlon Brando, Kim Hunter, Karl Malden, Rudy Bond, Nick Dennis. 125 mins.

Strike Up The Band (1940)

Oscars (1) best sound recording   Douglas Shearer

Judy Garland-Mickey Rooney musical about a group of high school youngsters who form their own juvenile band and rise to national fame on Paul Whiteman's nationwide radio show.

An MGM Picture, directed by Busby Berkeley. With Mickey Rooney, Judy Garland, Paul Whiteman, June Preisser, William Tracy, Larry Nunn. 120 mins.

The Subject was Roses (1968)

Oscars (1) best supporting actor   Jack Albertson

Adaptation of Frank Gilroy's prize-winning play about a young army veteran's return to his Bronx home and his increasingly strained relationship with his parents (Patricia Neal and Jack Albertson) who gradually poison him with their own bitterness. Martin Sheen features as the the young boy.

An MGM Picture, directed by Ulu Grosbard. With Patricia Neal, Jack Albertson, Martin Sheen, Don Saxon, Elaine Williams, Grant Gordon. Metrocolor. 107 mins.

Summer of 42 (1971)

Oscars (1) best original dramatic score Michel Legrand

Nostalgic, sentimental account of a young teenager's obsession with an attractive war bride (Jennifer O'Neill) during one lazy, idyllic summer on an island off the New England coast. Legrand's lushest of melancholy themes — one of the most romantic in years — won him the Academy Award for the best score of the year.

A Warner Bros. Picture, directed by Robert Mulligan. With Jennifer O'Neill, Gary Grimes, Jerry Houser, Oliver Conant, Katherine Allentuck. Technicolor. 104 mins.

Sundays and Cybele (1962)

Oscars (1) best foreign language film France

Delicate story of the strange, ultimately tragic friendship that develops between an ex-warplane pilot (Hardy Kruger) suffering from a guilt complex and loss of memory and the small girl in a convent school (Patricia Gozzi) whom he takes out with him on Sundays.

A Terra Film-Fides-Orsay Film/Les Films Trocadero, directed by Serge Bourguignon. With Hardy Kruger, Nicole Courcel, Patricia Gozzi, Daniel Ivernel, Michel de Re, Andre Oumansky. Transcope. 110 mins.

Sunrise (1927/28)

Oscars (3)	best actress	Janet Gaynor
	best cinematography	Charles Rosher & Karl Struss
	best artistic quality of production	Fox Studio

F. W. Murnau's drama of a young farmer, happily married with a wife and young child, who suddenly becomes infatuated by a temptress from the city and is almost enticed to murder. Tremendously stylish film, marvellously acted by Gaynor (as the wife), George O'Brien as the husband and Margaret Livingston as the other woman. The Oscars for Struss and Rosher were the first to be awarded for cinematography; Gaynor's portrayal was the third for which she was named best actress of the year (see also *Street Angel* and *Seventh Heaven*).

A Fox Picture, directed by F. W. Murnau. With George O'Brien, Janet Gaynor, Bodil Rossing, Margaret Livingston, J. Farrell MacDonald, Ralph Sipperly. 10-11 reels.

Sunset Boulevard (1950)

Oscars (3)	best story & screenplay	Charles Brackett, Billy Wilder & D. M. Marshman Jr.
	best art direction	Hans Dreier & John Meehan
	set decoration	Sam Comer & Ray Moyer
	best music score of a drama or comedy	Franz Waxman

Billy Wilder's ruthless story of a down-and-out screen-writer (William Holden) who is persuaded by a faded silent movie queen (Gloria Swanson) to be her gigolo and write the screenplay for her 'comeback' film. Another case of 'if only it had been released another year.' As it was, it clashed with *All About Eve*, a six-Oscar winner, and had to be content with the runner up position on presentations night. It remains however one of the finest movies about Hollywood and one of the best never to win a best picture Oscar.

A Paramount Picture, directed by Billy Wilder. With William Holden, Gloria Swanson, Erich Von Stroheim, Nancy Olson, Fred Clark, Jack Webb. 110 mins.

The Sunshine Boys (1975)

Oscars (1) best supporting actor   George Burns

The trials and tribulations of a harassed young theatrical agent (Richard Benjamin) when he tries to bring together two veteran vaudeville comics (Walter Matthau and George Burns) who haven't spoken to each other personally or professionally for eleven years. George Burns, at 80, remains the oldest acting winner in the Academy's history.

An MGM Picture, directed by Herbert Ross. With Walter Matthau, George Burns, Richard Benjamin, Lee Meredith, Carol Arthur, Rosetta Le Noire. Metrocolor. 111 mins.

Suspicion (1941)

Oscars (1) best actress   Joan Fontaine

Stylish Hitchcock thriller with wealthy young wife Joan Fontaine believing that her irresponsible playboy husband (Cary Grant) is trying to murder her. Very reminiscent of Hitch's British thrillers of the 30's and containing the only performance in a Hitchcock film ever to be awarded an Oscar.

An RKO Picture, directed by Alfred Hitchcock. With Cary Grant, Joan Fontaine, Cedric Hardwicke, Nigel Bruce, Dame May Whitty, Isabel Jeans, Heather Angel. 99 mins.

Sweet Bird of Youth (1962)

Oscars (1) best supporting actor   Ed Begley

Tennessee Williams drama about a tarnished Southern apollo (Paul Newman) who brings a load of trouble with him when he returns to his home town in the company of dissipated, drunken movie queen

Geraldine Page. In a film full of fine performances Ed Begley's corrupt town boss who goes after Newman to 'fix him for ruining his daughter' stands out.

An MGM Picture, directed by Richard Brooks. With Paul Newman, Geraldine Page, Shirley Knight, Ed Begley, Rip Torn, Mildred Dunnock, Madeleine Sherwood. CinemaScope/Metrocolor. 120 mins.

Swing Time (1936)

Oscars (1)   best song   'The Way You Look Tonight'
                                          Jerome Kern, music:
                                          Dorothy Fields, lyrics

Astaire and Rogers sixth film together, containing the usual boy and girl romance, one of Astaire's all-time top dancing routines — 'Bojangles of Harlem' — and the Academy Award winning song 'The Way You Look Tonight.'

An RKO Picture, directed by George Stevens. With Fred Astaire, Ginger Rogers, Victor Moore, Helen Broderick, Eric Blore, Betty Furness. 103 mins.

Tabu (1930/31)

Oscars (1) best cinematography Floyd Crosby

A simple tale of two young Polynesian lovers who defy the ancient tabu of their tribe. Filmed by Murnau and Flaherty in Tahiti and Bora Bora with a locally recruited non-professional cast.

A Paramount Picture, directed by F. W. Murnau and Robert Flaherty. With Reri, Matahi, Hitu, Jean, Jules, Kong Ah. 81 mins.

Telling the World (1927/28)

Oscars (1) best title writing Joseph Farnham

William Haines comedy-drama about an eager young newspaper reporter (Haines) who finds romance with chorus girl Anita Page plus adventure in the remote corners of China. One of three films (see also *The Fair Co-Ed* and *Laugh, Clown, Laugh*) for which Farnham won his title writing Oscar.

An MGM Picture, directed by Sam Wood. With William Haines, Anita Page, Eileen Percy, Frank Currier, Polly Moran, Bert Roach. 8 reels.

The Tempest (1927/28)

Oscars (1) best art direction William Cameron Menzies

John Barrymore as a Russian peasant who, during the Revolution of 1917, becomes an officer in the Russian Army and finds himself controlling the fate of the beautiful princess (Camilla Horn) who had earlier spurned him. Cameron Menzies was also named for his work on *The Dove* in his Oscar award.

A United Artists Picture, directed by Sam Taylor. With John Barrymore, Camilla Horn, Louis Wolheim, Boris De Fas, George Fawcett. 10 reels.

The Ten Commandments (1956)

Oscars (1) best special effects   John Fulton

DeMille's massive biblical epic (his last) about the life of Moses from his birth and abandonment as a baby to the eventual time he led the Israelites out of Egypt. Charlton Heston stars as Moses, Yul Brynner as Rameses II, Anne Baxter as Nefrititi. The parting of the Red Sea sequence earned the film its special effects award.

A Paramount Picture, directed by Cecil B. DeMille. With Charlton Heston, Yul Brynner, Anne Baxter, Edward G. Robinson, Yvonne De Carlo, Debra Paget, John Derek, Cedric Hardwicke, Nina Foch, Martha Scott, Judith Anderson, Vincent Price. Vista Vision. Technicolor. 219 mins.

That Hamilton Woman (1941)

(*Original U.K. title: Lady Hamilton*)

Oscars (1) best sound recording   Jack Whitney

Romanticised version of the life of humble-born blacksmith's daughter, Emma Hart (Vivien Leigh) — her marriage to Sir William Hamilton, Ambassador at the British Embassy in Naples, her notorious love affair with England's naval hero Horatio Nelson (Laurence Olivier) and her poverty-stricken old age as a wrinkled old thief scrounging a living in the quayside cafes of Calais.

A United Artist Picture, directed by Alexander Korda. With Vivien Leigh, Laurence Olivier, Alan Mowbray, Sara Allgood, Gladys Cooper, Henry Wilcoxon. 128 mins.

They Shoot Horses Don't They? (1969)

Oscars (1) best supporting actor   Gig Young

The hopes, fears and disillusionments of some of the entrants in one of Hollywood's dance marathons of the Depression 30's. Gig Young won his Oscar for his oily MC of the gruelling contest having been nominated in the supporting category twice earlier in his career — in Cagney's *Come Fill The Cup* and in Gable's *Teachers Pet*.

A Palomar-Cinerama Picture, directed by Sydney Pollack. With Jane Fonda, Michael Sarrazin, Susannah York, Gig Young, Red Buttons, Bonnie Bedelia, Michael Conrad, Bruce Dern. Panavision/De Luxe Color. 129 mins.

The Thief of Bagdad (1940)

Oscars (3)   best colour cinematography Georges Perinal
            best colour art direction   Vincent Korda
            best special effects   Lawrence Butler, photographic
                                          Jack Whitney, sound

Arabian Nights fantasy with Sabu as the wily native boy who outwits the wicked Grand Vizier of Bagdad. Superior Technicolor special effects including a deadly combat with a giant spider.

A London Films Production, directed by Michael Powell, Ludwig Berger and Tim Whelan. With Conrad Veidt, Sabu, June Duprez, John Justin, Rex Ingram, Miles Malleson. Technicolor. 106 mins.

The Third Man (1950)

Oscars (1) best b/w cinematography   Robert Krasker

Black marketeering in post-war Vienna with Orson Welles in one of his most famous roles as Harry Lime, infamous racketeer in watered-down penicillin. The famous zither score by Anton Karas did not win an Oscar nor even a nomination. Robert Krasker's sombre images of a ruined city in all its moods did — and deservedly so!

A London Films Production, directed by Carol Reed. With Joseph Cotten, Alida Valli, Orson Welles, Trevor Howard, Paul Hoerbiger, Ernst Deutsch, Bernard Lee, Wilfrid Hyde White. 104 mins.

Thirty Seconds Over Tokyo (1944)

Oscars (1) best special effects   A. Arnold Gillespie, Donald
                                         Jahraus & Warren Newcombe
                                         (photographic)
                                         Douglas Shearer (sound)

Semi-documentary account of the first American bomber attack on Japan in World War II. The movie covered the preparations for the raid, the take-off from the aircraft carriers, the raid itself and the return to ship. Spencer Tracy guested as Colonel Doolittle, commander-in-chief of the attack.

An MGM Picture, directed by Mervyn LeRoy. With Spencer Tracy, Van Johnson, Robert Walker, Phyllis Thaxter, Tim Murdock, Scott McKay, Gordon MacDonald, Don DeFore, Robert Mitchum. 138 mins.

This Above All (1942)

Oscars (1) best b/w art direction   Richard Day & Joseph Wright
                    int. decoration   Thomas Little

British wartime deserter Tyrone Power, disillusioned and bitter with the war, regains his courage through the love of gentle W.A.A.F. girl Joan Fontaine. 1940's propaganda movie taken from the novel by Eric Knight.
    A 20th Century-Fox Picture, directed by Anatole Litvak. With Tyrone Power, Joan Fontaine, Thomas Mitchell, Henry Stephenson, Nigel Bruce, Gladys Cooper. 110 mins.

This Is The Army (1943)

Oscars (1) best scoring of a musical   Ray Heindorf

Technicolor film version of the Irving Berlin stage hit which contained 350 World War II soldiers in its chorus, a morale booster in its message for millions of American fighting men and hit numbers like 'Oh, How I Hate To Get Up In The Morning' and 'I Left My Heart At The Stage Door Canteen.'
    A Warner Bros. Picture, directed by Michael Curtiz. With Irving Berlin as himself, George Murphy, Joan Leslie, George Tobias, Alan Hale, Charles Butterworth, Rosemary De Camp, Dolores Costello, Una Merkel. Technicolor. 121 mins.

This Land is Mine (1943)

Oscars (1) best sound recording   Stephen Dunn

Meek French schoolteacher Charles Laughton suddenly emerges as a figure of stature when his country is overrun by the Nazis in World War II. One of the five films made by Renoir in America during the war period.
    An RKO Picture, directed by Jean Renoir. With Charles Laughton, Maureen O'Hara, George Sanders, Walter Slezak, Kent Smith, Una O'Connor. 103 mins.

The Thomas Crown Affair (1968)

Oscars (1) best song   'The Windmills Of Your Mind'
                                 Michel Legrand, music;
                                 Alan & Marilyn Bergman, lyrics

The romantic, intellectual duel between a successful Boston business tycoon (Steve McQueen) who has successfully organised a spectacular bank raid withour revealing his identity and the attractive insurance investigator (Faye Dunaway) sent to look into the case. An already lush and romantic film is made even lusher by the Academy Award winning song 'The Windmills Of Your Mind' sung by Noel Harrison.

A United Artists Picture, directed by Norman Jewison. With Steve McQueen, Faye Dunaway, Paul Burke, Jack Weston, Biff McGuire, Yaphet Kotto. Panavision/De Luxe Color. 102 mins.

Thoroughly Modern Millie (1967)

Oscars (1) best music score　　　　　Elmer Bernstein

Spoof musical of the 20's with Julie Andrews and Mary Tyler Moore as a couple of innocent flapper girls neatly avoiding the clutches of homicidal Chinese white slave trader Beatrice Lillie. Elmer Bernstein's Oscar for his musical work on the film remains his only one to date, something of a surprise when one considers he composed scores of the calibre of *The Magnificent Seven, The Ten Commandments* and *To Kill A Mockingbird*.

A Universal Picture, directed by George Roy Hill. With Julie Andrews, Mary Tyler Moore, Carol Channing, James Fox, John Gavin, Beatrice Lillie. Technicolor. 138 mins.

A Thousand Clowns (1965)

Oscars (1) best supporting actor　　　Martin Balsam

Screen adaptation of Herb Gardner's play about a hack TV gag writer (Jason Robards) who, fed up with writing scripts for the terrible comedian on his show, determines that his young nephew will not finish up the same way and go to work like a thousand clowns. Martin Balsam's Oscar was for his portrayal of Robards' go-getting agent brother.

A United Artists Picture, directed by Fred Coe. With Jason Robards, Barbara Harris, Martin Balsam, Barry Gordon, Gene Saks, William Daniels. 118 mins.

Three Coins in the Fountain (1954)

Oscars (2) best colour cinematography Milton Krasner
　　　　　　best song　　　　　　　　'Three Coins In The Fountain'
　　　　　　　　　　　　　　　　　Jule Styne, music:
　　　　　　　　　　　　　　　　　Sammy Cahn, lyrics

Early CinemaScope production about three American secretaries (McGuire, Peters, McNamara) who journey to Rome primarily to find themselves attractive husbands. Clifton Webb, Louis Jourdan and Rossano Brazzi prove themselves the most likely candidates. Milton Krasner's staggeringly beautiful shots of the Eternal City earned him his only Oscar award.

A 20th Century-Fox Picture, directed by Jean Negulesco. With Clifton Webb, Dorothy McGuire, Jean Peters, Louis Jourdan, Maggie McNamara, Rossano Brazzi. CinemaScope/De Luxe Color. 102 mins.

The Three Faces of Eve (1957)

Oscars (1) best actress   Joanne Woodward

Supposedly true story of a young American housewife who finds she is a schizophrenic with three contrasting personalities. A *tour-de-force* performance by the then unknown Joanne Woodward in the leading role put her in the front rank of leading actresses. Lee J. Cobb featured as the psychiatrist whose patience and probing eventually helped the woman to lead a normal life.

A 20th Century-Fox Picture, directed by Nunnally Johnson. With Joanne Woodward, David Wayne, Lee J. Cobb, Nancy Kulp, Vince Edwards. CinemaScope. 91 mins.

Through a Glass Darkly (1961)

Oscars (1) best foreign language film   Sweden

Ingmar Bergman raises questions about the significance of God and the meaning of life as he traces a few days in the lives of four people — a just-released mental patient, her husband, her dissatisfied novelist-father and her younger brother — when they spend a summer together on a bleak island in the Baltic.

Svensk Filmindustri Production, directed by Ingmar Bergman. With Harriet Andersson, Max Von Sydow, Gunnar Bjornstrand, Lars Pass-gard. 91 mins.

Thunderball (1965)

Oscars (1) best special visual effects John Stears

Fourth Bond adventure with 007 attempting to find who is holding the world to ransom with two hi-jacked nuclear bombs. One-eyed Adolfo Celi is the man behind it all. Long underwater sequences at the film's climax earned it a special effects award.

A United Artists Picture, directed by Terence Young. With Sean Connery, Claudine Auger, Adolfo Celi, Luciana Paluzzi, Rik Van Nutter, Bernard Lee. Panavision/Technicolor. 132 mins.

The Time Machine (1960)

Oscars (1) best special effects   Gene Warren, Tim Barr: visual
                                                    effects

H. G. Wells' novel about a young Victorian (Rod Taylor) who invents a scientific machine that will take him into the distant future — through two world wars and into a time when strange beings inhabit the earth. The fifth George Pal production to win in the special effects category.

An MGM Picture, directed by George Pal. With Rod Taylor, Alan Young, Yvette Mimieux, Sebastian Cabot, Tom Helmore, Whit Bissell. Metroscope/Metrocolor. 103 mins.

Tin Pan Alley (1940)

Oscars (1) best music score   Alfred Newman

Formula Fox musical of the early 40's following the adventures of two songwriters (John Payne, Jack Oakie) and their girl friends (Alice Faye and Betty Grable) in the years immediately preceding and during World War I.

A 20th Century-Fox Picture, directed by Walter Lang. With Alice Faye, Betty Grable, Jack Oakie, John Payne, Allen Jenkins, Esther Ralston. 94 mins.

Titanic (1953)

Oscars (1) best story & screenplay   Charles Brackett, Walter Reisch
                                                    & Richard Breen

Story of the doomed maiden voyage of the 'Titanic' concentrating for most of its length on the private lives and fears of selected passengers — captain Brian Aherne, estranged American couple Clifton Webb and Barbara Stanwyck, young lovers Robert Wagner and Audrey Dalton, wisecracking wealthy widow Thelma Ritter and drunken, unfrocked priest Richard Basehart.

A 20th Century-Fox Picture, directed by Jean Negulesco. With Clifton Webb, Barbara Stanwyck, Robert Wagner, Audrey Dalton, Thelma Ritter, Brian Aherne, Richard Basehart, Allyn Joslyn. 98 mins.

To Catch a Thief (1955)

Oscars (1) best colour cinematography Robert Burks

Hitchcock on the French Riviera with debonair Cary Grant as a former cat burglar forced out of retirement to catch a new thief who is copying his methods. Grace Kelly (her last picture for Hitch) adds cool blonde beauty and slick repartee. Note: cameraman Robert Burks made twelve films for Hitchcock starting with *Strangers On A Train* in 1951 and ending with *Marnie* in 1964. This was the only time he figured among the Oscar winners.

A Paramount Picture, directed by Alfred Hitchcock. With Cary Grant, Grace Kelly, Jessie Royce Landis, John Williams, Charles Vanel, Brigitte Auber. Vista Vision/Technicolor. 97 mins.

To Each His Own (1946)

Oscars (1) best actress   Olivia de Havilland

Movie with a weepie theme used by Hollywood since the silent days — that of an unwed mother (Olivia de Havilland) who gives up her baby for fear of scandal and then watches him growing to manhood, pretending to be his aunt in order to be near him. The first of de Havilland's two Oscars (see *The Heiress*); John Lund featured in a dual role, that of de Havilland's husband and son, both of whom become air aces, the first in World War I, the second in World War II.

A Paramount Picture, directed by Mitchell Leisen. With Olivia de Havilland, John Lund, Mary Anderson, Roland Culver, Phillip Terry, Bill Goodwin. 100 mins.

To Kill a Mockingbird (1962)

Oscars (3) best actor   Gregory Peck
            best screenplay   Horton Foote
            best b/w art direction Alexander Golitzen &
                                    Henry Bumstead
            set decoration   Oliver Emert

Harper Lee's prizewinning tale of two motherless children growing up with their widowed lawyer father (Gregory Peck) amid racial prejudice in a small Southern town during the Depression. One of the most effective of Hollywood's films about race relations and one that finally earned Peck his Academy Award after many years of nominations — *The Keys Of The Kingdom* (45), *The Yearling* (46), *Gentleman's*

Agreement (47) and *Twelve O'Clock High* (49). His defence of a black man, unjustly accused of murder, at the film's climax is a *tour-de-force*.

A Universal Picture, directed by Robert Mulligan. With Gregory Peck, Mary Badham, Philip Alford, John Megna, Frank Overton, Rosemary Murphy, Ruth White, Brock Peters. 129 mins.

Tom Jones (1963)

Oscars (4) best film   Tony Richardson (producer)
            best direction   Tony Richardson
            best screenplay   John Osborne
            best music score   John Addison

Henry Fielding's tale of life in bawdy 18th century England, with Albert Finney as the illegitimate son of a servant girl who is fostered by a kindly country squire and then pursued lasciviously by every beautiful woman he meets on his way to manhood. The first entirely British made best picture winner since *Hamlet* and the only film in the history of the Academy to boast three supporting actress nominees in its cast — Diane Cilento as a wild gamekeeper's daugher, Edith Evans as Miss Western and Joyce Redman as a lady of easy virtue who seduces Tom over a large tavern meal. None of them won, Margaret Rutherford taking the award for her performance in the *V.I.P's*. Finney and Hugh Griffith as Squire Western also won nominations.

A Woodfall Production (released through United Artists), directed by Tony Richardson. With Albert Finney, Susannah York, Hugh Griffith, Edith Evans, Joan Greenwood, Diane Cilento, Joyce Redman. Eastman Color. 128 mins.

Tom Thumb (1958)

Oscars (1) best special effects   Tom Howard

Tiny boy Russ Tamblyn becomes the adopted son of childless woodland couple Bernard Miles and Jessie Matthews but is exploited by villainous robbers Terry-Thomas and Peter Sellers. Minor children's fantasy which earned an Academy Award for its mixture of live and animated special effects.

An MGM Picture, directed by George Pal. With Russ Tamblyn, Alan Young, Terry-Thomas, Peter Sellers, June Thorburn, Jessie Matthews, Bernard Miles. Eastman Color. 92 mins.

Topkapi (1964)

Oscars (1) best supporting actor   Peter Ustinov

Jules (*Rififi*) Dassin puts another gang of thieves through their paces as he sends a raffish group of criminals to Istanbul to steal the emerald-studded dagger from the famous Topkapi museum. Messrs Schell, Mercouri and Morley all participate although it is Peter Ustinov, employed by the gang for his strength rather than his brains, who comes out ahead from the acting point of view.

A United Artists Picture, directed by Jules Dassin. With Melina Mercouri, Peter Ustinov, Maximilian Schell, Robert Morley, Akim Tamiroff. Technicolor. 120 mins.

Tora! Tora! Tora! (1970)

Oscars (1) best special visual effects   A. D. Flowers & L. B. Abbott

The full story of the Japanese attack on Pearl Harbour on December 7, 1941, told from both points of view with the scenes of American intelligence officers code-breaking in Washington being intercut with those of Japanese strategists preparing their offensive. The title, when translated, means 'Tiger, Tiger, Tiger — Attack launched.'

A 20th Century-Fox Picture, directed by Richard Fleischer. With Martin Balsam, Soh Yamamura, Jason Robards, Joseph Cotten, Tatsuya Mihashi, E. G. Marshall, Takahiro Tamura, James Whitmore. Panavision/ De Luxe Color. 144 mins.

A Touch of Class (1973)

Oscars (1) best actress   Glenda Jackson

Mel Frank comedy about a well-heeled married insurance agent (George Segal) who drifts into an innocent affair with a smart rag-trade pirate (Glenda Jackson) then finds himself becoming over-romatically involved. Glenda Jackson's second Oscar (see also *Women In Love*) was for the first out-and-out female comedy performance since Judy Holliday's Billie Dawn in *Born Yesterday* twenty-three years earlier.

An Avco Embassy Picture, directed by Melvin Frank. With George Segal, Glenda Jackson, Paul Sorvino, Hildegard Neil, Cec Linder. Panavision/Technicolor. 106 mins.

The Towering Inferno (1974)

Oscars (3)	best cinematography	Fred Koenekamp & Joseph Biroc
	best editing	Harold F. Kress & Carl Kress
	best song	'We May Never Love Like This Again'
		music & lyrics by Al Kasha & Joel Hirschhorn

Massive disaster movie about the fight to save hundreds of people trapped by fire on the top floor of the world's tallest building — a 138 storey tower block — on the day of its inauguration ceremony in San Francisco. Fire chief Steve McQueen and designer-architect Paul Newman are the super heroes who help many of the trapped guests escape.

A 20th Century-Fox—Warner Bros. Picture, directed by John Guillermin. With Steve McQueen, Paul Newman, William Holden, Faye Dunaway, Fred Astaire, Susan Blakely, Richard Chamberlain, Jennifer Jones, O. J. Simpson, Robert Vaughn, Robert Wagner. Panavision/De Luxe Color. 165 mins.

Transatlantic (1931/32)

| Oscars (1) | best art direction | Gordon Wiles |

Conventional Hollywood melodrama set on board an Atlantic liner and centering on a master-gambler (Edmund Lowe) who comes up against a gang of crooks trying to engineer a robbery on board ship. Lois Moran adds female decoration; Gordon Wiles excellent Oscar-winning art direction that takes in nearly every aspect of the liner from deck to boiler room.

A Fox Picture, directed by William K. Howard. With Edmund Lowe, Lois Moran, John Halliday, Greta Nissen, Jean Hersholt, Myrna Loy, Earle Fox. 74 mins.

Travels With My Aunt (1972)

| Oscars (1) | best costume design | Anthony Powell |

Straight-laced bank manager (Alec McCowen) is swept into the crazy world of his eccentric aunt Augusta (Maggie Smith) who takes him all over Europe and involves him in a shady scheme to smuggle illegal currency into Turkey — a ransom payment for the only real love in her life, Robert Stephens. From the novel by Graham Greene.

An MGM Picture, directed by George Cukor. With Maggie Smith, Alec McCowen, Lou Gossett, Robert Stephens, Cindy Williams, Jose Luis Lopez Vasquez. Panavision/Metrocolor. 109 mins.

The Treasure of the Sierra Madre (1948)

Oscars (3) best direction   John Huston
            best supporting actor Walter Huston
            best screenplay   John Huston

The effects of greed on three penniless prospectors (Bogart, Huston, Holt) when they strike it rich in the bandit infested mountains of the Sierra Madre. Set in Mexico in the 1920's, the film was John Huston's first since the end of World War II and marked the only time in Academy history that father and son both won major Oscars in the same year for the same film.

A Warner Bros. Picture, directed by John Huston. With Humphrey Bogart, Walter Huston, Tim Holt, Bruce Bennet, Barton MacLane, Alfonso Bedoya. 126 mins.

A Tree Grows in Brooklyn (1945)

Oscars (1) best supporting actor   James Dunn

The childhood of a young girl (Peggy Ann Garner) and her relationships with her friends, neighbours and Irish parents as she grows up in a Brooklyn tenement in the 1900's. Dorothy McGuire is the mother constantly struggling to make ends meet, Oscar winner James Dunn the weak, casual worker-steady drunkard father. Director Elia Kazan's first film, adapted from the best-seller by Betty Smith.

A 20th Century-Fox Picture, directed by Elia Kazan. With Dorothy McGuire, Joan Blondell, James Dunn, Lloyd Nolan, Peggy Ann Garner, Ted Donaldson, James Gleason, Ruth Nelson. 128 mins.

True Grit (1969)

Oscars (1) best actor   John Wayne

John Wayne's Oscar performance (he had been nominated once before for the war movie Sands Of Iwo Jima) as the one-eyed, over-the-hill marshall Rooster Cogburn who is hired by a young teenage girl (Kim Darby) to hunt down the killers of her father. From the novel by Charles Portis.

A Paramount Picture, directed by Henry Hathaway. With John Wayne, Glen Campbell, Kim Darby, Jeremy Slate, Robert Duvall, Dennis Hopper, Alfred Ryder, Strother Martin. Technicolor. 128 mins.

Twelve O'Clock High (1949)

Oscars (2) best supporting actor   Dean Jagger
            best sound recording   Thomas T. Moulton

Gregory Peck as a ruthless American c.o. sent from headquarters in
World War II to rebuild a heavy bomber group whose morale has
cracked under heavy losses. Set in England during the early days of day-
light precision bombing over Germany, the film co-starred Gary Merrill,
Millard Mitchell and Dean Jagger as a middle-aged adjutant who
remembers the events in flashback from a deserted airfield after the war.

    A 20th Century-Fox Picture, directed by Henry King. With Gregory
Peck, Hugh Marlowe, Gary Merrill, Millard Mitchell, Dean Jagger,
Robert Arthur, Paul Stewart. 132 mins.

20,000 Leagues Under the Sea (1954)

Oscars (2) best colour art direction   John Meehan
                         set decoration Emile Kuri
            best special effects   Disney Studios

Jules Verne's 19th century science-fiction adventure about the mysterious, society-hating Captain Nemo (James Mason) and his underwater submarine Nautilus which is propelled by 'the dynamic force of
the Universe.' The special effects award was primarily for the brilliantly
filmed underwater fight between the sub and a giant squid.

    A Walt Disney Picture, directed by Richard Fleischer. With Kirk
Douglas, James Mason, Paul Lukas, Peter Lorre, Robert J. Wilke,
Carleton Young, Ted de Corsia. CinemaScope/Technicolor. 126 mins.

Two Arabian Knights (1927/28)

Oscars (1) best comedy direction   Lewis Milestone

William Boyd and Louis Wolheim as two brawling U.S. soldiers who
escape from German captivity in World War I by posing as Arabs and
head for Jaffa where they become rivals for the hand of Arab girl Mary
Astor. Milestone's award for comedy direction for his work on this film
was the only time an Oscar of this kind was presented.

    A United Artists Picture, directed by Lewis Milestone. With William
Boyd, Mary Astor, Louis Wolheim, Michael Vavitch, Ian Keith, DeWitt
Jennings. 9 reels.

2001: A Space Odyssey (1968)

Oscars (1) best special visual effects   Stanley Kubrick

Spectacular movie prediction of the future revolving round the discovery of a centuries old monolith on the moon and the subsequent journey by a group of astronauts to Jupiter in search of extra-terrestrial life. Breathtaking special effects by Kubrick and his team earned the film an Academy Award in that department although for many it deserved to win many of the major awards as well. For the record the film was nominated in the following categories: – best direction, art direction, story and screenplay and special effects.

An MGM Picture, directed by Stanley Kubrick. With Keir Dullea, Gary Lockwood, William Sylvester, Daniel Richter, Douglas Rain, Leonard Rossiter. Cinerama/Metrocolor. 141 mins.

Two Women (1961)

Oscars (1) best actress   Sophia Loren

Sophia Loren as a young widowed mother who, with her 13-year-old daughter, is raped by a howling mob of Moroccan troops during the dark days of battle in Italy in 1943. Harrowing drama, taken from the novel by Alberto Moravia.

A Gala Films-Champion (Rome)/Les Films Marceau-Cocinor/S.G.C. (Paris) co-production, directed by Vittoria De Sica. With Sophia Loren, Eleanora Brown, Raf Vallone, Jean-Paul Belmondo, Renato Salvatori. CinemaScope. 110 mins.

Underworld (1927/28)

Oscars (1) best original story   Ben Hecht

Revenge story starring George Bancroft as a big time underworld hoodlum, Evelyn Brent as his moll 'Feathers' and Clive Brook as an alcoholic lawyer. One of the very first major gangster films; Ben Hecht's original story Oscar was the first of its kind awarded by the Academy.

A Paramount Picture, directed by Josef von Sternberg. With George Bancroft, Clive Brook, Evelyn Brent, Larry Semon, Fred Kohler, Helen Lynch. 8 reels.

Vacation from Marriage (1946)

(Original U.K. title: Perfect Strangers)

Oscars (1) best original story   Clemence Dane

Mild young English couple, Robert Donat and Deborah Kerr, jolted out of their rut by the war — he joins the navy, she becomes a Wren — find they are each rejuvenated by wartime romance and then have to adjust once more to marriage at the war's close.

A London Films-MGM Picture, directed by Alexander Korda. With Robert Donat, Deborah Kerr, Glynis Johns, Ann Todd, Roland Culver. 102 mins.

The V.I.P.'s (1963)

Oscars (1) best supporting actress   Margaret Rutherford

'Grand Hotel' at London Airport with a set of high class passengers stranded for hours at the terminal because their flight has been delayed by fog. Elizabeth Taylor, Richard Burton, Louis Jourdan, Orson Welles, head the big guns but they're spiked by Oscar winner Margaret Rutherford as an eccentric duchess on her first flight. From an original script by Terence Rattigan.

An MGM Picture, directed by Anthony Asquith. With Elizabeth Taylor, Richard Burton, Louis Jourdan, Elsa Martinelli, Margaret Rutherford, Maggie Smith, Rod Taylor, Linda Christian, Orson Welles. Panavision/Metrocolor. 119 mins.

The Virgin Spring (1960)

Oscars (1) best foreign language film   Sweden

Ingmar Bergman in the fourteenth century, retelling a dramatic fable

174

about a young virgin who is raped and murdered by three herdsmen whilst on a holy errand, avenged by her grief stricken father and then miraculously commemorated by a magical spring which suddenly flows from the spot where she met her death.

Svensk Filmindustri, directed by Ingmar Bergman. With Max Von Sydow, Birgitta Valberg, Gunnel Lindblom, Birgitta Pettersson, Axel Duberg, Tor Isedal. 88 mins.

Viva Villa (1934)

Oscars (1) best assistant direction   John Waters

Part fact, part fiction adventure of the revolutionary bandit Pancho Villa (Wallace Beery) who led the fight for Madero's Mexican republic. Begun by Howard Hawks the film was completed by and credited to Jack Conway.

An MGM Picture, directed by Jack Conway. With Wallace Beery, Fay Wray, Leo Carrillo, Donald Cook, Stuart Erwin, George E. Stone, Joseph Schildkraut, Henry B. Walthall. 115 mins.

Viva Zapata (1952)

Oscars (1) best supporting actor   Anthony Quinn

Biography of another Mexican revolutionary, Emiliano Zapata (Marlon Brando) who fought for Madero at the same time as Villa and rose to almost legendary stature before being assassinated by soldiers of the Mexican Army. Steinbeck wrote the original screenplay; Oscar winner Anthony Quinn played Zapata's brother Eufemio.

A 20th Century-Fox Picture, directed by Elia Kazan. With Marlon Brando, Jean Peters, Anthony Quinn, Joseph Wiseman, Arnold Moss, Alan Reed, Margo, Lou Gilbert, Harold Gordon, Mildred Dunnock. 113 mins.

Waikiki Wedding (1937)

Oscars (1) best song   'Sweet Leilani'
                                         Harry Owens, music & lyrics

Early Crosby comedy musical with Bing as a press agent promoting
Shirley Ross as a pineapple queen in Hawaii. Among Bing's songs:
'Blue Hawaii' and the Academy Award winning 'Sweet Leilani'.

A Paramount Picture, directed by Frank Tuttle. With Bing Crosby,
Bob Burns, Martha Raye, Shirley Ross, George Barbier, Leif Erikson.
89 mins.

War and Peace (1968)

Oscars (1) best foreign language film   U.S.S.R.

Russia's mammoth six hour-plus version of Tolstoy's classic novel,
spanning the years 1805-1812 and following the fortunes of several
aristocratic families during the tremendous upheaval in the war with
France and Napoleon's attack and retreat from Moscow. Ludmila
Savelyeva is the young adolescent Natasha who grows to tragic womanhood, Vyacheslav Tikhonov features as Prince Andrei and Sergie
Bondarchuk, who also directed, is the clumsy idealist Pierre.

MosFilm (Russia), directed by Sergie Bondarchuk. With Ludmila
Savelyeva, Sergei Bondarchuk, Vyacheslav Tikhonov, Anastasia Vertin-
skaya, Vasily Lanovoi, Viktor Stanitsin. Sovcolor/70mm. 373 mins.

The War of the Worlds (1953)

Oscars (1) best special effects   Paramount Studios

Producer George Pal transfers H. G. Wells' novel of a deadly Martian
invasion from England to the USA, updating the story to the post-war
era and even using nuclear weapons against the invaders — without

success. Brilliant special effects of the alien spacecraft, their war machines and, in one brief sequence, the Martians themselves.

A Paramount Picture, directed by Byron Haskin. With Gene Barry, Ann Robinson, Les Tremayne, Bob Cornthwaite, Sandra Giglio, Lewis Martin. Technicolor. 85 mins.

Watch on the Rhine (1943)

Oscars (1) best actor   Paul Lukas

Version of Lillian Hellman's World War II play about an important member of the anti-Nazi underground movement (Paul Lukas) who escapes with his wife (Bette Davis) to Washington only to find himself being blackmailed and harried by Nazi agents in the States. Lukas' Oscar remains one of the most forgotten in the history of the awards.

A Warner Bros. Picture, directed by Herman Schumlin. With Bette Davis, Paul Lukas, Geraldine Fitzgerald, Lucile Watson, Beulah Bondi, George Coulouris, Donald Woods, Henry Daniell. 114 mins.

The Way of All Flesh (1927/28)

Oscars (1) best actor   Emil Jannings

The demoralisation and complete downfall of an elderly German-American bank cashier (Emil Jannings) who sinks to vagrancy after being accosted on a train journey by a femme fatale and relieved of the bank bonds he is carrying for his employers. Jannings' first U.S. feature and one of the two films (see also *The Last Command*) for which he won his Oscar.

A Paramount Picture, directed by Victor Fleming. With Emil Jannings, Belle Bennett, Phyllis Haver, Donald Keith, Fred Kohler, Philippe De Lacey. 9 reels.

The Way We Were (1973)

Oscars (2) best original dramatic   Marvin Hamlisch
            score
            best song   'The Way We Were'
                                       Marvin Hamlisch, music:
                                       Alan & Marilyn Bergman, lyrics

The story of a tempestuous, doomed love affair between two irreconcilable opposites — she (Barbra Streisand), an outspoken aggressive Jewish activist who retains her ideals throughout her life, he (Robert

Redford) the all-American golden haired college boy who after becoming a successful novelist switches to Hollywood to become a screenwriter. Expertly made weepie covering the period from the late 30's to the early 50's and containing in its melancholy score just the right ingredients to accompany the tear soaked events.

A Columbia Picture, directed by Sydney Pollack. With Barbra Streisand, Robert Redford, Bradford Dillman, Lois Chiles, Patrick O'Neal, Viveca Lindfors, Murray Hamilton. Panavision/Eastman Color. 118 mins.

The Westerner (1940)

Oscars (1) best supporting actor   Walter Brennan

Goldwyn-Wyler western about the battle between the cattlemen – the original settlers on the land – and the homesteaders in Texas in the rip-roaring days of the 1880's. Brennan's performance as the real-life character Judge Roy Bean, leader of the cattlemen and 'the sole law west of the Pecos', earned him his third supporting Oscar in five years, a record that still stands to this day.

A Sam Goldwyn Production (released through United Artists), directed by William Wyler. With Gary Cooper, Walter Brennan, Doris Davenport, Fred Stone, Paul Hurst, Chill Wills, Charles Halton, Forrest Tucker. 99 mins.

West Side Story (1961)

Oscars (10)		
best film	Robert Wise (producer)	
best direction	Robert Wise & Jerome Robbins	
best supporting actor	George Chakiris	
best supporting actress	Rita Moreno	
best colour cinematography	Daniel L. Fapp	
best colour art direction	Boris Leven	
set decoration	Victor A. Gangelin	
best colour costume design	Irene Sharaff	
best sound	Fred Hynes & Gordon E. Sawyer	
best editing	Thomas Stanford	
best scoring of a musical	Saul Chaplin, Johnny Green, Sid Ramin & Irwin Kostal	

A musical updating of Shakespeare's *Romeo And Juliet* to the slums of New York with Richard Beymer and Natalie Wood trying to find peace and love despite the gang wars – between the immigrant Puerto Ricans (The Sharks) and the native New Yorkers (The Jets) – going on around them. Chakiris and Moreno as a pair of young Puerto Rican lovers proved to be the only winners in the acting categories but the film itself emerged as the biggest musical best picture winner of all time and with ten awards stands second only to the Oscar record-holder *Ben-Hur*. Wise and Robbins shared the director's award (the first time in Oscar history) and Robbins was also voted a special award for his outstanding choreography.

A United Artists Picture, directed by Robert Wise and Jerome Robbins. With Natalie Wood, Richard Beymer, Russ Tamblyn, Rita Moreno, George Chakiris. Panavision 70/Technicolor. 155 mins.

Whatever Happened to Baby Jane? (1962)

Oscars (1) best b/w costume design   Norma Koch

Grand Guignol from Robert Aldrich with Bette Davis as a drunken, demented ex-child star getting her kicks by slowly torturing her crippled sister Joan Crawford in the decaying Hollywood mansion in which they live. The first time that the two former Warner stars appeared together with only Davis receiving an Academy nomination.

A Warner Bros Picture, directed by Robert Aldrich. With Joan Crawford, Bette Davis, Victor Buono, Marjorie Bennett, Maidie Norman, Anna Lee, Barbara Merrill 132 mins.

When Tomorrow Comes (1939)

Oscars (1) best sound recording   Bernard B. Brown

Lush tearjerker with world-famous concert pianist Charles Boyer falling in love with beautiful waitress Irene Dunne. The snag? The usual one in Hollywood films of its type and period. He's married!

A Universal Picture, directed by John M. Stahl. With Charles Boyer, Irene Dunne, Barbara O'Neil, Onslow Stevens, Mydia Westman, Fritz Feld. 90 mins.

When Worlds Collide (1951)

Oscars (1) best special effects   Paramount Studios

Another of George Pal's science-fiction fantasies of the early 50's with the planet earth about to be destroyed by a giant star hurtling towards it. Richard Derr and Barbara Rush lead the group of people racing against time to build a rocketship that will take them to a new planet and a new life. The Technicolored special effects, as always in Pal's films, were far superior to those in other science fiction films of the period.

A Paramount Picture, directed by Rudoph Mate. With Richard Derr, Barbara Rush, Peter Hanson, Judith Ames, John Hoyt. Technicolor. 81 mins.

White Shadows in the South Seas (1928/29)

Oscars (1) best cinematography   Clyde De Vinna

The first MGM sound film — synchronized sound effects and music were added after the film's completion — about a drunken doctor (Monte Blue) who tries to defend a tribe of South Seas natives from the machinations of unscrupulous trader Robert Anderson. Raquel Torres co-stars as a native girl. Photographed entirely on location in the Marquesas Islands.

An MGM Picture, directed by W. S. Van Dyke. With Monte Blue, Raquel Torres, Robert Anderson. 9 reels.

Who's Afraid of Virginia Woolf? (1966)

Oscars (5) best actress   Elizabeth Taylor
            best supporting actress   Sandy Dennis
            best b/w cinematography Haskell Wexler
            best b/w art direction   Richard Sylbert
                    set decoration   George James Hopkins
            best b/w costume design Irene Sharaff

The desperate infighting between a University Professor (Richard Burton) and his blowsy, shrewish wife (Elizabeth Taylor) and the innocent young faculty couple (George Segal, Sandy Dennis) they invite to join them for one of their vicious no-holds-barred evenings of marital fun and games. All four of the principal performers earned Oscar nominations although it was only the women who eventually came out the winners on awards night. Based on the play by Edward Albee.

A Warner Bros. Picture, directed by Mike Nichols. With Elizabeth Taylor, Richard Burton, George Segal, Sandy Dennis. 131 mins.

Wilson (1944)

Oscars (5) best original screenplay   Lamar Trotti
            best colour cinematography Leon Shamroy
            best colour art direction   Wiard Ihnen
                    int. decoration   Thomas Little
            best sound recording   E. H. Hansen
            best film editing   Barbara McLean

The prestige production of 1944 — a painstaking biography of America's 28th President Woodrow Wilson covering his period as a schoolteacher at Princeton and Governor of New Jersey, his election to the Presidency, his post-war fight for the League of Nations and his final illness and defeat. For all its production values and important themes it lost out to a much lighter vehicle, Crosby's *Going My Way*, as best picture of the year.

A 20th Century-Fox Picture, directed by Henry King. With Alexander Knox, Charles Coburn, Geraldine Fitzgerald, Thomas Mitchell, Cedric Hardwicke, Ruth Nelson, Vincent Price. Technicolor. 154 mins.

Wings (1927/28)

Oscars (2) best film   Lucien Hubbard (producer)
           best engineering effects   Roy Pomeroy

The first best picture winner, a routine World War I aviation story of two American pilots (Charles 'Buddy' Rogers and Richard Arlen) who find themselves rivals for the affections of small town girl Clara Bow. Turned into something special, however, by William Wellman's expertly staged action sequences — both in the air and on the ground. As well as being the first Oscar winner the picture was also the only non-speaking film to win the award, its only sound being synchronized music and sound effects. The following year's winner, *The Broadway Melody*, was a talkie. Other best picture nominees in that historic first year — *The Last Command, The Racket, The Way Of All Flesh* (all Paramount) and *Seventh Heaven* (Fox).

A Paramount Picture, directed by William A. Wellman. With Clara Bow, Charles 'Buddy' Rogers, Richard Arlen, Jobyna Ralston, Gary Cooper, Arlette Marchal. 13 reels.

With a Song in My Heart (1952)

Oscars (1) best scoring of a musical   Alfred Newman

The dramatic life of singer Jane Froman (Susan Hayward) who fought her way back to stardom after being badly crippled in a 'plane crash. Susan Hayward's third best actress nomination.

A 20th Century-Fox Picture, directed by Walter Lang. With Susan Hayward, Rory Calhoun, David Wayne, Thelma Ritter, Robert Wagner, Helen Westcott, Una Merkel. Technicolor. 117 mins.

With Byrd at the South Pole (1929/30)

Oscars (1) best cinematography   Willard Van Der Veer &
                                        Joseph T. Rucker

Documentary account of an incident packed expedition by Rear Admiral Richard E. Byrd and his men to the South Pole. Blizzards, storms at sea, battles with Antarctic icepacks, all handsomely photographed by the two Oscar winning cameramen.

   A Paramount Picture, synchronized narration by Floyd Gibbons. 8 reels.

The Wizard of Oz (1939)

Oscars (2) best original score   Herbert Stothart
            best song   'Over The Rainbow'
                                        Harold Arlen, music:
                                        E. Y. Harburg, lyrics

The Disney films apart, the most famous children's classic of the screen — a part Technicolor, part monochrome recreation of Frank Baum's magical land of Oz with Judy Garland as the lost little Kansas girl making her way to the Emerald City in the company of scarecrow Ray Bolger, tin man Jack Haley and cowardly lion Bert Lahr.

   An MGM Picture, directed by Victor Fleming. With Judy Garland, Frank Morgan, Ray Bolger, Bert Lahr, Jack Haley, Billie Burke, Margaret Hamilton, Charley Grapewin. Technicolor. 101 mins.

Woman of the Year (1942)

Oscars (1) best original screenplay   Ring Lardner Jr. &
                                        Michael Kanin

The first teaming of Tracy and Hepburn, he a down-to-earth baseball correspondent, she a world-famous international affairs journalist. Their resulting marriage produced a script on the husband versus career wife theme that has rarely, if ever, been bettered.

   An MGM Picture, directed by George Stevens. With Spencer Tracy, Katharine Hepburn, Fay Bainter, Reginald Owen, Minor Watson, William Bendix. 112 mins.

Women in Love (1970)

Oscars (1) best actress   Glenda Jackson

D. H. Lawrence's powerful novel of two less than peaceful love affairs in a small midlands colliery town in the early twenties. Glenda Jackson and Jennie Linden star as the two emancipated Brangwen sisters, Oliver Reed as Gerald Crich, the vigorous son of a local mine-owner and Alan Bates as the less exuberant but equally passionate school inspector Rupert Birkin.

A United Artists Picture, directed by Ken Russell. With Alan Bates, Oliver Reed, Glenda Jackson, Jennie Linden, Eleanor Bron, Michael Gough. De Luxe Color. 130 mins.

The Wonderful World of the Brothers Grimm (1962)

Oscars (1) best colour costume design Mary Wills

A combination of historical fact and fantasy, retelling the lives of the famous children's writers as well as some of the stories that made them famous. The second Cinerama movie to tell a story; George Pal directed the fantasy sequences, Henry Levin the main story line.

An MGM Picture, directed by Henry Levin. With Laurence Harvey, Karl Boehm, Claire Bloom, Walter Slezak, Barbara Eden, Oscar Homolka. Cinerama/Technicolor. 135 mins.

Wonder Man (1945)

Oscars (1) best special effects   John Fulton, photographic:
                                          Arthur W. Johns, sound

Danny Kaye's second movie, a special effects bonanza with Kaye as a quiet, bespectacled bookworm taking the place of his night club entertainer twin brother when the latter is bumped off by gangsters. The trick photography occurs when the bookworm is constantly bothered by his brother's frolicsome ghost.

A Sam Goldwyn Production (released through RKO), directed by Bruce Humberstone. With Danny Kaye, Virginia Mayo, Vera-Ellen, Allen Jenkins, Edward S. Brophy, S. Z. Sakall, Steve Cochran. Technicolor. 98 mins.

Written on the Wind (1956)

Oscars (1) best supporting actress   Dorothy Malone

Texas melodrama which gave Dorothy Malone her chance to win an Oscar as the nymphomaniac sister of multi-millionaire Robert Stack, a woman who almost manages to destroy both her brother and the man she sets out to get — Rock Hudson. Lauren Bacall as Stack's wife makes up the melodramatic quartet.

   A Universal International Picture, directed by Douglas Sirk. With Rock Hudson, Lauren Bacall, Robert Stack, Dorothy Malone, Robert Keith, Grant Williams, Robert J. Wilke. Technicolor. 99 mins.

Wuthering Heights (1939)

Oscars (1) best b/w cinematography   Gregg Toland

Goldwyn's favourite among all his pictures, an atmospheric production of Emily Bronte's brooding love story of the Yorkshire moors with Laurence Olivier as the wild Heathcliff and Merle Oberon as his tragic love, Cathy. Gregg Toland, for many people the finest cameraman Hollywood has ever produced, won his only Academy Award for this film although he was also nominated for *Les Miserables* (35), *Dead End* (37), *The Long Voyage Home* (40) and *Citizen Kane* (41) before his untimely death in 1948, aged 44.

   A Sam Goldwyn Production (released through United Artists), directed by William Wyler. With Merle Oberon, Laurence Olivier, David Niven, Donald Crisp, Flora Robson, Hugh Williams, Geraldine Fitzgerald, Cecil Kellaway, Leo G. Carroll. 103 mins.

Yankee Doodle Dandy (1942)

Oscars (3) best actor   James Cagney
           best sound recording   Nathan Levinson
           best scoring of a musical Ray Heindorf & Heinz Roemheld

James Cagney, sheer dynamite as the immortal George M. Cohan, one of the most popular American composer-entertainers of the early 1900's. Walter Huston features as Cohan Sr.; songs include 'Yankee Doodle Boy', 'Give My Regards To Broadway' and 'Over There.'
    A Warner Bros. Picture, directed by Michael Curtiz. With James Cagney, Joan Leslie, Walter Huston, Richard Whorf, George Tobias, Irene Manning, Rosemary De Camp, S. Z. Sakall. 126 mins.

The Yearling (1946)

Oscars (2) best colour cinematography Charles Rosher, Leonard Smith
                                       & Arthur Arling
           best colour art direction Cedric Gibbons & Paul Groesse
               int. decoration   Edwin B. Willis

Marjorie Kinnan Rawlings' story of a young boy's love for his pet fawn, an animal which has to be destroyed because it is gradually eating the crops on which his farmer parents depend for their living. Set in the Florida backwoods and handsomely photographed by three of Hollywood's top cameramen.
    An MGM Picture, directed by Clarence Brown. With Gregory Peck, Jane Wyman, Claude Jarman Jr., Chill Wills, Clem Bevans. Technicolor. 134 mins.

Yesterday, Today and Tomorrow (1964)

Oscars (1) best foreign language film   Italy

One of the lightest vehicles ever to win the best foreign film award, an

Italian comedy made up of three different stories all featuring Sophia
Loren. In the first she appears as a permanently pregnant slum black
marketer; in the second as the elegant wife of a rich Milan industrialist;
in the third as a call girl having an affair with Bologna playboy Marcello
Mastroianni.

A Champion/Concordia Production (Italy), directed by Vittorio De
Sica. With Sophia Loren, Marcello Mastroianni, Aldo Giuffre, Armando
Trovajoli, Giovanni Ridolfi. Techniscope/Technicolor. 119 mins.

You Can't Take it With You (1938)

Oscars (2) best film   Frank Capra (producer)
            best direction   Frank Capra

Frank Capra's third Oscar of the thirties, an adaptation of the Pulitzer
Prize winning Moss Hart-George Kaufman play about the zany
Vanderhof family who believe in doing just what they like and to hell
with the consequences. Leader of the clan is father Lionel Barrymore
who decided one day that he had earned enough money and would
spend the next thirty years having fun. Up against him — Wall Street
business tycoon Edward Arnold who needs to demolish the Vanderhof
home as part of his plans to expand his business plant.

A Columbia Picture, directed by Frank Capra. With Jean Arthur,
Lionel Barrymore, James Stewart, Edward Arnold, Mischa Auer, Ann
Miller, Spring Byington, Samuel S. Hinds, Donald Meek, H. B. Warner.
127 mins.

You Light Up My Life (1977)

Oscars (1) best song   'You Light Up My Life.' (Joseph
                                 Brooks, music and lyrics)

Character study of a former child star (DiDi Conn) who tries to leave
her past behind her and become a top recording artist in the pop music
business. A selfish, second-rate comedian father, a dull fiancée and
a faithless sponsor all leave her a sadder, single and wiser person.

A Columbia Picture, directed by Joseph Brooks. With DiDi Conn,
Joe Silver, Michael Zaslow, Stephen Nathan, Melanie Mayron, Jerry
Keller, Lisa Reeves. Technicolor. 91 mins.

Z (1969)

Oscars (2) best foreign language film   Algeria
            best editing   Francoise Bonnot

Chilling political thriller, set in an unidentified Mediterranean country, about a young district magistrate who, when investigating the death of an influential pacifist leader, finds it has been engineered by official-dom and the country's military authorities. Based on the true life incident of the 1963 assassination of a left wing Greek deputy.

Reggane Film (Paris)-O.N.C.I.C. (Algiers), directed by Costa-Gavras. With Yves Montand, Jean-Louis Trintignant, Jacques Perrin, Francois Perier, Irene Papas, Georges Geret, Charles Denner. Eastman Color. 127 mins.

Zorba the Greek (1964)

Oscars (3) best supporting actress   Lila Kedrova
            best b/w cinematography   Walter Lassally
            best b/w art direction   Vassilis Photopoulos

Anthony Quinn in perhaps his most famous role as a big-hearted, grizzled old Greek who befriends a quiet young Englishman (Alan Bates) when he attempts to reopen the Cretan mine left him by his father. Quinn, however, had to be content with just a nomination, the acting award in the film being stolen from under his nose by Lila Kedrova as a pathetic ageing whore living out her last days with only her memories for company.

An International Classics Picture (released by 20th Century-Fox), directed by Michael Cacoyannis. With Anthony Quinn, Alan Bates, Irene Papas, Lila Kedrova, George Foundas. 142 mins.

Appendix One

A year order list of the major Oscars presented by the Academy of Motion Picture Arts and Sciences in Hollywood, from 1927 to the present day.

1927/28
Production   Wings (Paramount)
Actor   Emil Jannings in *The Way Of All Flesh* and *The Last Command*.
Actress   Janet Gaynor in *Seventh Heaven, Street Angel* and *Sunrise*
Direction   Frank Borzage for *Seventh Heaven*
Note: Lewis Milestone was voted best comedy direction for *Two Arabian Knights,* an award not given after this first year.

1928/29
Production   The Broadway Melody (MGM)
Actor   Warner Baxter in *In Old Arizona*
Actress   Mary Pickford in *Coquette*
Direction   Frank Lloyd for *The Divine Lady*

1929/30
Production   All Quiet on The Western Front (Universal)
Actor   George Arliss in *Disraeli*
Actress   Norma Shearer in *The Divorcee*
Direction   Lewis Milestone for *All Quiet On The Western Front*

1930/31
Production   Cimarron (RKO)
Actor   Lionel Barrymore in *A Free Soul*
Actress   Marie Dressler in *Min And Bill*
Direction   Norman Taurog for *Skippy*

1931/32
Production   Grand Hotel (MGM)
Actor   Fredric March in *Dr. Jekyll And Mr. Hyde* and
    Wallace Beery in *The Champ*
Actress   Helen Hayes in *The Sin Of Madelon Claudet*
Direction   Frank Borzage for *Bad Girl*

1932/33
Production   Cavalcade (Fox)
Actor   Charles Laughton in *The Private Life Of Henry VIII*
Actress   Katharine Hepburn in *Morning Glory*
Direction   Frank Lloyd for *Cavalcade*

1934
Production   It Happened One Night (Columbia)
Actor   Clark Gable in *It Happened One Night*
Actress   Claudette Colbert in *It Happened One Night*
Direction   Frank Capra for *It Happened One Night*

1935
Production   Mutiny On The Bounty (MGM)
Actor   Victor McLaglen in *The Informer*
Actress   Bette Davis in *Dangerous*
Direction   John Ford for *The Informer*

1936
Production   The Great Ziegfeld (MGM)
Actor   Paul Muni in *The Story Of Louis Pasteur*
Actress   Luise Rainer in *The Great Ziegfeld*
Supp. Actor   Walter Brennan in *Come And Get It*
Supp. Actress   Gale Sondergaard in *Anthony Adverse*
Direction   Frank Capra for *Mr. Deeds Goes To Town*

1937
Production   The Life Of Emile Zola (Warner Bros.)
Actor   Spencer Tracy in *Captains Courageous*
Actress   Luise Rainer in *The Good Earth*
Supp. Actor   Joseph Schildkraut in *The Life Of Emile Zola*
Supp. Actress   Alice Brady in *In Old Chicago*
Direction   Leo McCarey for *The Awful Truth*

1938
Production   You Can't Take It With You (Columbia)
Actor   Spencer Tracy in *Boys Town*

Actress	Bette Davis in *Jezebel*
Supp. Actor	Walter Brennan in *Kentucky*
Supp. Actress	Fay Bainter in *Jezebel*
Direction	Frank Capra for *You Can't Take It With You*

1939

Production	Gone With The Wind (Selznick-MGM)
Actor	Robert Donat in *Goodbye Mr. Chips*
Actress	Vivien Leigh in *Gone With The Wind*
Supp. Actor	Thomas Mitchell in *Stagecoach*
Supp. Actress	Hattie McDaniel in *Gone With The Wind*
Direction	Victor Fleming for *Gone With The Wind*

1940

Production	Rebecca (Selznick-United Artists)
Actor	James Stewart in *The Philadelphia Story*
Actress	Ginger Rogers in *Kitty Foyle*
Supp. Actor	Walter Brennan in *The Westerner*
Supp. Actress	Jane Darwell in *The Grapes Of Wrath*
Direction	John Ford for *The Grapes Of Wrath*

1941

Production	How Green Was My Valley (20th Century-Fox)
Actor	Gary Cooper in *Sergeant York*
Actress	Joan Fontaine in *Suspicion*
Supp. Actor	Donald Crisp in *How Green Was My Valley*
Supp. Actress	Mary Astor in *The Great Lie*
Direction	John Ford for *How Green Was My Valley*

1942

Production	Mrs. Miniver (MGM)
Actor	James Cagney in *Yankee Doodle Dandy*
Actress	Greer Garson in *Mrs. Miniver*
Supp. Actor	Van Heflin in *Johnny Eager*
Supp. Actress	Teresa Wright in *Mrs. Miniver*
Direction	William Wyler for *Mrs. Miniver*

1943

Production	Casablanca (Warner Bros.)
Actor	Paul Lukas in *Watch On The Rhine*
Actress	Jennifer Jones in *The Song Of Bernadette*
Supp. Actor	Charles Coburn in *The More The Merrier*
Supp. Actress	Katina Paxinou in *For Whom The Bell Tolls*
Direction	Michael Curtiz for *Casablanca*

1944

Production	Going My Way (Paramount)
Actor	Bing Crosby in *Going My Way*
Actress	Ingrid Bergman in *Gaslight*
Supp. Actor	Barry Fitzgerald in *Going My Way*
Supp. Actress	Ethel Barrymore in *None But The Lonely Heart*
Direction	Leo McCarey for *Going My Way*

1945

Production	The Lost Weekend (Paramount)
Actor	Ray Milland in *The Lost Weekend*
Actress	Joan Crawford in *Mildred Pierce*
Supp. Actor	James Dunn in *A Tree Grows In Brooklyn*
Supp. Actress	Anne Revere in *National Velvet*
Direction	Billy Wilder for *The Lost Weekend*

1946

Production	The Best Years Of Our Lives (Goldwyn-RKO)
Actor	Fredric March in *The Best Years Of Our Lives*
Actress	Olivia de Havilland in *To Each His Own*
Supp. Actor	Harold Russell in *The Best Years Of Our Lives*
Supp. Actress	Anne Baxter in *The Razor's Edge*
Direction	William Wyler for *The Best Years Of Our Lives*

1947

Production	Gentleman's Agreement (20th Century-Fox)
Actor	Ronald Colman in *A Double Life*
Actress	Loretta Young in *The Farmer's Daughter*
Supp. Actor	Edmund Gwenn in *Miracle On 34th Street*
Supp. Actress	Celeste Holm in *Gentleman's Agreement*
Direction	Elia Kazan for *Gentleman's Agreement*

1948

Production	Hamlet (Two-Cities)
Actor	Laurence Olivier in *Hamlet*
Actress	Jane Wyman in *Johnny Belinda*
Supp. Actor	Walter Huston in *Treasure Of The Sierra Madre*
Supp. Actress	Claire Trevor in *Key Largo*
Direction	John Huston for *Treasure Of The Sierra Madre*

1949

Production	All The King's Men (Columbia)
Actor	Broderick Crawford in *All The King's Men*
Actress	Olivia de Havilland in *The Heiress*

Supp. Actor	Dean Jagger in *Twelve O'Clock High*
Supp. Actress	Mercedes McCambridge in *All The King's Men*
Direction	Joseph L. Mankiewicz for *A Letter To Three Wives*

1950

Production	All About Eve (20th Century-Fox)
Actor	Jose Ferrer in *Cyrano de Bergerac*
Actress	Judy Holliday in *Born Yesterday*
Supp. Actor	George Sanders in *All About Eve*
Supp. Actress	Josephine Hull in *Harvey*
Direction	Joseph L. Mankiewicz for *All About Eve*

1951

Production	An American in Paris (MGM)
Actor	Humphrey Bogart in *The African Queen*
Actress	Vivien Leigh in *A Streetcar Named Desire*
Supp. Actor	Karl Malden in *A Streetcar Named Desire*
Supp. Actress	Kim Hunter in *A Streetcar Named Desire*
Direction	George Stevens for *A Place In The Sun*

1952

Production	The Greatest Show On Earth (Paramount)
Actor	Gary Cooper in *High Noon*
Actress	Shirley Booth in *Come Back, Little Sheba*
Supp. Actor	Anthony Quinn in *Viva Zapata*
Supp. Actress	Gloria Grahame in *The Bad And The Beautiful*
Direction	John Ford for *The Quiet Man*

1953

Production	From Here To Eternity (Columbia)
Actor	William Holden in *Stalag 17*
Actress	Audrey Hepburn in *Roman Holiday*
Supp. Actor	Frank Sinatra in *From Here To Eternity*
Supp. Actress	Donna Reed in *From Here To Eternity*
Direction	Fred Zinnemann for *From Here To Eternity*

1954

Production	On The Waterfront (Columbia)
Actor	Marlon Brando in *On The Waterfront*
Actress	Grace Kelly in *The Country Girl*
Supp. Actor	Edmond O'Brien in *The Barefoot Contessa*
Supp. Actress	Eva Marie Saint in *On The Waterfront*
Direction	Elia Kazan for *On The Waterfront*

1955

Production	Marty (United Artists)
Actor	Ernest Borgnine in *Marty*
Actress	Anna Magnani in *The Rose Tattoo*
Supp. Actor	Jack Lemmon in *Mister Roberts*
Supp. Actress	Jo Van Fleet in *East Of Eden*
Direction	Delbert Mann for *Marty*

1956

Production	Around The World In 80 Days (United Artists)
Actor	Yul Brynner in *The King And I*
Actress	Ingrid Bergman in *Anastasia*
Supp. Actor	Anthony Quinn in *Lust For Life*
Supp. Actress	Dorothy Malone in *Written On The Wind*
Direction	George Stevens for *Giant*

1957

Production	The Bridge On The River Kwai (Columbia)
Actor	Alec Guinness in *The Bridge On The River Kwai*
Actress	Joanne Woodward in *The Three Faces Of Eve*
Supp. Actor	Red Buttons in *Sayonara*
Supp. Actress	Miyoshi Umeki in *Sayonara*
Direction	David Lean for *The Bridge On The River Kwai*

1958

Production	Gigi (MGM)
Actor	David Niven in *Separate Tables*
Actress	Susan Hayward in *I Want To Live*
Supp. Actor	Burl Ives in *The Big Country*
Supp. Actress	Wendy Hiller in *Separate Tables*
Direction	Vincente Minnelli for *Gigi*

1959

Production	Ben-Hur (MGM)
Actor	Charlton Heston in *Ben-Hur*
Actress	Simone Signoret in *Room At The Top*
Supp. Actor	Hugh Griffith in *Ben-Hur*
Supp. Actress	Shelley Winters in *The Diary Of Anne Frank*
Direction	William Wyler for *Ben-Hur*

1960

Production	The Apartment (United Artists)
Actor	Burt Lancaster in *Elmer Gantry*
Actress	Elizabeth Taylor in *Butterfield 8*

Supp. Actor	Peter Ustinov in *Spartacus*
Supp. Actress	Shirley Jones in *Elmer Gantry*
Direction	Billy Wilder for *The Apartment*

1961

Production	West Side Story (United Artists)
Actor	Maximilian Schell in *Judgment At Nuremberg*
Actress	Sophia Loren in *Two Women*
Supp. Actor	George Chakiris in *West Side Story*
Supp. Actress	Rita Moreno in *West Side Story*
Direction	Robert Wise and Jerome Robbins for *West Side Story*

1962

Production	Lawrence Of Arabia (Columbia)
Actor	Gregory Peck in *To Kill A Mockingbird*
Actress	Anne Bancroft in *The Miracle Worker*
Supp. Actor	Ed Begley in *Sweet Bird Of Youth*
Supp. Actress	Patty Duke in *The Miracle Worker*
Direction	David Lean for *Lawrence Of Arabia*

1963

Production	Tom Jones (Woodfall-United Artists)
Actor	Sidney Poitier in *Lilies Of The Field*
Actress	Patricia Neal in *Hud*
Supp. Actor	Melvyn Douglas in *Hud*
Supp. Actress	Margaret Rutherford in *The V.I.P.s*
Direction	Tony Richardson for *Tom Jones*

1964

Production	My Fair Lady (Warner Bros.)
Actor	Rex Harrison in *My Fair Lady*
Actress	Julie Andrews in *Mary Poppins*
Supp. Actor	Peter Ustinov in *Topkapi*
Supp. Actress	Lila Kedrova in *Zorba The Greek*
Direction	George Cukor for *My Fair Lady*

1965

Production	The Sound Of Music (20th Century-Fox)
Actor	Lee Marvin in *Cat Ballou*
Actress	Julie Christie in *Darling*
Supp. Actor	Martin Balsam in *A Thousand Clowns*
Supp. Actress	Shelley Winters in *A Patch Of Blue*
Direction	Robert Wise for *The Sound Of Music*

1966
Production | A Man For All Seasons (Columbia)
Actor | Paul Scofield in *A Man For All Seasons*
Actress | Elizabeth Taylor in *Who's Afraid Of Virginia Woolf?*
Supp. Actor | Walter Matthau in *The Fortune Cookie*
Supp. Actress | Sandy Dennis in *Who's Afraid Of Virginia Woolf?*
Direction | Fred Zinnemann for *A Man For All Seasons*

1967
Production | In The Heat Of The Night (United Artists)
Actor | Rod Steiger in *In The Heat Of The Night*
Actress | Katharine Hepburn in *Guess Who's Coming To Dinner?*
Supp. Actor | George Kennedy in *Cool Hand Luke*
Supp. Actress | Estelle Parsons in *Bonnie And Clyde*
Direction | Mike Nichols for *The Graduate*

1968
Production | Oliver! (Columbia)
Actor | Cliff Robertson in *Charly*
Actress | Katharine Hepburn in *The Lion In Winter* and Barbra Streisand in *Funny Girl*
Supp. Actor | Jack Albertson in *The Subject Was Roses*
Supp. Actress | Ruth Gordon in *Rosemary's Baby*
Direction | Carol Reed for *Oliver!*

1969
Production | Midnight Cowboy (United Artists)
Actor | John Wayne in *True Grit*
Actress | Maggie Smith in *The Prime Of Miss Jean Brodie*
Supp. Actor | Gig Young in *They Shoot Horses, Don't They?*
Supp. Actress | Goldie Hawn in *Cactus Flower*
Direction | John Schlesinger for *Midnight Cowboy*

1970
Production | Patton (20th Century-Fox)
Actor | George C. Scott in *Patton*
Actress | Glenda Jackson in *Women In Love*
Supp. Actor | John Mills in *Ryan's Daughter*
Supp. Actress | Helen Hayes in *Airport*
Direction | Franklin J. Schaffner for *Patton*

1971
Production | The French Connection (20th Century-Fox)
Actor | Gene Hackman in *The French Connection*

Actress	Jane Fonda in *Klute*
Supp. Actor	Ben Johnson in *The Last Picture Show*
Supp. Actress	Cloris Leachman in *The Last Picture Show*
Direction	William Friedkin for *The French Connection*

1972

Production	The Godfather (Paramount)
Actor	Marlon Brando in *The Godfather*
Actress	Liza Minnelli in *Cabaret*
Supp. Actor	Joel Grey in *Cabaret*
Supp. Actress	Eileen Heckart in *Butterflies Are Free*
Direction	Bob Fosse for *Cabaret*

1973

Production	The Sting (Universal)
Actor	Jack Lemmon in *Save The Tiger*
Actress	Glenda Jackson in *A Touch Of Class*
Supp. Actor	John Houseman in *The Paper Chase*
Supp. Actress	Tatum O'Neal in *Paper Moon*
Direction	George Roy Hill for *The Sting*

1974

Production	The Godfather Part II (Paramount)
Actor	Art Carney in *Harry And Tonto*
Actress	Ellen Burstyn in *Alice Doesn't Live Here Anymore*
Supp. Actor	Robert De Niro in *The Godfather Part II*
Supp. Actress	Ingrid Bergman in *Murder On The Orient Express*
Direction	Francis Ford Coppola for *The Godfather Part II*

1975

Production	One Flew Over The Cuckoo's Nest (United Artists)
Actor	Jack Nicholson in *One Flew Over The Cuckoo's Nest*
Actress	Louise Fletcher in *One Flew Over The Cuckoo's Nest*
Supp. Actor	George Burns in *The Sunshine Boys*
Supp. Actress	Lee Grant in *Shampoo*
Direction	Milos Forman for *One Flew Over The Cuckoo's Nest*

1976

Production	Rocky (United Artists)
Actor	Peter Finch in *Network*
Actress	Faye Dunaway in *Network*
Supp. Actor	Jason Robards in *All The President's Men*
Supp. Actress	Beatrice Straight in *Network*
Direction	John Avildsen for *Rocky*

1977

Production	Annie Hall (United Artists)
Actor	Richard Dreyfuss in *The Goodbye Girl*
Actress	Diane Keaton in *Annie Hall*
Supp. Actor	Jason Robards in *Julia*
Supp. Actress	Vanessa Redgrave in *Julia*
Direction	Woody Allen for *Annie Hall*

Appendix Two

A companion year order list of all acting, directing and best film nominees from 1927 to the present.

1927/28

Production	*The Last Command* (Paramount); *The Racket* (Paramount); *Seventh Heaven* (Fox); *The Way Of All Flesh* (Paramount); *Wings* (Paramount).
Actor	Richard Barthelmess in *The Noose*; Richard Barthelmess in *The Patent Leather Kid*; Charles Chaplin in *The Circus*; Emil Jannings in *The Last Command*; Emil Jannings in *The Way Of All Flesh*
Actress	Louise Dresser in *A Ship Comes In*; Janet Gaynor in *Seventh Heaven*; Janet Gaynor in *Street Angel*; Janet Gaynor in *Sunrise*; Gloria Swanson in *Sadie Thompson*
Direction	Frank Borzage for *Seventh Heaven*; Herbert Brenon for *Sorrell And Son*; King Vidor for *The Crowd*
	Comedy Direction (Not given after this year): Charles Chaplin for *The Circus*; Lewis Milestone for *Two Arabian Knights*; Ted Wilde for *Speedy*

1928/29

Production	*Alibi* (United Artists); *The Broadway Melody* (MGM); *Hollywood Revue* (MGM); *In Old Arizona* (Fox); *The Patriot* (Paramount)
Actor	Warner Baxter in *In Old Arizona*; Chester Morris in *Alibi*; Paul Muni in *The Valiant*; George Bancroft in *Thunderbolt*; Lewis Stone in *The Patriot*

Actress	Ruth Chatterton in *Madame X*; Betty Compson in *The Barker*; Jeanne Eagels in *The Letter*; Bessie Love in *The Broadway Melody*; Mary Pickford in *Coquette*
Direction	Lionel Barrymore for *Madame X*; Harry Beaumont for *The Broadway Melody*; Irving Cummings for *In Old Arizona*; Frank Lloyd for *The Divine Lady*; Frank Lloyd for *Weary River*; Frank Lloyd for *Drag*; Ernst Lubitsch for *The Patriot*

1929/30

Production	*All Quiet On The Western Front* (Universal); *The Big House* (MGM); *Disraeli* (Warner Bros.); *The Divorcee* (MGM); *The Love Parade* (Paramount)
Actor	George Arliss in *Disraeli*; George Arliss in *The Green Goddess*; Wallace Beery in *The Big House*; Maurice Chevalier in *The Love Parade*; Maurice Chevalier in *The Big Pond*; Ronald Colman in *Bulldog Drummond*; Ronald Colman in *Condemned*; Lawrence Tibbett in *The Rogue Song*
Actress	Nancy Carroll in *The Devil's Holiday*; Ruth Chatterton in *Sarah And Son*; Greta Garbo in *Anna Christie*; Greta Garbo in *Romance*; Norma Shearer in *The Divorcee*; Norma Shearer in *Their Own Desire*; Gloria Swanson in *The Trespasser*
Direction	Clarence Brown for *Anna Christie*; Clarence Brown for *Romance*; Robert Z. Leonard for *The Divorcee*; Ernst Lubitsch for *The Love Parade*; Lewis Milestone for *All Quiet On The Western Front*; King Vidor for *Hallelujah*

1930/31

Production	*Cimarron* (RKO Radio); *East Lynne* (Fox); *The Front Page* (United Artists); *Skippy* (Paramount); *Trader Horn* (MGM)
Actor	Lionel Barrymore in *A Free Soul*; Jackie Cooper in *Skippy*; Richard Dix in *Cimarron*; Fredric March in *The Royal Family Of Broadway*; Adolphe Menjou in *The Front Page*

Actress	Marlene Dietrich in *Morocco*; Marie Dressler in *Min And Bill*; Irene Dunne in *Cimarron*; Ann Harding in *Holiday*; Norma Shearer in *A Free Soul*
Direction	Clarence Brown for *A Free Soul*; Lewis Milestone for *The Front Page*; Wesley Ruggles for *Cimarron*; Josef von Sternberg for *Morocco*; Norman Taurog for *Skippy*

1931/32

Production	*Arrowsmith* (United Artists); *Bad Girl* (Fox); *The Champ* (MGM); *Five Star Final* (First National); *Grand Hotel* (MGM); *One Hour With You* (Paramount); *Shanghai Express* (Paramount); *The Smiling Lieutenant* (Paramount)
Actor	Wallace Beery in *The Champ*; Alfred Lunt in *The Guardsman*; Fredric March in *Dr. Jekyll And Mr. Hyde*
Actress	Marie Dressler in *Emma*; Lynne Fontanne in *The Guardsman*; Helen Hayes in *The Sin of Madelon Claudet*
Direction	Frank Borzage for *Bad Girl*; King Vidor for *The Champ*; Josef von Sternberg for *Shanghai Express*

1932/33

Production	*Cavalcade* (Fox); *A Farewell To Arms* (Paramount); *Forty-Second Street* (Warner Bros.); *I Am A Fugitive From A Chain Gang* (Warner Bros.); *Lady For A Day* (Columbia); *Little Women* (RKO Radio); *The Private Life Of Henry VIII* (London Films); *She Done Him Wrong* (Paramount); *Smilin' Thru* (MGM); *State Fair* (Fox)
Actor	Leslie Howard in *Berkeley Square*; Charles Laughton in *The Private Life Of Henry VIII*; Paul Muni in *I Am A Fugitive From A Chain Gang*
Actress	Katharine Hepburn in *Morning Glory*; May Robson in *Lady For A Day*; Diana Wynyard in *Cavalcade*
Direction	Frank Capra for *Lady For A Day*; George Cukor for *Little Women*; Frank Lloyd for *Cavalcade*

1934

Production	*The Barretts Of Wimpole Street* (MGM); *Cleopatra*

(Paramount); *Flirtation Walk* (First National); *The Gay Divorcee* (RKO Radio); *Here Comes The Navy* (Warner Bros.); *The House Of Rothschild* (Twentieth Century); *Imitation Of Life* (Universal); *It Happened One Night* (Columbia); *One Night Of Love* (Columbia); *The Thin Man* (MGM); *Viva Villa* (MGM); *The White Parade* (Fox)

Actor	Clark Gable in *It Happened One Night*; Frank Morgan in *Affairs Of Cellini*; William Powell in *The Thin Man*
Actress	Claudette Colbert in *It Happened One Night*; Grace Moore in *One Night Of Love*; Norma Shearer in *The Barretts Of Wimpole Street*
Direction	Frank Capra for *It Happened One Night*; Victor Schertzinger for *One Night Of Love*; W. S. Van Dyke for *The Thin Man*

1935

Production	*Alice Adams* (RKO Radio); *The Broadway Melody Of 1936* (MGM); *Captain Blood* (Warner Bros.); *David Copperfield* (MGM); *The Informer* (RKO Radio); *Les Miserables* (Twentieth Century); *Lives Of A Bengal Lancer* (Paramount); *A Midsummer Night's Dream* (Warner Bros.); *Mutiny On The Bounty* (MGM); *Naughty Marietta* (MGM); *Ruggles Of Red Gap* (Paramount); *Top Hat* (RKO Radio)
Actor	Clark Gable in *Mutiny On The Bounty*; Charles Laughton in *Mutiny On The Bounty*; Victor McLaglen in *The Informer*; Franchot Tone in *Mutiny On The Bounty*
Actress	Elisabeth Bergner in *Escape Me Never*; Claudette Colbert in *Private Worlds*; Bette Davis in *Dangerous*; Katharine Hepburn in *Alice Adams*; Miriam Hopkins in *Becky Sharp*; Merle Oberon in *The Dark Angel*
Direction	John Ford for *The Informer*; Henry Hathaway for *Lives Of A Bengal Lancer*; Frank Lloyd for *Mutiny On The Bounty*

1936

Production	*Anthony Adverse* (Warner Bros.); *Dodsworth* (Goldwyn UA); *The Great Ziegfeld* (MGM);

	Libeled Lady (MGM); *Mr. Deeds Goes To Town* (Columbia); *Romeo And Juliet* (MGM); *San Francisco* (MGM); *The Story Of Louis Pasteur* (Warner Bros.); *A Tale Of Two Cities* (MGM); *Three Smart Girls* (Universal)
Actor	Gary Cooper in *Mr. Deeds Goes To Town*; Walter Huston in *Dodsworth*; Paul Muni in *The Story Of Louis Pasteur*; William Powell in *My Man Godfrey*; Spencer Tracy in *San Francisco*
Actress	Irene Dunne in *Theodora Goes Wild*; Gladys George in *Valiant Is The Word For Carrie*; Carole Lombard in *My Man Godfrey*; Luise Rainer in *The Great Ziegfeld*; Norma Shearer in *Romeo And Juliet*
Supporting Actor	Mischa Auer in *My Man Godfrey*; Walter Brennan in *Come And Get It*; Stuart Erwin in *Pigskin Parade*; Basil Rathbone in *Romeo And Juliet*; Akim Tamiroff in *The General Died At Dawn*
Supporting Actress	Beulah Bondi in *The Gorgeous Hussy*; Alice Brady in *My Man Godfrey*; Bonita Granville in *These Three*; Maria Ouspenskaya in *Dodsworth*; Gale Sondergaard in *Anthony Adverse*
Direction	Frank Capra for *Mr. Deeds Goes To Town*; Gregory LaCava for *My Man Godfrey*; Robert Z. Leonard for *The Great Ziegfeld*; W. S. Van Dyke for *San Francisco*; William Wyler for *Dodsworth*

1937

Production	*The Awful Truth* (Columbia); *Captains Courageous* (MGM); *Dead End* (Goldwyn, UA); *The Good Earth* (MGM); *In Old Chicago* (20th Century-Fox); *The Life Of Emile Zola* (Warner Bros.); *Lost Horizon* (Columbia); *One Hundred Men And A Girl* (Universal); *Stage Door* (RKO Radio); *A Star is Born* (Selznick International, UA)
Actor	Charles Boyer in *Conquest*; Fredric March in *A Star Is Born*; Robert Montgomery in *Night Must Fall*; Paul Muni in *The Life Of Emile Zola*; Spencer Tracy in *Captains Courageous*
Actress	Irene Dunne in *The Awful Truth*; Greta Garbo in *Camille*; Janet Gaynor in *A Star Is Born*; Luise Rainer in *The Good Earth*; Barbara Stanwyck in *Stella Dallas*

202

Supporting Actor	Ralph Bellamy in *The Awful Truth*; Thomas Mitchell in *The Hurricane*; Joseph Schildkraut in *The Life Of Emile Zola*; H. B. Warner in *Lost Horizon*; Roland Young in *Topper*
Supporting Actress	Alice Brady in *In Old Chicago*; Andrea Leeds in *Stage Door*; Anne Shirley in *Stella Dallas*; Claire Trevor in *Dead End*; Dame May Whitty in *Night Must Fall*
Direction	William Dieterle for *The Life Of Emile Zola*; Sidney Franklin for *The Good Earth*; Gregory LaCava for *Stage Door*; Leo McCarey for *The Awful Truth*; William Wellman for *A Star is Born*

1938

Production	*The Adventures Of Robin Hood* (Warner Bros.); *Alexander's Ragtime Band* (20th Century-Fox); *Boys Town* (MGM); *The Citadel* (MGM); *Four Daughters* (Warner Bros.); *La Grande Illusion* (France); *Jezebel* (Warner Bros.); *Pygmalion* (MGM); *Test Pilot* (MGM); *You Can't Take It With You* (Columbia)
Actor	Charles Boyer in *Algiers*; James Cagney in *Angels With Dirty Faces*; Robert Donat in *The Citadel*; Leslie Howard in *Pygmalion*; Spencer Tracy in *Boys Town*
Actress	Fay Bainter in *White Banners*; Bette Davis in *Jezebel*; Wendy Hiller in *Pygmalion*; Norma Shearer in *Marie Antoinette*; Margaret Sullivan in *Three Comrades*
Supporting Actor	Walter Brennan in *Kentucky*; John Garfield in *Four Daughters*; Gene Lockhart in *Algiers*; Robert Morley in *Marie Antoinette*; Basil Rathbone in *If I Were King*
Supporting Actress	Fay Bainter in *Jezebel*; Beulah Bondi in *Of Human Hearts*; Spring Byington in *You Can't Take It With You*; Billie Burke in *Merrily We Live*; Miliza Korjus in *The Great Waltz*
Direction	Frank Capra for *You Can't Take It With You*; Michael Curtiz for *Angels With Dirty Faces*; Michael Curtiz for *Four Daughters*; Norman Taurog for *Boys Town*; King Vidor for *The Citadel*

1939

Production	*Dark Victory* (Warner Bros.); *Gone With The Wind* (Selznick/MGM); *Goodbye Mr. Chips* (MGM); *Love Affair* (RKO Radio); *Mr. Smith Goes To Washington* (Columbia); *Ninotchka* (MGM); *Of Mice And Men* (United Artists); *Stagecoach* (United Artists); *The Wizard Of Oz* (MGM); *Wuthering Heights* (Goldwyn, UA)
Actor	Robert Donat in *Goodbye, Mr. Chips*; Clark Gable in *Gone With The Wind*; Laurence Olivier in *Wuthering Heights*; Mickey Rooney in *Babes In Arms*; James Stewart in *Mr. Smith Goes To Washington*
Actress	Bette Davis in *Dark Victory*; Irene Dunne in *Love Affair*; Greta Garbo in *Ninotchka*; Greer Garson in *Goodbye, Mr. Chips*; Vivien Leigh in *Gone With The Wind*
Supporting Actor	Brian Aherne in *Juarez*; Harry Carey in *Mr. Smith Goes To Washington*; Brian Donlevy in *Beau Geste*; Thomas Mitchell in *Stagecoach*; Claude Rains in *Mr. Smith Goes To Washington*
Supporting Actress	Olivia de Havilland in *Gone With The Wind*; Geraldine Fitzgerald in *Wuthering Heights*; Hattie McDaniel in *Gone With The Wind*; Edna May Oliver in *Drums Along The Mohawk*; Maria Ouspenskaya in *Love Affair*
Direction	Frank Capra for *Mr. Smith Goes To Washington*; Victor Fleming for *Gone With The Wind*; John Ford for *Stagecoach*; Sam Wood for *Goodbye, Mr. Chips*; William Wyler for *Wuthering Heights*

1940

Production	*All This, And Heaven Too* (Warner Bros.); *Foreign Correspondent* (United Artists); *The Grapes Of Wrath* (20th Century-Fox); *The Great Dictator* (United Artists); *Kitty Foyle* (RKO Radio); *The Letter* (Warner Bros.); *The Long Voyage Home* (United Artists); *Our Town* (United Artists); *The Philadelphia Story* (MGM); *Rebecca* (Selznick, United Artists)
Actor	Charles Chaplin in *The Great Dictator*; Henry Fonda in *The Grapes Of Wrath*; Raymond Massey in *Abe Lincoln In Illinois*; Laurence Olivier in *Rebecca*; James Stewart in *The Philadelphia Story*

Actress	Bette Davis in *The Letter*; Joan Fontaine in *Rebecca*; Katharine Hepburn in *The Philadelphia Story*; Ginger Rogers in *Kitty Foyle*; Martha Scott in *Our Town*
Supporting Actor	Albert Basserman in *Foreign Correspondent*; Walter Brennan in *The Westerner*; William Gargan in *They Knew What They Wanted*; Jack Oakie in *The Great Dictator*; James Stephenson in *The Letter*
Supporting Actress	Judith Anderson in *Rebecca*; Jane Darwell in *The Grapes Of Wrath*; Ruth Hussey in *The Philadelphia Story*; Barbara O'Neil in *All This, And Heaven Too*; Marjorie Rambeau in *Primrose Path*
Direction	George Cukor for *The Philadelphia Story*; John Ford for *The Grapes Of Wrath*; Alfred Hitchcock for *Rebecca*; Sam Wood for *Kitty Foyle*; William Wyler for *The Letter*

1941

Production	*Blossoms In The Dust* (MGM); *Citizen Kane* (RKO Radio); *Here Comes Mr. Jordan* (Columbia); *Hold Back The Dawn* (Paramount); *How Green Was My Valley* (20th Century-Fox); *The Little Foxes* (Goldwyn, RKO Radio); *The Maltese Falcon* (Warner Bros.); *One Foot In Heaven* (Warner Bros.) *Sergeant York* (Warner Bros.); *Suspicion* (RKO Radio)
Actor	Gary Cooper in *Sergeant York*; Cary Grant in *Penny Serenade*; Walter Huston in *All That Money Can Buy*; Robert Montgomery in *Here Comes Mr. Jordan*; Orson Welles in *Citizen Kane*
Actress	Bette Davis in *The Little Foxes*; Joan Fontaine in *Suspicion*; Greer Garson in *Blossoms In The Dust*; Olivia de Havilland in *Hold Back The Dawn*; Barbara Stanwyck in *Ball Of Fire*
Supporting Actor	Walter Brennan in *Sergeant York*; Charles Coburn in *The Devil And Miss Jones*; Donald Crisp in *How Green Was My Valley*; James Gleason in *Here Comes Mr. Jordan*; Sydney Greenstreet in *The Maltese Falcon*
Supporting Actress	Sara Allgood in *How Green Was My Valley*; Mary Astor in *The Great Lie*; Patricia Collinge in *The Little Foxes*; Teresa Wright in *The Little Foxes*; Margaret Wycherly in *Sergeant York*

Direction	John Ford for *How Green Was My Valley*; Alexander Hall for *Here Comes Mr. Jordan*; Howard Hawks for *Sergeant York*; Orson Welles for *Citizen Kane*; William Wyler for *The Little Foxes*

1942

Production	*The Invaders* (British — GB *The 49th Parallel*); *Kings Row* (Warner Bros.); *The Magnificent Ambersons* (RKO Radio); *Mrs. Miniver*(MGM); *The Pied Piper*((20th Century-Fox); *The Pride Of The Yankees* (Goldwyn, RKO); *Random Harvest* (MGM); *The Talk Of The Town* (Columbia); *Wake Island* (Paramount); *Yankee Doodle Dandy* (Warner Bros.)
Actor	James Cagney in *Yankee Doodle Dandy*; Ronald Colman in *Random Harvest*; Gary Cooper in *The Pride Of The Yankees*; Walter Pidgeon in *Mrs. Miniver*; Monty Woolley in *The Pied Piper*
Actress	Bette Davis in *Now, Voyager*; Greer Garson in *Mrs. Miniver*; Katharine Hepburn in *Woman Of The Year*; Rosalind Russell in *My Sister Eileen*; Teresa Wright in *The Pride Of The Yankees*
Supporting Actor	William Bendix in *Wake Island*; Van Heflin in *Johnny Eager*; Walter Huston in *Yankee Doodle Dandy*; Frank Morgan in *Tortilla Flat*; Henry Travers in *Mrs. Miniver*
Supporting Actress	Gladys Cooper in *Now, Voyager*; Agnes Moorehead in *The Magnificent Ambersons*; Susan Peters in *Random Harvest*; Dame May Whitty in *Mrs. Miniver*; Teresa Wright in *Mrs. Miniver*
Direction	Michael Curtiz for *Yankee Doodle Dandy*; John Farrow for *Wake Island*; Mervyn LeRoy for *Random Harvest*; Sam Wood for *Kings Row*; William Wyler for *Mrs. Miniver*

1943

Production	*Casablanca* (Warner Bros.); *For Whom The Bell Tolls* (Paramount); *Heaven Can Wait* (20th Century-Fox); *The Human Comedy* (MGM); *In Which We Serve* (British); *Madame Curie* (MGM); *The More The Merrier* (Columbia); *The Ox-Bow Incident* (20th Century-Fox); *The Song Of Bernadette* (20th Century-Fox); *Watch On The Rhine* (Warner Bros.)

Actor	Humphrey Bogart in *Casablanca*; Gary Cooper in *For Whom The Bell Tolls*; Paul Lukas in *Watch On The Rhine*; Walter Pidgeon in *Madame Curie*; Mickey Rooney in *The Human Comedy*
Actress	Jean Arthur in *The More The Merrier*; Ingrid Bergman in *For Whom The Bell Tolls*; Joan Fontaine in *The Constant Nymph*; Greer Garson in *Madame Curie*; Jennifer Jones in *The Song Of Bernadette*
Supporting Actor	Charles Bickford in *The Song Of Bernadette*; Charles Coburn in *The More The Merrier*; J. Carrol Naish in *Sahara*; Claude Rains in *Casablanca*; Akim Tamiroff in *For Whom The Bell Tolls*
Supporting Actress	Gladys Cooper in *The Song Of Bernadette*; Paulette Goddard in *So Proudly We Hail*; Katina Paxinou in *For Whom The Bell Tolls*; Anne Revere in *The Song Of Bernadette*; Lucile Watson in *Watch On The Rhine*
Direction	Clarence Brown for *The Human Comedy*; Michael Curtiz for *Casablanca*; Henry King for *The Song Of Bernadette*; Ernst Lubitsch for *Heaven Can Wait*; George Stevens for *The More The Merrier*

1944

Production	*Double Indemnity* (Paramount); *Gaslight* (MGM); *Going My Way* (Paramount); *Since You Went Away* (Selznick International, UA); *Wilson* (20th Century-Fox)
Actor	Charles Boyer in *Gaslight*; Bing Crosby in *Going My Way*; Barry Fitzgerald in *Going My Way*; Cary Grant in *None But The Lonely Heart*; Alexander Knox in *Wilson*
Actress	Ingrid Bergman in *Gaslight*; Claudette Colbert in *Since You Went Away*; Bette Davis in *Mr. Skeffington*; Greer Garson in *Mrs. Parkington*; Barbara Stanwyck in *Double Indemnity*
Supporting Actor	Hume Cronyn in *The Seventh Cross*; Barry Fitzgerald in *Going My Way*; Claude Rains in *Mr. Skeffington*; Clifton Webb in *Laura*; Monty Woolley in *Since You Went Away*
Supporting Actress	Ethel Barrymore in *None But The Lonely Heart*; Jennifer Jones in *Since You Went Away*;

Angela Lansbury in *Gaslight*; Aline MacMahon in *Dragon Seed*; Agnes Moorehead in *Mrs. Parkington*

Direction   Alfred Hitchcock for *Lifeboat*; Henry King for *Wilson*; Leo McCarey for *Going My Way*; Otto Preminger for *Laura*; Billy Wilder for *Double Indemnity*

1945
Production   *Anchors Aweigh* (MGM); *The Bells Of St. Mary's* (RKO Radio); *The Lost Weekend* (Paramount); *Mildred Pierce* (Warner Bros.); *Spellbound* (Selznick International, UA)

Actor   Bing Crosby in *The Bells Of St. Mary's*; Gene Kelly in *Anchors Aweigh*; Ray Milland in *The Lost Weekend*; Gregory Peck in *The Keys Of The Kingdom*; Cornel Wilde in *A Song To Remember*

Actress   Ingrid Bergman in *The Bells Of St. Mary's*; Joan Crawford in *Mildred Pierce*; Greer Garson in *The Valley Of Decision*; Jennifer Jones in *Love Letters*; Gene Tierney in *Leave Her To Heaven*

Supporting Actor   Michael Chekhov in *Spellbound*; John Dall in *The Corn Is Green*; James Dunn in *A Tree Grows In Brooklyn*; Robert Mitchum in *The Story Of G.I. Joe*; J. Carrol Naish in *A Medal For Benny*

Supporting Actress   Eve Arden in *Mildred Pierce*; Ann Blyth in *Mildred Pierce*; Angela Lansbury in *The Picture Of Dorian Gray*; Joan Lorring in *The Corn Is Green*; Anne Revere in *National Velvet*

Direction   Clarence Brown for *National Velvet*; Alfred Hitchcock for *Spellbound*; Leo McCarey for *The Bells Of St. Mary's*; Jean Renoir for *The Southerner*; Billy Wilder for *The Lost Weekend*

1946
Production   *The Best Years Of Our Lives* (Goldwyn, RKO); *Henry V* (Rank/Two Cities/British); *It's A Wonderful Life* (RKO Radio); *The Razor's Edge* (20th Century-Fox); *The Yearling* (MGM)

Actor   Fredric March in *The Best Years Of Our Lives*; Laurence Oliver in *Henry V*; Larry Parks in *The Jolson Story*; Gregory Peck in *The Yearling*; James Stewart in *It's A Wonderful Life*

Actress	Olivia de Havilland in *To Each His Own*; Celia Johnson in *Brief Encounter*; Jennifer Jones in *Duel In The Sun*; Rosalind Russell in *Sister Kenny*; Jane Wyman in *The Yearling*
Supporting Actor	Charles Coburn in *The Green Years*; William Demarest in *The Jolson Story*; Claude Rains in *Notorious*; Harold Russell in *The Best Years Of Our Lives*; Clifton Webb in *The Razor's Edge*
Supporting Actress	Ethel Barrymore in *The Spiral Staircase*; Anne Baxter in *The Razor's Edge*; Lillian Gish in *Duel In The Sun*; Flora Robson in *Saratoga Trunk* Gale Sondergaard in *Anna And The King Of Siam*
Direction	Clarence Brown for *The Yearling*; Frank Capra for *It's A Wonderful Life*; David Lean for *Brief Encounter*; Robert Siodmak for *The Killers*; William Wyler for *The Best Years Of Our Lives*

1947

Production	*The Bishop's Wife* (Goldwyn, RKO); *Crossfire* (RKO Radio); *Gentleman's Agreement* (20th Century-Fox); *Great Expectations* (Rank-Cineguild/British); *Miracle On 34th Street* (20th Century-Fox)
Actor	Ronald Colman in *A Double Life*; John Garfield in *Body And Soul*; Gregory Peck in *Gentleman's Agreement*; William Powell in *Life With Father*; Michael Redgrave in *Mourning Becomes Electra*
Actress	Joan Crawford in *Possessed*; Susan Hayward in *Smash-Up — The Story Of A Woman*; Dorothy McGuire in *Gentleman's Agreement*; Rosalind Russell in *Mourning Becomes Electra*; Loretta Young in *The Farmer's Daughter*
Supporting Actor	Charles Bickford in *The Farmer's Daughter*; Thomas Gomez in *Ride The Pink Horse*; Edmund Gwenn in *Miracle On 34th Street*; Robert Ryan in *Crossfire*; Richard Widmark in *Kiss Of Death*
Supporting Actress	Ethel Barrymore in *The Paradine Case*; Gloria Grahame in *Crossfire*; Celeste Holm in *Gentleman's Agreement*; Marjorie Main in *The Egg And I*; Anne Revere in *Gentleman's Agreement*
Direction	George Cukor for *A Double Life*; Edward Dmytryk for *Crossfire*; Elia Kazan for *Gentleman's Agreement*; Henry Koster for *The Bishop's Wife*; David Lean for *Great Expectations*

1948

Production	*Hamlet* (Rank-Two Cities/British); *Johnny Belinda* (Warner Bros.); *The Red Shoes* (Rank-Archers/ British); *The Snake Pit* (20th Century-Fox); *Treasure Of The Sierra Madre* (Warner Bros.)
Actor	Lew Ayres in *Johnny Belinda*; Montgomery Clift in *The Search*; Dan Dailey in *When My Baby Smiles At Me*; Laurence Olivier in *Hamlet*; Clifton Webb in *Sitting Pretty*
Actress	Ingrid Bergman in *Joan Of Arc*; Olivia de Havilland in *The Snake Pit* Irene Dunne in *I Remember Mama*; Barbara Stanwyck in *Sorry, Wrong Number*; Jane Wyman in *Johnny Belinda*
Supporting Actor	Charles Bickford in *Johnny Belinda*; Jose Ferrer in *Joan Of Arc*; Oscar Homolka in *I Remember Mama*; Walter Huston in *Treasure Of The Sierra Madre*; Cecil Kellaway in *The Luck Of The Irish*
Supporting Actress	Barbara Bel Geddes in *I Remember Mama*; Ellen Corby in *I Remember Mama*; Agnes Moorehead in *Johnny Belinda*; Jean Simmons in *Hamlet*; Claire Trevor in *Key Largo*
Direction	John Huston for *Treasure Of The Sierra Madre*; Anatole Litvak for *The Snake Pit*; Jean Negulesco for *Johnny Belinda*; Laurence Olivier for *Hamlet*; Fred Zinnemann for *The Search*

1949

Production	*All The King's Men* (Columbia); *Battleground* (MGM); *The Heiress* (Paramount); *A Letter To Three Wives* (20th Century-Fox); *Twelve O'Clock High* (20th Century-Fox)
Actor	Broderick Crawford in *All The King's Men*; Kirk Douglas in *Champion*; Gregory Peck in *Twelve O'Clock High*; Richard Todd in *The Hasty Heart*; John Wayne in *Sands Of Iwo Jima*
Actress	Jeanne Crain in *Pinky*; Olivia de Havilland in *The Heiress*; Susan Hayward in *My Foolish Heart*; Deborah Kerr in *Edward, My Son*; Loretta Young in *Come To The Stable*
Supporting Actor	John Ireland in *All The King's Men*; Dean Jagger in *Twelve O'Clock High*; Arthur Kennedy in *Champion*; Ralph Richardson in *The Heiress*; James Whitmore in *Battleground*

Supporting Actress	Ethel Barrymore in *Pinky*; Celeste Holm in *Come To The Stable*; Elsa Lanchester in *Come To The Stable*; Mercedes McCambridge in *All The King's Men*; Ethel Waters in *Pinky*
Direction	Joseph L. Mankiewicz for *A Letter To Three Wives*; Carol Reed for *The Fallen Idol*; Robert Rossen for *All The King's Men*; William A. Wellman for *Battleground*; William Wyler for *The Heiress*

1950

Production	*All About Eve* (20th Century-Fox); *Born Yesterday* (Columbia); *Father Of The Bride* (MGM); *King Solomon's Mines* (MGM); *Sunset Boulevard* (Paramount)
Actor	Louis Calhern in *The Magnificent Yankee*; Jose Ferrer in *Cyrano de Bergerac*; William Holden in *Sunset Boulevard*; James Stewart in *Harvey*; Spencer Tracy in *Father Of The Bride*
Actress	Anne Baxter in *All About Eve*; Bette Davis in *All About Eve*; Judy Holliday in *Born Yesterday*; Eleanor Parker in *Caged*; Gloria Swanson in *Sunset Boulevard*
Supporting Actor	Jeff Chandler in *Broken Arrow*; Edmund Gwenn in *Mister 880*; Sam Jaffe in *The Asphalt Jungle*; George Sanders in *All About Eve*; Erich Von Stroheim in *Sunset Boulevard*
Supporting Actress	Hope Emerson in *Caged*; Celeste Holm in *All About Eve*; Josephine Hull in *Harvey*; Nancy Olson in *Sunset Boulevard*; Thelma Ritter in *All About Eve*
Direction	George Cukor for *Born Yesterday*; John Huston for *The Asphalt Jungle*; Joseph L. Mankiewicz for *All About Eve*; Carol Reed for *The Third Man*; Billy Wilder for *Sunset Boulevard*

1951

Production	*An American In Paris* (MGM); *Decision Before Dawn* (20th Century-Fox); *A Place In The Sun* (Paramount); *Quo Vadis* (MGM); *A Streetcar Named Desire* (Warner Bros.)
Actor	Humphrey Bogart in *The African Queen*; Marlon Brando in *A Streetcar Named Desire*; Montgomery Clift in *A Place In The Sun*; Arthur Kennedy in *Bright Victory*; Fredric March in *Death Of A Salesman*

Actress	Katharine Hepburn in *The African Queen*; Vivien Leigh in *A Streetcar Named Desire*; Eleanor Parker in *Detective Story*; Shelley Winters in *A Place In The Sun*; Jane Wyman in *The Blue Veil*
Supporting Actor	Leo Genn in *Quo Vadis*; Karl Malden in *A Streetcar Named Desire*; Kevin McCarthy in *Death Of A Salesman*; Peter Ustinov in *Quo Vadis*; Gig Young in *Come Fill The Cup*
Supporting Actress	Joan Blondell in *The Blue Veil*; Mildred Dunnock in *Death Of A Salesman*; Lee Grant in *Detective Story*; Kim Hunter in *A Streetcar Named Desire*; Thelma Ritter in *The Mating Season*
Direction	John Huston for *The African Queen*; Vincente Minnelli for *An American In Paris*; William Wyler for *Detective Story*; George Stevens for *A Place In The Sun*; Elia Kazan for *A Streetcar Named Desire*

1952

Production	*The Greatest Show On Earth* (Paramount); *High Noon* (United Artists); *Ivanhoe* (MGM); *Moulin Rouge* (United Artists); *The Quiet Man* (Republic)
Actor	Marlon Brando in *Viva Zapata*; Gary Cooper in *High Noon*; Kirk Douglas in *The Bad And The Beautiful*; Jose Ferrer in *Moulin Rouge*; Alec Guinness in *The Lavender Hill Mob*
Actress	Shirley Booth in *Come Back Little Sheba*; Joan Crawford in *Sudden Fear*; Bette Davis in *The Star*; Julie Harris in *The Member Of The Wedding*; Susan Hayward in *With A Song In My Heart*
Supporting Actor	Richard Burton in *My Cousin Rachel*; Arthur Hunnicutt in *The Big Sky*; Victor McLaglen in *The Quiet Man*; Jack Palance in *Sudden Fear*; Anthony Quinn in *Viva Zapata*
Supporting Actress	Gloria Grahame in *The Bad And The Beautiful*; Jean Hagen in *Singin' In The Rain*; Colette Marchand in *Moulin Rouge*; Terry Moore in *Come Back Little Sheba*; Thelma Ritter in *With A Song In My Heart*
Direction	Cecil B. DeMille for *The Greatest Show On Earth*; John Ford for *The Quiet Man*; John Huston for *Moulin Rouge*; Joseph L. Mankiewicz for *Five Fingers*; Fred Zinnemann for *High Noon*

1953

Production	*From Here To Eternity* (Columbia); *Julius Caesar* (MGM); *The Robe* (20th Century-Fox); *Roman Holiday* (Paramount); *Shane* (Paramount)
Actor	Marlon Brando in *Julius Caesar*; Richard Burton in *The Robe*; Montgomery Clift in *From Here To Eternity*; William Holden in *Stalag 17*; Burt Lancaster in *From Here To Eternity*
Actress	Leslie Caron in *Lili*; Ava Gardner in *Mogambo*; Audrey Hepburn in *Roman Holiday*; Deborah Kerr in *From Here To Eternity*; Maggie McNamara in *The Moon Is Blue*
Supporting Actor	Eddie Albert in *Roman Holiday*; Brandon De Wilde in *Shane*; Jack Palance in *Shane*; Frank Sinatra in *From Here To Eternity*; Robert Strauss in *Stalag 17*
Supporting Actress	Grace Kelly in *Mogambo*; Geraldine Page in *Hondo*; Marjorie Rambeau in *Torch Song*; Donna Reed in *From Here To Eternity*; Thelma Ritter in *Pickup On South Street*
Direction	George Stevens for *Shane*; Charles Walters for *Lili*; Billy Wilder for *Stalag 17*; William Wyler for *Roman Holiday*; Fred Zinnemann for *From Here To Eternity*

1954

Production	*The Caine Mutiny* (Columbia); *The Country Girl* Paramount); *On The Waterfront* (Columbia); *Seven Brides For Seven Brothers* (MGM); *Three Coins In The Fountain* (20th Century-Fox)
Actor	Humphrey Bogart in *The Caine Mutiny*; Marlon Brando in *On The Waterfront*; Bing Crosby in *The Country Girl*; James Mason in *A Star Is Born*; Dan O'Herlihy in *The Adventures Of Robinson Crusoe*
Actress	Dorothy Dandridge in *Carmen Jones*; Judy Garland in *A Star Is Born*; Audrey Hepburn in *Sabrina*; Grace Kelly in *The Country Girl*; Jane Wyman in *Magnificent Obsession*
Supporting Actor	Lee J. Cobb in *On The Waterfront*; Karl Malden in *On The Waterfront*; Edmond O'Brien in *The Barefoot Contessa*; Rod Steiger in *On The Waterfront*; Tom Tully in *The Caine Mutiny*

Supporting Actress	Nina Foch in *Executive Suite*; Katy Jurado in *Broken Lance*; Eva Marie Saint in *On The Waterfront*; Jan Sterling in *The High And The Mighty*; Claire Trevor in *The High And The Mighty*
Direction	Alfred Hitchcock for *Rear Window*; Elia Kazan for *On The Waterfront*; George Seaton for *The Country Girl*; William A. Wellman for *The High And The Mighty*; Billy Wilder for *Sabrina*

1955

Production	*Love Is A Many-Splendoured Thing* (20th Century-Fox); *Marty* (United Artists); *Mister Roberts* (Warner Bros.); *Picnic* (Columbia); *The Rose Tattoo* (Paramount)
Actor	Ernest Borgnine in *Marty*; James Cagney in *Love Me Or Leave Me*; James Dean in *East Of Eden*; Frank Sinatra in *The Man With The Golden Arm*; Spencer Tracy in *Bad Day At Black Rock*
Actress	Susan Hayward in *I'll Cry Tomorrow*; Katharine Hepburn in *Summertime*; Jennifer Jones in *Love Is A Man-Splendoured Thing*; Anna Magnani in *The Rose Tattoo*; Eleanor Parker in *Interrupted Melody*
Supporting Actor	Arthur Kennedy in *Trial*; Jack Lemmon in *Mister Roberts*; Joe Mantell in *Marty*; Sal Mineo in *Rebel Without A Cause*; Arthur O'Connell in *Picnic*
Supporting Actress	Betsy Blair in *Marty*; Peggy Lee in *Pete Kelly's Blues*; Marisa Pavan in *The Rose Tattoo*; Jo Van Fleet in *East Of Eden*; Natalie Wood in *Rebel Without A Cause*
Direction 1956	Elia Kazan for *East Of Eden*; David Lean for *Summertime*; Joshua Logan for *Picnic*; Delbert Mann for *Marty*; John Sturges for *Bad Day At Black Rock*

1956

Production	*Around The World In 80 Days* (United Artists); *Friendly Persuasion* (Allied Artists); *Giant* (Warner Bros.); *The King And I* (20th Century-Fox); *The Ten Commandments* (Paramount)
Actor	Yul Brynner in *The King And I*; James Dean in *Giant*; Kirk Douglas in *Lust For Life*; Rock Hudson in *Giant*; Laurence Oliver in *Richard III*

Actress	Carroll Baker in *Baby Doll*; Ingrid Bergman in *Anastasia*; Katharine Hepburn in *The Rainmaker*; Nancy Kelly in *The Bad Seed*; Deborah Kerr in *The King And I*
Supporting Actor	Don Murray in *Bus Stop*; Anthony Perkins in *Friendly Persuasion*; Anthony Quinn in *Lust For Life*; Mickey Rooney in *The Bold And The Brave*; Robert Stack in *Written On The Wind*
Supporting Actress	Mildred Dunnock in *Baby Doll*; Eileen Heckart in *The Bad Seed*; Mercedes McCambridge in *Giant*; Patty McCormack in *The Bad Seed*; Dorothy Malone in *Written On The Wind*
Direction	Michael Anderson for *Around The World In 80 Days*; William Wyler for *Friendly Persuasion*; George Stevens for *Giant*; Walter Lang for *The King And I*; King Vidor for *War And Peace*

1957

Production	*The Bridge On The River Kwai* (Columbia); *Peyton Place* (20th Century-Fox); *Sayonara* (Warner Bros.); *Twelve Angry Men* (United Artists); *Witness For The Prosecution* (United Artists)
Actor	Marlon Brando in *Sayonara*; Anthony Franciosa in *A Hatful Of Rain*; Alec Guinness in *The Bridge On The River Kwai*; Charles Laughton in *Witness For The Prosecution*; Anthony Quinn in *Wild Is The Wind*
Actress	Deborah Kerr in *Heaven Knows, Mr. Allison*; Anna Magnani in *Wild Is The Wind*; Elizabeth Taylor in *Raintree County*; Lana Turner in *Peyton Place*; Joanne Woodward in *The Three Faces Of Eve*
Supporting Actor	Red Buttons in *Sayonara*; Vittorio De Sica in *A Farewell To Arms*; Sessue Hayakawa in *The Bridge On The River Kwai*; Arthur Kennedy in *Peyton Place*; Russ Tamblyn in *Peyton Place*
Supporting Actress	Carolyn Jones in *The Bachelor Party*; Elsa Lanchester in *Witness For The Prosecution*; Hope Lange in *Peyton Place*; Miyoshi Umeki in *Sayonara*; Diane Varsi in *Peyton Place*
Direction	David Lean for *The Bridge On The River Kwai*; Mark Robson for *Peyton Place*; Joshua Logan for *Sayonara*; Sidney Lumet for *Twelve Angry Men*; Billy Wilder for *Witness For The Prosecution*

1958

Production	*Auntie Mame* (Warner Bros.); *Cat On A Hot Tin Roof* (MGM); *The Defiant Ones* (United Artists); *Gigi* (MGM); *Separate Tables* (United Artists)
Actor	Tony Curtis in *The Defiant Ones*; Paul Newman in *Cat On A Hot Tin Roof*; David Niven in *Separate Tables*; Sidney Poitier in *The Defiant Ones*; Spencer Tracy in *The Old Man And The Sea*
Actress	Susan Hayward in *I Want To Live*; Deborah Kerr in *Separate Tables*; Shirley MacLaine in *Some Came Running*; Rosalind Russell in *Auntie Mame*; Elizabeth Taylor in *Cat On A Hot Tin Roof*
Supporting Actor	Theodore Bikel in *The Defiant Ones*; Lee J. Cobb in *The Brothers Karamazov*; Burl Ives in *The Big Country*; Arthur Kennedy in *Some Came Running*; Gig Young in *Teacher's Pet*
Supporting Actress	Peggy Cass in *Auntie Mame*; Wendy Hiller in *Separate Tables*; Martha Hyer in *Some Came Running*; Maureen Stapleton in *Lonelyhearts*; Cara Williams in *The Defiant Ones*
Direction	Richard Brooks for *Cat On A Hot Tin Roof*; Stanley Kramer for *The Defiant Ones*; Vincente Minnelli for *Gigi*; Robert Wise for *I Want To Live*; Mark Robson for *The Inn Of The Sixth Happiness*

1959

Production	*Anatomy Of A Murder* (Columbia); *Ben-Hur* (MGM); *The Diary Of Anne Frank* (20th Century-Fox); *The Nun's Story* (Warner Bros.); *Room At The Top* (Romulus Films/British)
Actor	Laurence Harvey in *Room At The Top*; Charlton Heston in *Ben-Hur*; Jack Lemmon in *Some Like It Hot*; Paul Muni in *The Last Angry Man*; James Stewart in *Anatomy Of A Murder*
Actress	Doris Day in *Pillow Talk*; Audrey Hepburn in *The Nun's Story*; Katharine Hepburn in *Suddenly, Last Summer*; Simone Signoret in *Room At The Top*; Elizabeth Taylor in *Suddenly, Last Summer*
Supporting Actor	Hugh Griffith in *Ben-Hur*; Arthur O'Connell in *Anatomy Of A Murder*; George C. Scott in *Anatomy Of A Murder*; Robert Vaughn in *The Young Philadelphians*; Ed Wynn in *The Diary Of Anne Frank*

Supporting Actress	Hermione Baddeley in *Room At The Top*; Susan Kohner in *Imitation Of Life*; Juanita Moore in *Imitation Of Life*; Thelma Ritter in *Pillow Talk*; Shelley Winters in *The Diary Of Anne Frank*
Direction	William Wyler for *Ben-Hur*; George Stevens for *The Diary Of Anne Frank*; Fred Zinnemann for *The Nun's Story*; Jack Clayton for *Room At The Top*; Billy Wilder for *Some Like It Hot*

1960

Production	*The Alamo* (United Artists); *The Apartment* (United Artists); *Elmer Gantry* (United Artists); *Sons And Lovers* (20th Century-Fox); *The Sundowners* (Warner Bros.)
Actor	Trevor Howard in *Sons And Lovers*; Burt Lancaster in *Elmer Gantry*; Jack Lemmon in *The Apartment*; Laurence Olivier in *The Entertainer*; Spencer Tracy in *Inherit The Wind*
Actress	Greer Garson in *Sunrise At Campobello*; Deborah Kerr in *The Sundowners*; Shirley MacLaine in *The Apartment*; Melina Mercouri in *Never On Sunday*; Elizabeth Taylor in *Butterfield 8*
Supporting Actor	Peter Falk in *Murder Inc.*; Jack Kruschen in *The Apartment*; Sal Mineo in *Exodus*; Peter Ustinov in *Spartacus*; Chill Wills in *The Alamo*
Supporting Actress	Glynis Johns in *The Sundowners*; Shirley Jones in *Elmer Gantry*; Shirley Knight in *The Dark At The Top Of The Stairs*; Janet Leigh in *Psycho*; Mary Ure in *Sons And Lovers*
Direction	Jack Cardiff for *Sons And Lovers*; Jules Dassin for *Never On Sunday*; Alfred Hitchcock for *Psycho*; Billy Wilder for *The Apartment*; Fred Zinnemann for *The Sundowners*

1961

Production	*Fanny* (Warner Bros.); *The Guns Of Navarone* (Columbia); *The Hustler* (20th Century-Fox); *Judgment At Nuremberg* (United Artists); *West Side Story* (United Artists)
Actor	Charles Boyer in *Fanny*; Paul Newman in *The Hustler*; Maximilian Schell in *Judgment At Nuremberg*; Spencer Tracy in *Judgment At Nuremberg*; Stuart Whitman in *The Mark*

Actress	Audrey Hepburn in *Breakfast At Tiffany's*; Piper Laurie in *The Hustler*; Sophia Loren in *Two Women*; Geraldine Page in *Summer And Smoke*; Natalie Wood in *Splendour In The Grass*
Supporting Actor	George Chakiris in *West Side Story*; Montgomery Clift in *Judgment At Nuremberg*; Peter Falk in *Pocketful Of Miracles*; Jackie Gleason in *The Hustler*; George C. Scott in *The Hustler*
Supporting Actress	Fay Bainter in *The Children's Hour*; Judy Garland in *Judgment At Nuremberg*; Lotte Lenya in *The Roman Spring Of Mrs. Stone*; Una Merkel in *Summer And Smoke*; Rita Moreno in *West Side Story*
Direction	J. Lee Thompson for *The Guns Of Navarone*; Robert Rossen for *The Hustler*; Stanley Kramer for *Judgment At Nuremberg*; Federico Fellini for *La Dolce Vita*; Robert Wise and Jerome Robbins for *West Side Story*

1962

Production	*Lawrence Of Arabia* (Columbia); *The Longest Day* (20th Century-Fox); *The Music Man* (Warner Bros.); *Mutiny On The Bounty* (MGM); *To Kill A Mockingbird* (Universal-International)
Actor	Burt Lancaster in *Birdman Of Alcatraz*; Jack Lemmon in *Days Of Wine And Roses*; Marcello Mastroianni in *Divorce Italian Style*; Peter O'Toole in *Lawrence Of Arabia*; Gregory Peck in *To Kill A Mockingbird*
Actress	Anne Bancroft in *The Miracle Worker*; Bette Davis in *What Ever Happened To Baby Jane?*; Katharine Hepburn in *Long Day's Journey Into Night*; Geraldine Page in *Sweet Bird Of Youth*; Lee Remick in *Days Of Wine And Roses*
Supporting Actor	Ed Begley in *Sweet Bird Of Youth*; Victor Buono in *What Ever Happened To Baby Jane?*; Telly Savalas in *Birdman Of Alcatraz*; Omar Sharif in *Lawrence Of Arabia*; Terence Stamp in *Billy Budd*
Supporting Actress	Mary Badham in *To Kill A Mockingbird*; Patty Duke in *The Miracle Worker*; Shirley Knight in *Sweet Bird Of Youth*; Angela Lansbury in *The Manchurian Candidate*; Thelma Ritter in *Birdman Of Alcatraz*

Direction	Frank Perry for *David And Lisa*; Pietro Germi for *Divorce Italian Style*; David Lean for *Lawrence Of Arabia*; Arthur Penn for *The Miracle Worker*; Robert Mulligan for *To Kill A Mockingbird*

1963

Production	*Tom Jones* (United Artists); *America, America* (Warner Bros.); *Cleopatra* (20th Century-Fox); *How The West Was Won* (MGM); *Lilies Of The Field* (United Artists)
Actor	Albert Finney in *Tom Jones*; Richard Harris in *This Sporting Life*; Rex Harrison in *Cleopatra*; Paul Newman in *Hud*; Sidney Poitier in *Lilies Of The Field*
Actress	Leslie Caron in *The L-Shaped Room*; Shirley MacLaine in *Irma La Douce*; Patricia Neal in *Hud*; Rachel Roberts in *This Sporting Life*; Natalie Wood in *Love With The Proper Stranger*
Supporting Actor	Nick Adams in *Twilight Of Honour*; Bobby Darin in *Captain Newman MD*; Melvyn Douglas in *Hud*; Hugh Griffith in *Tom Jones*; John Huston in *The Cardinal*
Supporting Actress	Diane Cilento in *Tom Jones*; Edith Evans in *Tom Jones*; Joyce Redman in *Tom Jones*; Margaret Rutherford in *The V.I.P.s*; Lilia Skala in *Lilies Of The Field*
Direction	Tony Richardson for *Tom Jones*; Elia Kazan for *America, America*; Otto Preminger for *The Cardinal*; Federico Fellini for *8½*; Martin Ritt for *Hud*

1964

Production	*Becket* (Paramount); *Dr. Strangelove* (Columbia); *Mary Poppins* (Walt Disney); *My Fair Lady* (Warner Bros.); *Zorba The Greek* (20th Century-Fox)
Actor	Rex Harrison in *My Fair Lady*; Peter O'Toole in *Becket*; Anthony Quinn in *Zorba The Greek*; Peter Sellers in *Dr. Strangelove*; Richard Burton in *Becket*
Actress	Julie Andrews in *Mary Poppins*; Anne Bancroft in *The Pumpkin Eater*; Sophia Loren in *Marriage-Italian Style*; Debbie Reynolds in *The Unsinkable Molly Brown*; Kim Stanley in *Seance On A Wet Afternoon*

Supporting Actor	John Gielgud in *Becket*; Stanley Holloway in *My Fair Lady*; Edmond O'Brien in *Seven Days In May*; Lee Tracy in *The Best Man*; Peter Ustinov in *Topkapi*
Supporting Actress	Gladys Cooper in *My Fair Lady*; Edith Evans in *The Chalk Garden*; Grayson Hall in *Night Of The Iguana*; Lila Kedrova in *Zorba The Greek*; Agnes Moorehead in *Hush...Hush, Sweet Charlotte*
Direction	Peter Glenville for *Becket*; Stanley Kubrick for *Dr. Strangelove*; Robert Stevenson for *Mary Poppins*; George Cukor for *My Fair Lady*; Michael Cacoyannis for *Zorba The Greek*

1965

Production	*Darling* (Embassy/British); *Dr. Zhivago* (MGM); *Ship Of Fools* (Columbia); *The Sound Of Music* (20th Century-Fox); *A Thousand Clowns* (United Artists)
Actor	Richard Burton in *The Spy Who Came In From The Cold*; Lee Marvin in *Cat Ballou*; Laurence Olivier in *Othello*; Rod Steiger in *The Pawnbroker*; Oskar Werner in *Ship Of Fools*
Actress	Julie Andrews in *The Sound Of Music*; Julie Christie in *Darling*; Samantha Eggar in *The Collector*; Elizabeth Hartman in *A Patch Of Blue*; Simone Signoret in *Ship Of Fools*
Supporting Actor	Martin Balsam in *A Thousand Clowns*; Ian Bannen in *Flight Of The Phoenix*; Tom Courtenay in *Dr. Zhivago*; Michael Dunn in *Ship Of Fools*; Frank Finlay in *Othello*
Supporting Actress	Ruth Gordon in *Inside Daisy Clover*; Joyce Redman in *Othello*; Maggie Smith in *Othello*; Shelley Winters in *A Patch Of Blue*; Peggy Wood in *The Sound Of Music*
Direction	William Wyler for *The Collector*; John Schlesinger for *Darling*; David Lean for *Dr. Zhivago*; Robert Wise for *The Sound Of Music*; Hiroshi Teshigahara for *Woman Of The Dunes*

1966

Production	*Alfie* (Paramount/British); *A Man For All Seasons* (Columbia); *The Russians Are Coming, The Russians Are Coming* (United Artists); *The Sand Pebbles* (20th Century-Fox); *Who's Afraid Of Virgina Woolf?* (Warner Bros.)

Actor	Alan Arkin in *The Russians Are Coming, The Russians Are Coming*; Richard Burton in *Who's Afraid Of Virginia Woolf?*; Michael Caine in *Alfie*; Steve McQueen in *The Sand Pebbles*; Paul Scofield in *A Man For All Seasons*
Actress	Anouk Aimee in *A Man And A Woman*; Ida Kaminska in *The Shop On Main Street*; Lynn Redgrave in *Georgy Girl*; Vanessa Redgrave in *Morgan: A Suitable Case For Treatment*; Elizabeth Taylor in *Who's Afraid Of Virginia Woolf?*
Supporting Actor	Mako in *The Sand Pebbles*; James Mason in *Georgy Girl*; Walter Matthau in *The Fortune Cookie*; George Segal in *Who's Afraid Of Virginia Woolf?* Robert Shaw in *A Man For All Seasons*
Supporting Actress	Sandy Dennis in *Who's Afraid Of Virginia Woolf?*; Wendy Hiller in *A Man For All Seasons*; Jocelyn LaGarde in *Hawaii*; Vivien Merchant in *Alfie*; Geraldine Page in *You're A Big Boy Now*
Direction	Michelangelo Antonioni for *Blow Up*; Claude Lelouch for *A Man And A Woman*; Fred Zinnemann for *A Man For All Seasons*; Richard Brooks for *The Professionals*; Mike Nichols for *Who's Afraid Of Virginia Woolf?*

1967

Production	*Bonnie And Clyde* (Warner Bros.); *Doctor Dolittle* (20th Century-Fox); *The Graduate* (United Artists); *Guess Who's Coming To Dinner?* (Columbia); *In The Heat Of The Night* (United Artists)
Actor	Warren Beatty in *Bonnie And Clyde*; Dustin Hoffman in *The Graduate*; Paul Newman in *Cool Hand Luke*; Rod Steiger in *In The Heat Of The Night*; Spencer Tracy in *Guess Who's Coming To Dinner?*
Actress	Anne Bancroft in *The Graduate*; Faye Dunaway in *Bonnie And Clyde*; Edith Evans in *The Whisperers*; Audrey Hepburn in *Wait Until Dark*; Katharine Hepburn in *Guess Who's Coming To Dinner?*
Supporting Actor	John Cassavetes in *The Dirty Dozen*; Gene Hackman in *Bonnie And Clyde*; Cecil Kellaway in *Guess Who's Coming To Dinner?*; George Kennedy in *Cool Hand Luke*; Michael J. Pollard in *Bonnie And Clyde*

Supporting Actress	Carol Channing in *Thoroughly Modern Millie*; Mildred Natwick in *Barefoot In The Park*; Estelle Parsons in *Bonnie And Clyde*; Beah Richards in *Guess Who's Coming To Dinner?*; Katharine Ross in *The Graduate*
Direction	Arthur Penn for *Bonnie And Clyde*; Mike Nichols for *The Graduate*; Stanley Kramer for *Guess Who's Coming To Dinner*; Richard Brooks for *In Cold Blood*; Norman Jewison for *In The Heat Of The Night*

1968

Production	*Funny Girl* (Columbia); *The Lion In Winter* (Avco Embassy); *Oliver!* (Columbia); *Rachel, Rachel* (Warner Bros.); *Romeo And Juliet* (Paramount)
Actor	Alan Arkin in *The Heart Is A Lonely Hunter*; Alan Bates in *The Fixer*; Ron Moody in *Oliver!*; Peter O'Toole in *The Lion In Winter*; Cliff Robertson in *Charly*
Actress	Katharine Hepburn in *The Lion In Winter*; Patricia Neal in *The Subject Was Roses*; Vanessa Redgrave in *Isadora*; Barbra Streisand in *Funny Girl*; Joanne Woodward in *Rachel, Rachel*
Supporting Actor	Jack Albertson in *The Subject Was Roses*; Seymour Cassel in *Faces*; Daniel Massey in *Star!*; Jack Wild in *Oliver!*; Gene Wilder in *The Producers*
Supporting Actress	Lynn Carlin in *Faces*; Ruth Gordon in *Rosemary's Baby*; Sondra Locke in *The Heart Is The Lonely Hunter*; Kay Medford in *Funny Girl*; Estelle Parsons in *Rachel, Rachel*
Direction	Gillo Pontecorvo for *The Battle Of Algiers*; Franco Zeffirelli for *Romeo And Juliet*; Anthony Harvey for *The Lion In Winter*; Carol Reed for *Oliver!*; Stanley Kubrick for *2001: A Space Odyssey*

1969

Production	*Anne Of The Thousand Days* (Universal); *Butch Cassidy And The Sundance Kid* (20th Century-Fox); *Hello, Dolly!* (20th Century-Fox); *Midnight Cowboy* (United Artists); *Z* (Algeria/France)

Actor	Richard Burton in *Anne Of The Thousand Days*; Dustin Hoffman in *Midnight Cowboy*; Peter O'Toole in *Goodbye, Mr. Chips*; Jon Voight in *Midnight Cowboy*; John Wayne in *True Grit*
Actress	Genevieve Bujold in *Anne Of The Thousand Days*; Jane Fonda in *They Shoot Horses, Don't They?*; Liza Minnelli in *The Sterile Cuckoo*; Jean Simmons in *The Happy Ending*; Maggie Smith in *The Prime Of Miss Jean Brodie*
Supporting Actor	Rupert Crosse in *The Reivers*; Elliott Gould in *Bob And Carol And Ted And Alice*; Jack Nicholson in *Easy Rider*; Anthony Quayle in *Anne Of The Thousand Days*; Gig Young in *They Shoot Horses, Don't They?*
Supporting Actress	Cathy Burns in *Last Summer*; Dyan Cannon in *Bob And Carol And Ted And Alice*; Goldie Hawn in *Cactus Flower*; Sylvia Miles in *Midnight Cowboy*; Susannah York in *They Shoot Horses, Don't They?*
Direction	Arthur Penn for *Alice's Restaurant*; George Roy Hill for *Butch Cassidy And The Sundance Kid*; John Schlesinger for *Midnight Cowboy*; Sydney Pollack for *They Shoot Horses, Don't They?*; Costa-Gavras for *Z*

1970

Production	*Airport* (Universal); *Five Easy Pieces* (Columbia); *Love Story* (Paramount); *M-A-S-H* (20th Century-Fox); *Patton* (20th Century-Fox)
Actor	Melvyn Douglas in *I Never Sang For My Father*; James Earl Jones in *The Great White Hope*; Jack Nicholson in *Five Easy Pieces*; Ryan O'Neal in *Love Story*; George C. Scott in *Patton*
Actress	Jane Alexander in *The Great White Hope*; Glenda Jackson in *Women In Love*; Ali MacGraw in *Love Story*; Sarah Miles in *Ryan's Daughter*; Carrie Snodgress in *Diary Of A Mad Housewife*
Supporting Actor	Richard Castellano in *Lovers And Other Strangers*; Chief Dan George in *Little Big Man*; Gene Hackman in *I Never Sang For My Father*; John Mills in *Ryan's Daughter*; John Marley in *Love Story*
Supporting Actress	Karen Black in *Five Easy Pieces*; Lee Grant in *The Landlord*; Helen Hayes in *Airport*; Sally Kellerman in *M-A-S-H*; Maureen Stapleton in *Airport*

Direction	Federico Fellini for *Satyricon*; Arthur Hiller for *Love Story*; Robert Altman for *M-A-S-H*; Franklin J. Schaffner for *Patton*; Ken Russell for *Women In Love*

1971

Production	*A Clockwork Orange* (Warner Bros.); *Fiddler On The Roof* (United Artists); *The French Connection* (20th Century-Fox); *The Last Picture Show* (Columbia); *Nicholas And Alexandra* (Columbia)
Actor	Peter Finch in *Sunday Bloody Sunday*; Gene Hackman in *The French Connection*; Walter Matthau in *Kotch*; George C. Scott in *The Hospital*; Topol in *Fiddler On The Roof*
Actress	Jane Fonda in *Klute*; Julie Christie in *McCabe And Mrs. Miller*; Glenda Jackson in *Sunday Bloody Sunday*; Vanessa Redgrave in *Mary, Queen of Scots*; Janet Suzman in *Nicholas and Alexandra*
Supporting Actor	Jeff Bridges in *The Last Picture Show*; Leonard Frey in *Fiddler On The Roof*; Richard Jaeckel in *Sometimes A Great Notion*; Ben Johnson in *The Last Picture Show*; Roy Scheider in *The French Connection*
Supporting Actress	Ellen Burstyn in *The Last Picture Show*; Barbara Harris in *Who Is Harry Kellerman?*; Cloris Leachman in *The Last Picture Show*; Margaret Leighton in *The Go-Between*; Ann-Margret in *Carnal Knowledge*
Direction	Stanley Kubrick for *A Clockwork Orange*; Norman Jewison for *Fiddler On The Roof*; William Friedkin for *The French Connection*; Peter Bogdanovich for *The Last Picture Show*; John Schlesinger for *Sunday Bloody Sunday*

1972

Production	*Cabaret* (Allied Artists); *Deliverance* (Warner Bros.); *The Emigrants* (Sweden); *The Godfather* (Paramount); *Sounder* (20th Century-Fox)
Actor	Marlon Brando in *The Godfather*; Michael Caine in *Sleuth*; Laurence Olivier in *Sleuth*; Peter O'Toole in *The Ruling Class*; Paul Winfield in *Sounder*
Actress	Liza Minnelli in *Cabaret*; Diana Ross in *Lady Sings The Blues*; Maggie Smith in *Travels With My Aunt*; Cicely Tyson in *Sounder*; Liv Ullmann in *The Emigrants*

Supporting Actor	Eddie Albert in *The Heartbreak Kid*; James Caan in *The Godfather*; Robert Duvall in *The Godfather*; Al Pacino in *The Godfather*; Joel Grey in *Cabaret*
Supporting Actress	Eileen Heckart in *Butterflies Are Free*; Geraldine Page in *Pete 'n' Tillie*; Susan Tyrrell in *Fat City*; Shelley Winters in *The Poseidon Adventure*; Jeannie Berlin in *The Heartbreak Kid*
Direction	Bob Fosse for *Cabaret*; John Boorman for *Deliverance*; Jan Troell for *The Emigrants*; Francis Ford Coppola for *The Godfather*; Joseph L. Mankiewicz for *Sleuth*

1973

Production	*American Graffiti* (Universal); *Cries And Whispers* (Sweden); *The Exorcist* (Warner Bros.); *The Sting* (Universal); *A Touch Of Class* (Avco Embassy)
Actor	Marlon Brando in *Last Tango In Paris*; Jack Lemmon in *Save The Tiger*; Jack Nicholson in *The Last Detail*; Al Pacino in *Serpico*; Robert Redford in *The Sting*
Actress	Ellen Burstyn in *The Exorcist*; Glenda Jackson in *A Touch Of Class*; Marcia Mason in *Cinderella Liberty*; Barbra Streisand in *The Way We Were*; Joanne Woodward in *Summer Wishes, Winter Dreams*
Supporting Actor	Vincent Gardenia in *Bang The Drum Slowly*; Jack Gilford in *Save The Tiger*; John Houseman in *The Paper Chase*; Jason Miller in *The Exorcist*; Randy Quaid in *The Last Detail*
Supporting Actress	Linda Blair in *The Exorcist*; Candy Clark in *American Graffiti*; Madeline Kahn in *Paper Moon*; Tatum O'Neal in *Paper Moon*; Sylvia Sidney in *Summer Wishes, Winter Dreams*
Direction	George Lucas for *American Graffiti*; Ingmar Bergman for *Cries And Whispers*; William Friedkin for *The Exorcist*; George Roy Hill for *The Sting*; Bernardo Bertolucci for *Last Tango In Paris*

1974

Production	*Chinatown* (Paramount); *The Conversation* (Paramount); *The Godfather, Part II* (Paramount);

	Lenny (United Artists); *The Towering Inferno* (20th Century-Fox/Warner Bros.)
Actor	Art Carney in *Harry And Tonto*; Albert Finney in *Murder On The Orient Express*; Dustin Hoffman in *Lenny*; Jack Nicholson in *Chinatown*; Al Pacino in *The Godfather, Part II*
Actress	Ellen Burstyn in *Alice Doesn't Live Here Anymore*; Diahann Carroll in *Claudine*; Faye Dunaway in *Chinatown*; Valerie Perrine in *Lenny*; Gena Rowlands in *A Woman Under The Influence*
Supporting Actor	Fred Astaire in *The Towering Inferno*; Jeff Bridges in *Thunderbolt And Lightfoot*; Robert De Niro in *The Godfather, Part II*; Michael V. Gazzo in *The Godfather, Part II*; Lee Strasberg in *The Godfather, Part II*
Supporting Actress	Ingrid Bergman in *Murder On The Orient Express*; Valentina Cortese in *Day For Night*; Madeline Kahn in *Blazing Saddles*; Diane Ladd in *Alice Doesn't Live Here Anymore*; Talia Shire in *The Godfather, Part II*
Direction	Roman Polanski for *Chinatown*; Francois Truffaut for *Day For Night*; Francis Ford Coppola for *The Godfather, Part II*; Bob Fosse for *Lenny*; John Cassavetes for *A Woman Under The Influence*

1975

Production	*Barry Lyndon* (Warner Bros.); *Dog Day Afternoon* (Warner Bros.); *Jaws* (Universal); *Nashville* (Paramount); *One Flew Over The Cuckoo's Nest* (United Artists)
Actor	Walter Matthau in *The Sunshine Boys*; Jack Nicholson in *One Flew Over The Cuckoo's Nest*; Al Pacino in *Dog Day Afternoon*; Maximilian Schell in *The Man In The Glass Booth*; James Whitmore in *"Give 'Em Hell, Harry"*
Actress	Isabelle Adjani in *The Story Of Adele H.*; Ann-Margret in *Tommy*; Louise Fletcher in *One Flew Over The Cuckoo's Nest*; Glenda Jackson in *Hedda*; Carol Kane in *Hester Street*
Supporting Actor	George Burns in *The Sunshine Boys*; Brad Dourif in *One Flew Over The Cuckoo's Nest*; Burgess Meredith in *The Day Of The Locust*; Chris Sarandon in *Dog Day Afternoon*; Jack Warden in *Shampoo*

Supporting Actress   Ronee Blakley in *Nashville*; Lee Grant in
                      Shampoo; Sylvia Miles in *Farewell My Lovely*;
                      Lily Tomlin in *Nashville*; Brenda Vaccaro in
                      Once Is Not Enough
Direction   Federico Fellini for *Amarcord*; Stanley Kubrick
                      for *Barry Lyndon*; Sidney Lumet for *Dog Day
                      Afternoon*; Robert Altman for *Nashville*; Milos
                      Forman for *One Flew Over The Cuckoo's Nest*

1976
Production   *All The President's Men* (Warner Bros.); *Bound
                      For Glory* (United Artists); *Network* (United
                      Artists); *Rocky* (United Artists); *Taxi Driver*
                      (Columbia)
Actor   Robert De Niro in *Taxi Driver*; Peter Finch in
                      Network; Giancarlo Giannini in *Seven Beauties*;
                      William Holden in *Network*; Sylvester Stallone
                      in *Rocky*
Actress   Marie-Christine Barrault in *Cousin, Cousine*;
                      Faye Dunaway in *Network*; Talia Shire in *Rocky*;
                      Sissy Spacek in *Carrie*; Liv Ullmann in *Face
                      To Face*
Supporting Actor   Ned Beatty in *Network*; Burgess Meredith in
                      Rocky; Laurence Olivier in *Marathon Man*; Jason
                      Robards in *All The President's Men*; Burt Young
                      in *Rocky*
Supporting Actress   Jane Alexander in *All The President's Men*; Jodie
                      Foster in *Taxi Driver*; Lee Grant in *Voyage Of
                      The Damned*; Piper Laurie in *Carrie*; Beatrice
                      Straight in *Network*
Direction   Alan J. Pakula for *All The President's Men*;
                      Ingmar Bergman for *Face To Face*; Sidney
                      Lumet for *Network*; John G. Avildsen for
                      Rocky; Lina Wertmuller for *Seven Beauties*

1977
Production   *Annie Hall* (United Artists); *The Goodbye Girl*
                      (MGM-Warner Bros.); *Julia* (20th Century-Fox);
                      Star Wars (20th Century-Fox); *The Turning
                      Point* (20th Century-Fox)
Actor   Woody Allen in *Annie Hall;* Richard Burton in
                      Equus; Richard Dreyfuss in *The Goodbye Girl;*
                      Marcello Mastroianni in *A Special Day;* John
                      Travolta in *Saturday Night Fever*

Actress	Anne Bancroft in *The Turning Point;* Jane Fonda in *Julia;* Diane Keaton in *Annie Hall;* Shirley MacLaine in *The Turning Point;* Marsha Mason in *The Goodbye Girl*
Supporting Actor	Mikhail Baryshnikov in *The Turning Point;* Peter Firth in *Equus;* Alec Guinness in *Star Wars;* Jason Robards in *Julia;* Maximilian Schell in *Julia;*
Supporting Actress	Leslie Browne in *The Turning Point;* Quinn Cummings in *The Goodbye Girl;* Melinda Dillon in *Close Encounters Of The Third Kind;* Vanessa Redgrave in *Julia;* Tuesday Weld in *Looking for Mr. Goodbar*
Direction	Woody Allen for *Annie Hall;* Steven Spielberg for *Close Encounters Of The Third Kind;* Fred Zinnemann for *Julia;* George Lucas for *Star Wars;* Herbert Ross for *The Turning Point*

Appendix Three

This book has been about the winners, the Oscar champions of the last fifty years. Taken as a whole they constitute a unique record of the changing taste in films over half-a-century, taking in thrillers, musicals, epics, westerns, comedies and just about every *genre* in the medium.

But there remains a small postscript to be added about the losers — not every loser, that would take another volume bigger even than this one — but those films which for one reason or another never won a single nomination. From the films that have fallen into this sad category I have selected 100 famous movies which were completely forgotten at Oscar nomination time and consequently never contenders in the 50 or so annual Oscar races. Not one of them won a nomination in *any* single category.

The list is an arbitrary one but all films are famous for one reason or another, either critically or commercially. And just like the 500 films that make up the core of this book they all have one thing in common. Only this time they aren't winners, they are losers. They all missed out on Oscar night! Read on and be surprised.

Note: The films listed below are followed (in parenthesis) by the names of their directors and also by their years of release.

Accident (Losey)	1967
Advise And Consent (Preminger)	1962
Applause (Mamoulian)	1929
The Big Heat (Lang)	1953
The Big Knife (Aldrich)	1955
The Big Sleep (Hawks)	1946
The Blue Angel (von Sternberg)	1930
Bluebeard's Eighth Wife (Lubitsch)	1938
Bringing-Up Baby (Hawks)	1938
The Browning Version (Asquith)	1951

Call Northside 777 (Hathaway)	1948
The Cincinatti Kid (Jewison)	1965
City Lights (Chaplin)	1931
City Streets (Mamoulian)	1931
Cul-de-Sac (Polanski)	1966
The Day The Earth Stood Still (Wise)	1951
Dirty Harry (Siegel)	1971
Don't Look Now (Roeg)	1973
Dracula (Browning)	1931
Fahrenheit 451 (Truffaut)	1966
Farewell My Lovely (Dmytryk)	1944
Frankenstein (Whale)	1931
The Front Page (Wilder)	1975
Gilda (Vidor, Charles)	1946
The Group (Lumet)	1966
Gunga Din (Stevens)	1939
Hell In The Pacific (Boorman)	1968
High Sierra (Walsh)	1941
The Hill (Lumet)	1965
His Girl Friday (Hawks)	1940
Hombre (Ritt)	1966
The Innocents (Clayton)	1961
Intruder In The Dust (Brown)	1949
Invasion Of The Body Snatchers (Siegel)	1956
The Invisible Man (Whale)	1933
Junior Bonner (Peckinpah)	1972
The Killing (Kubrick)	1956
Kind Hearts And Coronets (Hamer)	1948
King Kong (Cooper, Schoedsack)	1933
Kiss Me Deadly (Aldrich)	1955
The Lady From Shanghai (Welles)	1948
The Lady Vanishes (Hitchcock)	1938
The Last Hurrah (Ford)	1958
Letter From An Unknown Woman (Ophuls)	1948
Lonely Are The Brave (Miller)	1962
Love Me Tonight (Mamoulian)	1932

Major Dundee (Peckinpah)   1965
The Mask Of Dimitrios (Negulesco)   1944
Midnight (Leisen)   1939
The Misfits (Huston)   1961
Modern Times (Chaplin)   1936
Murder By Death (Moore)   1976
My Darling Clementine (Ford)   1946

Night Of The Hunter (Laughton)   1955
Nothing Sacred (Wellman)   1937

Oliver Twist (Lean)   1948
O Lucky Man (Anderson)   1972
Outcast Of The Islands (Reed)   1952

The Palm Beach Story (Sturges)   1942
The Passenger (Antonioni)   1975
Paths Of Glory (Kubrick)   1957
Performance (Roeg)   1970
The Plainsman (DeMille)   1936
Point Blank (Boorman)   1967
The Postman Always Rings Twice (Garnett)   1946

The Railway Children (Jeffries)   1970
The Red Badge Of Courage (Huston)   1951
Rio Bravo (Hawks)   1959
Riot In Cell Block 11 (Siegel)   1954
The Roaring Twenties (Walsh)   1939
Roxie Hart (Wellman)   1942

Saturday Night & Sunday Morning (Reisz)   1960
Scarface (Hawks)   1932
The Scarlet Empress (von Sternberg)   1934
Scarlet Street (Lang)   1945
The Searchers (Ford)   1956
The Servant (Losey)   1964
The Set-Up (Wise)   1949
Seven Women (Ford)   1966
Showboat (Whale)   1936
Silent Movie (Mel Brooks)   1976
Sullivan's Travels (Sturges)   1942
The Sun Shines Bright (Ford)   1953
The Sweet Smell Of Success (Mackendrick)   1957

They Won't Forget (LeRoy)	1937
The Thing (Nyby)	1951
Things To Come (Cameron Menzies)	1936
The Thirty Nine Steps (Hitchcock)	1935
This Gun For Hire (Tuttle)	1942
3.10 To Yuma (Daves)	1957
To Have And Have Not (Hawks)	1944
Touch Of Evil (Welles)	1958
Trouble In Paradise (Lubitsch)	1932
The Trouble With Harry (Hitchcock)	1956
Wagonmaster (Ford)	1950
A Walk In The Sun (Milestone)	1946
The Wild One (Benedek)	1953
Winchester 73 (Mann)	1950
The Women (Cukor)	1939
You Only Live Once (Lang)	1937

Appendix Four

Another group of movie deserves brief mention before this volume finally comes to a close. Like those in the preceding section the films in the following list are all losers and, in a way, are even more unlucky not to figure in the Oscar record book for all were nominated in their respective years. Yet despite many nominations against their names they won precisely nothing. Not one of them came out a winner in any category.

Again the list is an arbitrary one but all the films included are well-known and all could — or perhaps should — have won at least one Academy Award in their time.

The number of nominations won by each film is listed in the right hand column. If the picture was a best film nominee in its year of release it is marked with an asterisk. Directors and release dates are shown after each title.

For the record, the non-Oscar winner with the most nominations is *The Turning Point,* made in 1977 by Herbert Ross and starring Anne Bancroft and Shirley MacLaine.

*Alfie (Gilbert, 1966)	5
*Anatomy Of A Murder (Preminger, 1959)	7
Anna Christie (Brown, 1929/30)	3
The Asphalt Jungle (Huston, 1950)	4
Baby Doll (Kazan, 1956)	4
Bad Day At Black Rock (Sturges, 1955)	3
The Band Wagon (Minnelli, 1953)	3
Blackboard Jungle (Richard Brooks, 1955)	4
Blazing Saddles (Mel Brooks, 1974)	3
Brief Encounter (Lean, 1946)	3
*The Caine Mutiny (Dmytryk, 1954)	7
*Cat On A Hot Tin Roof (Richard Brooks, 1958)	6

*A Clockwork Orange (Kubrick, 1971)   4
*The Conversation (Coppola, 1974)   3
*Crossfire (Dmytryk, 1947)   5

*Dark Victory (Goulding, 1939)   3
*David Copperfield (Cukor, 1935)   2
*Dead End (Wyler, 1937)   4
 Death Of A Salesman (Benedek, 1951)   5
*Deliverance (Boorman, 1972)   3
 Detective Story (Wyler, 1951)   4
*Double Indemnity (Wilder, 1944)   7
*Dr. Strangelove (Kubrick, 1964)   4

 Easy Rider (Hopper, 1969)   2
 El Cid (Anthony Mann, 1961)   3
 Executive Suite (Wise, 1954)   4

 The Fallen Idol (Reed, 1949)   2
*Father Of The Bride (Minnelli, 1950)   3
*Five Easy Pieces (Rafelson, 1970)   4
*Foreign Correspondent (Hitchcock, 1940)   6
*42nd Street (Bacon, 1932/33)   2
*Friendly Persuasion (Wyler, 1956)   6
*The Front Page (Milestone, 1930/31)   3

*The Great Dictator (Chaplin, 1940)   5

 The Heart Is A Lonely Hunter (Miller, 1968)   2
*Henry V (Olivier, 1946)   4
 High Society (Walters, 1956)   3
 The Hunchback Of Notre Dame (Dieterle, 1939)   2

*I Am A Fugitive From A Chain Gang (LeRoy, 1932/33)   3
 In Cold Blood (Richard Brooks, 1967)   4
 Inherit The Wind (Kramer, 1960)   4
*It's A Wonderful Life (Capra, 1946)   5

 The Killers (Siodmak, 1946)   4
*King's Row (Wood, 1942)   3
 Kiss Of Death (Hathaway, 1947)   2

*Lady For A Day (Capra, 1932/33)   4
 Last Tango In Paris (Bertolucci, 1973)   2
*Lenny (Fosse, 1974)   6

*The Letter (Wyler, 1940)	7
Life With Father (Curtiz, 1947)	4
*The Little Foxes (Wyler, 1941)	9
*The Long Voyage Home (Ford, 1940)	6
*Love Affair (McCarey, 1939)	6
*The Love Parade (Lubitsch, 1929/30)	6
*Madame Curie (LeRoy, 1943)	7
*The Magnificent Ambersons (Welles, 1942)	4
*The Maltese Falcon (Huston, 1941)	3
The Manchurian Candidate (Frankenheimer, 1962)	2
The Man Who Shot Liberty Valance (Ford, 1962)	1
Meet Me In St. Louis (Minnelli, 1944)	4
Morocco (Von Sternberg, 1930/31)	4
*Mutiny On The Bounty (Milestone, 1962)	7
My Man Godfrey (LaCava, 1936)	6
*Ninotchka (Lubitsch, 1939)	4
North By Northwest (Hitchcock, 1959)	3
Notorious (Hitchcock, 1946)	2
*The Nun's Story (Zinnemann, 1959)	8
The Odd Couple (Saks, 1968)	2
Odd Man Out (Reed, 1947)	1
*Of Mice And Men (Milestone, 1939)	4
The Prisoner Of Zenda (Cromwell, 1937)	2
The Private Lives Of Elizabeth & Essex (Curtiz, 1939)	5
Psycho (Hitchcock, 1960)	4
*Quo Vadis (LeRoy, 1951)	8
*Random Harvest (LeRoy, 1942)	7
Rear Window (Hitchcock, 1954)	4
Rebel Without A Cause (Ray, 1955)	3
Red River (Hawks, 1948)	2
Sands Of Iwo Jima (Dwan, 1949)	4
The Sea Hawk (Curtiz, 1940)	4
Singin' In The Rain (Kelly/Donen, 1952)	2
Sleuth (Mankiewicz, 1972)	3
The Spiral Staircase (Siodmak, 1946)	1
The Spy Who Came In From The Cold (Ritt, 1965)	2
A Star Is Born (Cukor, 1954)	6

*State Fair (King, 1932/33)	2
The Story Of G.I. Joe (Wellmann, 1945)	4
Suddenly Last Summer (Mankiewicz, 1959)	3
Summertime (Lean, 1955)	2
Sunday Bloody Sunday (Schlesinger, 1971)	4
Taxi Driver (Scorsese, 1976)	4
*The Thin Man (Van Dyke, 1934)	4
*Top Hat (Sandrich, 1935)	4
*The Turning Point (Ross, 1977)	11
*Twelve Angry Men (Lumet, 1957)	3
Vertigo (Hitchcock, 1958)	2
*Wake Island (Farrow, 1942)	4
Waterloo Bridge (LeRoy, 1940)	2
White Heat (Walsh, 1949)	1
The Wild Bunch (Peckinpah, 1969)	2
*Witness For The Prosecution (Wilder, 1957)	6

Appendix Five

The Thalberg Award was established in 1937 and is voted by the Academy's Board of Governors only in those years in which the Board feels there is a deserving recipient. The Award is for 'outstanding motion picture production' and remains one of the most coveted of the Academy prizes.

Winners

1937	Darryl F. Zanuck
1938	Hal B. Wallis
1939	David O. Selznick
1941	Walt Disney
1942	Sidney Franklin
1943	Hal B. Wallis
1944	Darryl F. Zanuck
1946	Samuel Goldwyn
1948	Jerry Wald
1950	Darryl F. Zanuck
1951	Arthur Freed
1952	Cecil B. DeMille
1953	George Stevens
1956	Buddy Adler
1958	Jack L. Warner
1961	Stanley Kramer
1963	Sam Spiegel
1965	William Wyler
1966	Robert Wise
1967	Alfred Hitchcock
1970	Ingmar Bergman
1973	Lawrence Weingarten
1975	Mervyn LeRoy
1976	Pandro S. Berman
1977	Walter Mirisch

Jean Hersholt Humanitarian Award

First presented in 1956, the Hersholt Award is for 'reflecting credit on the industry, and like the Thalberg Award is voted by the Board of Governors. Again, it is awarded only in those years in which, in the Board's opinion, there is a deserving recipient.

Winners

1956	Y. Frank Freeman
1957	Samuel Goldwyn
1959	Bob Hope
1960	Sol Lesser
1961	George Seaton
1962	Steve Broidy
1965	Edmond L. DePatie
1966	George Bagnall
1967	Gregory Peck
1968	Martha Raye
1969	George Jessel
1970	Frank Sinatra
1972	Rosalind Russell
1973	Lew Wasserman
1974	Arthur B. Krim
1975	Dr. Jules Stein
1977	Charlton Heston

Special And Honorary Awards Presented By The Academy since 1927/28

1927/28	Warner Brothers for producing *The Jazz Singer*, the pioneer talking picture which has revolutionized the industry
	Charles Chaplin, for versatility and genius in writing, acting, directing and producing *The Circus*
1931/32	Walt Disney, for the creation of Mickey Mouse
1934	Shirley Temple, presented in grateful recognition of her outstanding contribution to screen entertainment during the year 1934
1935	David Wark Griffith, for his distinguished creative achievements as director and producer and his invaluable initiative and lasting contributions to the progress of the motion picture arts
1936	The March Of Time, for its significance to motion pictures and for having revolutionized one of the most important branches of the industry — the newsreel

W. Howard Greene and Harold Rosson, for the colour cinematography of the Selznick International production, *The Garden Of Allah*

1937   The Museum Of Modern Art Film Library, for making available to the public the means of studying the development of the motion picture as one of the major arts

Mack Sennett, for his lasting contribution to the comedy technique of the screen

Edgar Bergen, for his outstanding comedy creation, Charlie McCarthy

W. Howard Greene, for the colour cinematography of *A Star Is Born*

1938   Deanna Durbin and Mickey Rooney, for their significant contribution in bringing to the screen the spirit and personification of youth and as juvenile players setting a high standard of ability and achievement

Harry M. Warner, in recognition of patriotic service in the production of historical short subjects presenting significant episodes in the early struggle of the American people for liberty

Walt Disney for *Snow White And The Seven Dwarfs*, recognised as a significant screen innovation which has charmed millions and pioneered a great new entertainment field for the motion picture cartoon

J. Arthur Ball for outstanding contributions to the advancement of colour in motion picture photography.

Oliver Marsh and Allen Davey for the colour cinematography of *Sweethearts*

Special award to Paramount for outstanding achievement in creating the special photographic and sound effects in *Spawn Of The North*

1939   Douglas Fairbanks (Commemorative Award), recognizing the unique and outstanding contribution of Douglas Fairbanks, first President of the Academy, to the international development of the motion picture

The Technicolor Company, for its contributions in successfully bringing three-colour feature production to the screen

Motion Picture Relief Fund, acknowledging the outstanding services to the industry during the past year of the Motion Picture Relief Fund and its progressive leadership

Judy Garland, for her outstanding performance as a screen juvenile during the past year

William Cameron Menzies, for outstanding achievement in the use of colour for the enhancement of dramatic mood in the production of *Gone With The Wind*

1940   Bob Hope, in recognition of his unselfish services to the Motion Picture Industry

Colonel Nathan Levinson, for his outstanding services to the industry and the Army which made possible the present efficient mobilization of the Motion Picture Industry facilities for the production of Army training films

1941   *Churchill's Island*, Canadian National Film Board, citation for distinctive achievement

Rey Scott, for his extraordinary achievement in producing *Kukan*

The British Ministry Of Information, for *Target For Tonight*

Leopold Stokowski and his associates, for their unique achievement in the creation of a new form of visualized music in *Fantasia*

Walt Disney, William Garity, John N. A. Hawkins and the RCA Manufacturing Company, for their outstanding contribution to the advancement of the use of sound in motion pictures through the production of *Fantasia*

1942   Charles Boyer for his progressive cultural achievement in establishing the French Research Foundation in Los Angeles

Noel Coward for his outstanding production achievement in *In Which We Serve*

Metro-Goldwyn-Mayer Studio, for its achievement in representing the American Way Of Life in the production of the *Andy Hardy* series of films

1943   George Pal, for the development of novel methods and techniques in the production of short subjects known as Puppetoons

1944   Margaret O'Brien, outstanding child actress of 1944

Bob Hope, for his many services to the Academy, a Life Membership in the Academy of Motion Picture Arts and Sciences

1945   Walter Wanger, for his six years' service as President of the Academy Of Motion Picture Arts and Sciences

Peggy Ann Garner, outstanding child actress of 1945

The House I Live In, tolerance short subject; directed by Mervyn LeRoy and starring Frank Sinatra. Released by RKO Radio

1946 Laurence Olivier, for his outstanding achievement as actor, producer and director in bringing *Henry V* to the screen

Harold Russell, for bringing hope and courage to his fellow veterans through his appearance in *The Best Years Of Our Lives*

Ernst Lubitsch, for his distinguished contributions to the art of the motion picture

Claude Jarman Jr., outstanding child actor of 1946

1947 James Baskett, for his able and heart-warming characterization of Uncle Remus, friend and story teller to the children of the world

Bill And Coo in which artistry and patience blended in a novel and entertaining use of the medium of motion pictures

Shoe Shine (Italy) for the high quality of this film

Colonel William N. Selig, Albert E. Smith, Thomas Armat and George K. Spoor, film pioneers

1948 *Monsieur Vincent* (France), voted by the Academy Board of Governors as the most outstanding foreign language film released in the United States during 1948

Ivan Jandl, for the outstanding juvenile performance of 1948 in *The Search*

Sid Grauman, master showman, who raised the standard of exhibition of motion pictures

Adolph Zukor, a man who has been called the father of the feature film in America, for his services to the industry over a period of forty years

Walter Wanger, for distinguished service to the industry in adding to its moral stature in the world community by his production of the picture *Joan Of Arc*

1949 *The Bicycle Thief* (Italy), voted by the Academy Board of Governors as the most outstanding foreign language film released in the United States during 1949

Bobby Driscoll, as the outstanding juvenile actor of 1949

Fred Astaire, for his unique artistry and his contributions to the technique of musical pictures

Cecil B. DeMille, distinguished motion picture pioneer, for 37 years of brilliant showmanship

Jean Hersholt, for distinguished service to the Motion Picture Industry

1950 *The Walls Of Malapaga* (France-Italy), voted by the Board of Governors as the most outstanding foreign language film released in the United States in 1950

George Murphy, for his services in interpreting the film

industry to the country at large

Louis B. Mayer, for distinguished service to the motion picture industry

1951   *Rashomon* (Japan), voted by the Board of Governors as the most outstanding foreign language film released in the United States during 1951

Gene Kelly, in appreciation of his versatility as an actor, singer, director and dancer, and specially for his brilliant achievements in the art of choreography on film

1952   *Forbidden Games* (France), best foreign language film released in the United States during 1952

George Alfred Mitchell, for the design and development of the camera which bears his name and for his continued and dominant presence in the field of cinematography

Joseph M. Schenck for long and distinguished service to the motion picture industry

Merian C. Cooper, for his many innovations and contributions to the art of motion pictures

Harold Lloyd, master comedian and good citizen

Bob Hope, for his contribution to the laughter of the world

1953   Pete Smith, for his witty and pungent observations on the American scene in the series of *Pete Smith Specialities*

The 20th Century-Fox Film Corporation, in recognition of their imagination, showmanship and foresight in introducing the revolutionary process known as Cinema-Scope

Joseph I. Breen, for his conscientious, open-minded and dignified management of the Motion Picture Production Code

Bell and Howell Company, for their pioneering and basic achievements in the advancement of the Motion Picture Industry

1954   *Gate Of Hell* (Japan), best foreign language film of 1954

Bausch and Lomb Optical Company, for their contributions to the advancement of the motion picture industry

Kemp R. Niver, for the development of the Renovare Process

Greta Garbo, for unforgettable performances

Danny Kaye, for his unique talents, his service to the Academy, the motion picture industry, and the American people

Jon Whitely, for his outstanding juvenile performance in *The Little Kidnappers* (G.B. title *The Kidnappers*)

Vincent Winter, for his outstanding juvenile performance in *The Little Kidnappers*

1955   *Samurai* (Japan), best foreign language film of 1955

1956   Eddie Cantor, for distinguished service to the film industry

1957   Charles Brackett, for outstanding service to the Academy

B.B. Kahane, for distinguished service to the Motion Picture Industry

Gilbert M. ('Broncho Billy') Anderson, motion picture pioneer, for his contributions to the development of motion pictures as entertainment

The Society of Motion Picture and Television Engineers for their contributions to the advancement of the Motion Picture Industry

1958   Maurice Chevalier, for his contributions to the world of entertainment for more than half a century

1959   Lee de Forest, for his pioneering inventions which brought sound to motion pictures

Buster Keaton, for his unique talents which brought immortal comedies to the screen

1960   Gary Cooper, for his many memorable screen performances and the international recognition he, as an individual, has gained for the Motion Picture Industry

Stan Laurel, for his creative pioneering in the field of cinema comedy

Hayley Mills, for *Pollyanna*, the most outstanding juvenile performance during 1960

1961   William L. Hendricks, for his outstanding patriotic service in the conception, writing and production of the Marine Corps Film, *A Force In Readiness*, which has brought honour to the Academy and the Motion Picture Industry

Jerome Robbins, for his brilliant achievements in the art of choreography on film in *West Side Story*

Fred L. Metzler, for his dedication and outstanding service to the Academy of Motion Picture Arts and Sciences

1964   William Tuttle for his outstanding make-up work in the film *7 Faces Of Dr. Lao*

1965   Bob Hope for unique and distinguished service to the motion picture industry and the Academy

1966   Y. Frank Freeman, for unusual and outstanding service to the Academy during his thirty years in Hollywood

Yakima Canutt, for creating the profession of stuntman as it exists today and for the development of many safety devices used by stuntmen everywhere

1967   Arthur Freed, MGM producer for distinguished service to the Motion Picture Academy of Arts and Sciences in the production of six top-rated Awards telecasts

1968   Onna White for her choreography of *Oliver*

John Chambers for his creative makeup design for *Planet Of The Apes*

1969   Cary Grant, for his unique mastery of the art of screen acting with the respect and affection of his colleagues

1970   Lillian Gish and Orson Welles for their superlative and distinguished service in the making of motion pictures

1971   Charles Chaplin, for the incalculable effect he has had in making motion pictures the art form of this century

1972   Edward G. Robinson for his contribution to the acting art

Charles Boren, leader for 38 years of the industry's enlightened labour relations and architect of its policy of non-discrimination.

1973   Groucho Marx, for his brilliant creativity and for the unequalled achievements of the Marx Brothers in the art of motion picture comedy

Henri Langlois, for his untiring devotion to the art of film, for his massive contributions towards preserving its historical past and for his unswerving faith in its future

1974   Howard Hawks, a giant of the American cinema whose pictures taken as a whole represent one of the most consistent, vivid and varied bodies of work in world cinema

Jean Renoir, a film-maker who has worked with grace, responsibility and enviable competence through silent film, sound film, feature, documentary and television

1975   Mary Pickford, in recognition of her unique contributions to the film industry and the development of film as an artistic medium

1977   Margaret Booth, for 62 years of exceptionally distinguished service to the motion picture industry as a film editor.

Janet Gaynor, for her truly immeasurable contribution to the art of motion pictures and for the pleasure and entertainment her unique artistry has brought to millions of film fans around the globe.

Index

Winning Films

Winning People